"Leading from the Middle"

"Leading from the Middle," and Other Contrarian Essays on Library Leadership

JOHN LUBANS JR.

Beta Phi Mu Monograph Series

 LIBRARIES UNLIMITED

AN IMPRINT OF ABC-CLIO, LLC
Santa Barbara, California • Denver, Colorado • Oxford, England

Library of Congress Cataloging-in-Publication Data

Lubans, John.
  Leading from the middle and other contrarian essays on library
  leadership / John Lubans, Jr.
     p. cm. -- (Beta Phi Mu monograph series)
  Includes bibliographical references and index.
  ISBN 978-1-59884-577-8 (pbk. : acid-free paper) -- ISBN
978-1-59884-578-5 (ebook) 1. Library administration. 2. Library
personnel management. 3. Leadership. 4. Organizational effectiveness.
I. Title. II. Title: Leading from the middle.
  Z678.L83 2010
  025.1--dc22   2010014566

ISBN: 978-1-59884-577-8
EISBN: 978-1-59884-578-5

14 13 12 11 10   1 2 3 4 5

This book is also available on the World Wide Web as an eBook.
Visit www.abc-clio.com for details.

Libraries Unlimited
An Imprint of ABC-CLIO, LLC

ABC-CLIO, LLC
130 Cremona Drive, P.O. Box 1911
Santa Barbara, California 93116-1911

This book is printed on acid-free paper ∞
Manufactured in the United States of America

I dedicate this collection of writings in memory of Edward A. Chapman, Director of Libraries at Rensselaer Polytechnic Institute. He hired me and was a mentor and friend for much of my career. Mr. Chapman always encouraged me to be active in the profession, do research, publish, and attend conferences far and wide. His support was of paramount importance in my development as a leader, librarian, and writer.

Contents

Foreword

There have been very few published collections of columns in the field of librarianship, and many of these have had a humorous bent. With the appearance of John Lubans Jr.'s writings on library leadership and organizational dynamics, readers will have an opportunity to savor the informed musings of a master stylist of this brief, declarative format. Most of these chapters first appeared as columns in Library Leadership & Management (LL&M), the official journal of the Library Leadership and Management Association, a division of the American Library Association. They have been comprehensively revised for currency and relevance.

John brings multiple assets to the columnist's domain. He spent his entire career as a practicing academic librarian, much of the time in senior leadership positions. He is equally at home in the literature of organizational theory, communication paradigms, and literary classics. Never accepting conventional wisdom or the tug of the status quo, John frequently challenges the "how we do it good at our place" approach by reexamining goals, objectives, and evidence. Pragmatism is at the heart of his analysis. If a project or process is cost-effective, transparent, collaborative, and user-centered, then it should be embraced.

Librarianship is not the only focus of these columns. John makes rewarding forays into a variety of different fields. Here you will meet a symphonic conductor, the owners of a delicatessen, a women's basketball coach, and the leadership team of Southwest Airlines. In each of these settings, the author is looking for transportable leadership traits. He is clearly asserting that librarianship has much to learn from leaders outside of our own comfort zone. And in every instance, he elicits valuable insights from his subjects.

The role and value of the column as a distinct format has received little attention in the scholarly literature. William Pannapacker, writing under the pseudonym of Thomas H. Benton, recently reflected on his years of writing a column for the Chronicle of Higher Education:

> Columns are exploratory and impressionistic. . . . [T]he columnist who tries to be scrupulously correct—however laudable that might be—provokes little more than a shrug of affirmation. A columnist who is wrong—and maybe even a little warped— gives readers the pleasure of showing how right and sane they are by comparison. A column is an eccentric little dance; it's a shtick. An established column—like a comic strip—can linger for many years, while readers return, again and again, hoping for

a flash of whatever it was they once liked about the series, while the author tries to make the old new again. But with good will on both sides, the author-reader relationship can continue, like the conversations of long time colleagues.[1]

John Lubans Jr. in many respects fulfills this mission by inverting the conventional and seeking new directions.

Finally, we believe that the column has been almost completely overlooked as a source for the profession's research agenda. Leadership studies, especially, cannot begin and end in the groves of academe. Sustained practical experience, especially when it is recorded through the prism of a knowledgeable participant observer, should be analyzed for concepts and ideas to be tested through rigors of the scientific method. To do less is to confine ourselves to the limits of established wisdom.

Arthur P. Young
Northern Illinois University

Peter Hernon
Simmons College

NOTE

1. Thomas H. Benton (pseud. William Pannapacker), "50 Columns Later," *Chronicle of Higher Education* 53 (March 16, 2007): C1.

Preface

Warning: do not read this book if you do not want to change. Any serious book about leadership is a book about change. Maintaining the status quo does not require leaders; it requires keepers. "Leading from the Middle" will not help you become a better keeper; it will help you shatter the status quo.

Each of us has at least a modicum of accumulated wisdom, but few of us can call upon it in a way that allows us to pass it on. And so we frequently repeat the mistakes of our predecessors. One of the oldest, most enduring, and most powerful ways of passing on wisdom is through stories, something John Lubans Jr. knows. So here, using stories, John makes accessible a wealth of wisdom garnered from years of real-world experience. It is not a "how to" book, no three easy steps to becoming a leader. But if you read the stories and listen and ponder and think, you will find your self-awareness growing. And that growing self-awareness, stimulated by these carefully told stories, can be the beginning of mature leadership.

Leading, of course, cannot be done in isolation. So self-awareness is a good start but an insufficient finish. Leaders need followers. It is typically assumed that leading is done from the front of the line or the top of the pyramid, suggesting a particular power equation between leaders and followers. But imagine the audacity to suggest that leading possibly may be best done from among one's colleagues, from the middle, that coaching and consulting are essential to forging a highly motivated, effective workforce. This is a different power equation, one in which a leader must be equally aware of colleagues. Leading is about enabling, motivating colleagues to realize their highest potential.

If you are of my generation, you may ask yourself why you weren't fortunate enough to have this book when you were just beginning. And if you are a beginner, well, let's just say that you have a head start.

And as for change, if you do not fear new paradigms and are interested in a different leadership proposition, then keep reading. This is the book for you.

Jerry Campbell
President of Claremont School of Theology
Claremont, California

Introduction

My paradoxical title, *"Leading from the Middle,"* dates from mid-2004, when I used it to introduce an essay "Leading from the Middle: 'I'm the Boss.'" (Chapter 2 in this book.) Later that year the phrase was the title of my talk at the 3rd LAMA National Institute: "What It Takes to Take the Lead" in Palm Springs, California. At the time I thought I had coined the expression, but soon realized that it had had some currency before I juxtaposed those contradictory words. Etymology aside, the phrase is as apt now as it was then because much of what I write is about leading from the middle, about how nonleaders help an organization get better and how effective followers are essential to the best kind of leadership.

"Leading from the Middle" pretty much sums up my personal leadership philosophy. Whenever I've taken on leader roles, in the profession and the library, I have depended on followers who behaved like leaders in their own right: people who thought for themselves and whose vision more often than not aligned with mine. Some of my best days at work were when a colleague dropped by to tell me, "I've been thinking . . ." and then elaborated on an idea for improvement. Not all ideas were implemented. Many were. Those that were not adopted often led to better ways because their suggestion opened the door to rethinking what we were doing and why. It all started with the follower's "I've been thinking . . . ." When I write about individual leaders, I focus on whether they liberate followers. Do they support the good ideas of their staff to permit them to lead from the middle?

"Leading from the Middle" distills fifteen years' worth of leadership essays. These three dozen chapters draw from disparate realms: travel, sports, music, retail businesses, airlines, and libraries. All of the essays have been edited and revised and many have been updated extensively with new material and epilogues.

Some readers may find this collection idiosyncratic and contrarian, even quixotic. They are partly right, but I hope they can also see the pragmatic aspects and positive results. I learned early on that organizations outside of libraries can give libraries new, insightful perspectives on leadership. If the reader disagrees but in the process gains a better understanding of who he or she is as a leader or follower, all for the good. And if the reader finds a kindred spirit on these pages with whom to converse, all the better.

Each part of this book has a particular emphasis:

> Part 1: Leadership, Leading from the Middle, Teamwork, Empowerment, Followership
>
> Part 2: Leaders, Bosses, Challenges, Values
>
> Part 3: Coaching, Self-Management, Collaboration, Communication
>
> Part 4: Techniques and Tools, Productivity, Climate

A few of the terms I've used above are less self-explanatory than they could be. For example, self-management is about being open to ideas; it requires reflection, discipline, and taking part in learning and gaining skills from experience, from juxtapositions and misalignments. Self-management is being aware beyond just doing the job. It is noting why something may work or not and relating it to yourself.

One of my themes is empowerment of self and others. The term empowerment has been much weakened from overuse and misuse. My empowerment is about a staff member's confidence and competence. It grows exponentially when an organization permits, indeed expects, individuals to resolve problems without seeking permission first. I am always impressed when someone is proactive on my behalf. I want to know how that happens. Is it internal to the employee, or is it something expected and endorsed by the organization for all employees?

Another theme is less familiar than leadership: followership. I speak of the highly effective follower. How do organizations enable "many leaders," not just those with "provides leadership" in their job descriptions? How do leaders, aware they cannot do it alone, get followers to join in with trust, respect, and energy?

Why do I write about organizations outside of libraries? The wisdom in how one organization succeeds often provides clues to the success of other groups, including libraries. When I look at other organizations, I always ask, What can I learn and transfer from what I see?

"Leading from the Middle" targets three groups of readers. First there are the regular readers of my work, especially the On Managing and Leading from the Middle columns from over the past decade. For them, this compilation should be a convenient "go to" for locating some idea or topic that appealed to them. Because I have revised all of the columns, these same readers will find new material and ideas that do not exist anywhere else. It is my hope that this gathering of essays strengthens and illuminates my message for these readers.

A second group is librarians who rarely read management literature. These librarians, often in managerial positions, may value the convenience of a leadership compilation written by a librarian and founded on his experience. My personal missteps and the trials and errors in the doing often move me to write in hopes of adding to our understanding. On occasion I am guilty of the "do as I say, not as I do" peccadillo, but for the most part, my writing is indeed the way I think and work as influenced by personal experience—good and bad.

Library science students in management classes are my third target group. This compilation—with its discussion of management classics—can supplement their required reading and expose them to nontraditional thinking—with which they may well concur—about how organizations work. A professor's guided discussion of several chapters might engage these students to reconsider how groups are led and what works best. Clarity about what it means to lead and to follow can only help our new librarians as they enter this exciting and ever-evolving profession.

Finally, I want to thank my colleague and friend, Arthur P. Young, for proposing I do this collection for Beta Phi Mu under his editorship. Our first conversation about this was in January 2004 at the ALA Midwinter meeting in San Diego. As we delved into it, a fog bank rolled onto the restaurant's patio, and I could barely see Art across the table. In spite of what the fog might have portended, Art has stayed with me and this project.

Art and I first met early in our careers in New York State. We were proactive young librarians and no doubt agitated the gray heads of the New York Library Association with our propensity to first do and then, much later, ask permission. Among other positive outcomes, our NYLA work resulted in a standing-room-only conference and sold-out conference proceedings that gave a strong boost to the incipient national movement in library user education.

John Lubans Jr.
Greenknoll Lodge, Three Mile Pond
Windsor, Maine

PART 1

Leadership, Leading from the Middle,
Teamwork, Empowerment, Followership

CHAPTER 1

Balaam's Ass: Toward Proactive Leadership in Libraries

During a recent *summer of discontent* a convergence of events—conversations at June's ALA Annual Conference about leadership, influential summer reading, and some early-morning lakeside reflections on followership—moved me to consider library leadership, the reactive and the proactive. How can libraries become more proactive?

Part of my summer reading was a P. G. Wodehouse (2000) compendium of the Jeeves and Wooster saga. Besides much laughter, it gave me this essay's title. Even the endearingly fluffy-headed Bertram Wooster gets fed up. There comes a time when Bertie digs in his heels and takes a stand, like the biblical ass of Balaam. If you are a Wodehouse aficionado, you will recall that Bertie took great pride in winning his private school's Scripture Knowledge prize by correctly relating, *mirabile dictu,* Balaam's story. A reference to Balaam's ass was never far away whenever Bertie reached his personal guff limit, drawing a line in the sand, "We Woosters have our pride!"

The Balaam story is a metaphor for good leadership, a leadership that is made right by the follower, even when beaten for refusing to do his master's bidding. Because of potential beatings, playing the recalcitrant donkey is never easy. Erin McClam's (2005) recounting of a recent court ruling against Betty Vinson, a WorldCom executive who falsified accounts, suggests what happens when followers go along: "Ms. Vinson was among the least culpable members of the conspiracy at WorldCom"; still, "had Ms. Vinson refused to do what she was asked, it's possible this conspiracy might have been nipped in the bud."

Barbara Kellerman's *Bad Leadership* (2004) was far less fun than Wodehouse, but noteworthy because of her premise that bad leaders and bad followers spoil the leadership stew. Indeed her seven bad leader types include some I have run into in our profession—the callous, the incompetent, the insular, and the intemperate, each a treacherous reef beneath our seemingly placid library waters. Kellerman contends that bad leaders would not be so bad if followers

3

stood up to them, held them accountable, forced them to listen, and said no when told to do bad things.

Leadership is an equation, not a person. There are two elements to the left of the equals sign: leader and follower (L + F = Leadership). Leadership is not neutral; it is often good or bad, depending on the values leaders and followers bring to the mix. The two develop a relationship that influences each other as well as the organization and society. Leaders and followers do not do the same things, just as musicians and conductors do not, but they are both essential to the process of leadership. The musician is essential to the conductor; because conductors are silent, without the musician there is no sound.

James MacGregor Burns (1978, 100) defined leadership as "leaders inducing followers to act for certain goals that represent the values and the motivations . . . of both leaders and followers."

"HYPOCRISY ABOUNDS"

Kellerman's book underscored conversations at June's ALA Annual Conference. A friend labors at a prestigious university library, a learning organization professing openness and collaboration. I have long respected my friend's clear thinking, independence, and pragmatism. Just prior to the conference, the boss told my friend to muzzle her troops—no more questioning unilateral administrative decisions—and to align her staff with the administrative lead.

This admonition, and a recent unexplained relocation of her work group, dismissed my friend's and her staff's ability to work collaboratively toward good solutions. "Hypocrisy abounds" is how she sums up the difference between what this organization professes and what it practices.

Fortunately my friend has a sense of humor to assuage the *slings and arrows of outrageous fortune*. According to her, this is how many leaders view what they do: "Leaders have vision. Followers implement." In other words, there are two kinds of people, those *with* and those *without* vision, the few who have it and the many who do not.

My friend has another take: "Leaders have hallucinations. Followers have doubts!" Like many resilient followers saddled with callous or incompetent leaders, my friend developed hidden networks within and outside the library to cope and to get work done. That's a high-risk strategy, but essential for one's self-respect and for achieving one's personal vision. And since my friend, however battered, never lost sight of her personal value, she found a better job elsewhere. There she is a highly regarded member of a team. Her skills are no different. Her new leader values a strong follower; the previous leader and her coterie fear independent staff.

Kellerman's book offers a few pages (239–43) of additional strategies ("self-help" and "working with others") on what followers can do for themselves when confronted with a bad boss. Kellerman's advice also applies to any follower seeking to be as effective as possible.

At the June Annual Conference there also was disquieting news from the commercial side. A vendor colleague gave me a jaw-dropping report on his boss's temper tantrum at a sales meeting. When my friend politely asked a provocative question about the corporate vision, the sales manager hurled a volley of expletives and a glass of ice water at my friend's head. Behavior like this, in a firm known for its punctilious dignity, is as outrageous as would be Jeeves's mooning one of Bertie's aunts.

Moreover, I was bemused at the conference when a couple of respected library leaders told me that my notion of administratively letting go was OK as long as it didn't happen in their backyards. There were few, if any, librarians in their shops to make responsible decisions. Musically speaking, no way could their orchestras play without a conductor!

Are these stories little more than the office grumblings heard daily on commuter trains, airplanes, and shuttle vans from too delicate flowers swooning at the office hurly-burly? Perhaps, if we are content to accept the status quo ("work is hell") and the loss of innovation, initiative, and great customer service because of bad bosses and sheepish followers. The Brafmans' (2008, 161–68) recent book, *Sway*, is about the human tendency to err. The authors maintain that dissent is essential to limiting our wrongheadedness and that it is important to establish a climate that permits, even *empowers*, dissent. Airlines now train cockpit crews and hospital operating room teams in how to "block"—the term for getting in the way of irrational behavior—when a safety rule may be violated. Not only does dissent improve decision making, it can also save lives. Now, although the irrational behavior in libraries described above might not lose lives, it may well weaken the organization, lead to ineffective decisions, and undercut a library's potential to excel.

THE REACTIVE LIBRARY

Is your library proactive (doing) or reactive (being done to)? In my workshops, I hear a lot about the reactive variety, almost to the exclusion of the proactive. Looking back on the several leader and follower roles in my career, I count myself fortunate for the many proactive leaders I worked with. These leaders helped me, with their encouragement and trust, to be proactive personally and to achieve goals I set for myself. Ours was a proactive leadership.

But I have worked with a few leaders who were overly cautious and mistrustful of change initiatives. They were not necessarily incompetent; perhaps they simply lacked confidence in their vision. Whatever the reason, they preferred to play it safe, to be reactive rather than to anticipate new directions and services. After my ideas were rebuffed by them several times, my default was to let things take their course, to keep a low profile.

One is never alone in this reactive, languid flow—there were other library leaders and followers bobbing along with me. Drifting takes less energy and has less risk than proactively doing. Yes, there's something to be said for the comforts of the reactive life, unless being done to involves a poke with a sharp stick.

Consider this compelling story from Jim Shamp (2005). Two hospitals were involved in a mix-up of elevator hydraulic fluid with liquid soap used for sterilizing surgical instruments. Someone erroneously put hydraulic fluid into soap barrels. One hospital performed 3,800 surgeries with instruments washed in the hydraulic fluid. The other hospital did zero surgeries with instruments washed in the hydraulic fluid. Why?

This latter hospital has a policy of empowering staff to take action: "[A]nybody, at any time, if they have suspicions on something like this, they can just stop it." Significantly, "the people who sounded the alarm and stopped the cleaning process were instrument technicians, not high-ranking corporate officers."

The other hospital ignored its frontline staff's red flag that the surgical instruments were coming out tacky. That hospital, although it claims that the hydraulically bathed instruments were safe, faces lawsuits from several of the 3,800 patients who think otherwise.

Fortunately most of us don't need to face a lawsuit to change our ways. On a personal level, I recall my disappointment when a colleague did a 180-degree turn on his leader's compass. What jolted me out of my reactive stance was his accepting as normal a five-year gap between his reference department's observation that the Internet was siphoning off more than half of the reference question market share to actually doing something about it. In other words, it took this department half a decade to move from point A (behind the desk) to point B (outside the desk) in response to this highly visible shift in information-seeking behavior.

Not only was he reconciled to the long wait, he regretted his earlier impatience. Well, maybe my colleague was mellowing, but accommodating years of delay sounds more addled than mellow. Perhaps my colleague was accepting the reality of working in a classically reactive library, so his U-turn might have been a matter of survival—"if you can't beat 'em, join 'em."

What do I mean by proactive leadership? Being proactive is acting in advance to deal with an expected or observed difficulty. It requires followers to be engaged and concerned with what is happening, to be intelligent about the big picture. Librarians have been proactive—interlibrary loan, book mobiles, OCLC, user education, and the British Library's Document Supply at Boston Spa are early examples. Paraphrasing Burns, the proactive organization's genius is found in the ways leaders engage followers in an enterprise that builds on their own and their effective followers' values and motivations, just like those early library initiatives did.

When you think about it, Jeeves is the quintessential effective follower, never compromising his personal values while rescuing his leader in each comedic venture. Jeeves thinks independently and is a leader in the butler's pantry. And he is committed to a higher calling, the "feudal spirit to oblige." The point is that Jeeves has something external to himself—a philosophy, not a boss—guiding his actions.

Why the Reactive Stand?

For one thing, there is much suspicion in the not-for-profit sector about business strategies that seek to empower staff. Usually the strategy starts off wrong when it is imposed, top down, by administrators outside the library. Invariably these administrators exempt themselves from the strategy, at best a mixed message. When applied in this way, with inadequate funding, training, and explanation, the strategy falters and is easily sabotaged and legitimately criticized for being superficial. The new way of working soon falls to the wayside. It implodes not from any superior value in the hierarchy, but because of ambiguous goals and inadequate understanding and commitment.

The hierarchy—the pecking order—remains our dominant organizational structure, however dysfunctional. There's an undeniable inherent premise: everyone needs a supervisor. In other words, no one can be trusted too much. Although those at the top of the pecking order might fantasize otherwise, most people—especially skilled and well-trained staff—resent being told what to do, however subtle the order. Our chains of command, performance appraisal, and salary structure are control mechanisms.

And more than any other organizational structure, the top-down arrangement encourages a reactive followership. Hierarchies or bureaucracies do function—some quite well—but only with an extraordinary commitment to and understanding among managers about what employees want, according to the organizational researcher, Fred Emery:[1] adequate elbow room for decision making, variety and meaning in what they do, mutual support and respect, opportunities to learn on the job, and a desirable future. Managers who focus on cultivating this type of organizational environment help make hierarchies productive.

Unions and professional associations have made inroads toward a more participatory workplace; kudos to them. However, these agencies appear to be stuck on a plateau, more worried about giving up gains and not being pushed off the cliff than focused on staging an assault for greater democracy.

A PROACTIVE LEADERSHIP

We need more libraries that are encouraging workplaces with a commitment to bring out the best in each person; a workplace that is bold and collaborative in decision making and action taking, anticipative and responsive to our many challenges.

Much of my writing celebrates proactive leadership. My stories on Don Riggs, Simone Young, Saul Zabar, a women's basketball team, Herb Kelleher and Colleen Barrett, and the Orpheus Chamber Orchestra are about leaders and followers who leave the comfort zone and get it right. Because several of my cases are drawn from outside of libraries, you might ask, for example, "How can Zabar's (the world's best food store) have anything to offer libraries?" Well, we actually have much in common, and the different perspective gained through looking at how Zabar's achieves its mission helps us better understand how to achieve ours. Another agency's success in being proactive just might give us the confidence to give it a try.

Asking Jeeves

A Jeeves and Wooster story often turns when Bertie realizes he's in a predicament and looks beseechingly to Jeeves, he of the eyes "agleam with the light of pure intelligence" and size nine-and-a-quarter hat.

Now it's my turn to do the beseeching. I wonder out loud: "What would Jeeves tell us about moving an organization from reactive to proactive?"

Hearing his name, Jeeves shimmered in. "Indeed, I am pleased to oblige, sir. Permit me to suggest seven stratagems."

1. For new hires, stress credentials less, spirit and independent thinking more. A pool of credentialed but rigid applicants is hardly preferable to one including inexperienced applicants with positive attitudes.

2. Increase integrated decision making and decrease top-down decisions. The people doing the work meet with leaders and develop the best collaborative solutions. Solutions emerge when intelligent people engage in open and honest discussion.

3. Flatten the administration and spread out administrative responsibility. Reduce the number of administrators while upgrading the responsibility and authority of the unit heads or team leaders. Invest overhead savings into frontline staff and staff development.

4. If they are worthy, make clear your organizational values. These values relate to how people work together, how they treat each other, and what the library aspires to be. Say them, mean them, do them, every day.

5. Experiment more and spend less time in committees contemplating what might go wrong. Find out by doing. Make more mistakes in pursuit of best solutions.

6. Use self-managing teams or other constructs that require critical thinking and decision making by followers. Leader roles throughout the library should be fluid, with turn-taking every few years.

7. Increase staff development budgets to train everyone in soft and hard skills. Establish a staff development strategy and replace formal performance evaluation meetings with career development conversations. Rigorously evaluate staff development purpose and outcomes.

"You are a marvel, Jeeves!"

"I endeavour to give satisfaction, sir." And he trickled off.

Well, I've kicked up my heels, brayed loudly, and probably stepped in a hornet's nest or two. No doubt it is time to heed Bertie's wisdom when quoting the poet: "'Exit hurriedly, pursued by a bear.'"

CHAPTER 2

Leading from the Middle: "I'm the Boss."

A trip to San Francisco is never complete for me without a seafood dish at the Tadich Grill. Located at the bottom of California Street, with the trolley cars rumbling past, it is the city's oldest restaurant, family owned, dating back to 1849. What draws me there?

Good food? Of course, but good food abounds in San Francisco. The ambiance? True, there's the inviting glow from the 1940s-era chandeliers visible through the half-curtained window. But the dark, wood-paneled walls, the white tile floor, and the L-shaped wooden bar are anomalous in this city of way-out-there design.

What really pulls me there is the Tadich tradition. It's twofold. There's an ingratiating stodginess with its rules, like no reservations, always closed on Sunday, no singles at tables, no substitutions on the menu, and so on. That firmness turns off a few, but for 600 diners each day the apparent brusqueness is tempered by an old-world courtesy, attentive service, good food, and a prevailing camaraderie. Tadich's family have made a conscious decision to keep and improve what works well, uphold the traditional values, and be attentive to the details—those hundreds of little things that make dining out delightful, or deplorable when overlooked. The Tadich tradition is shared by the customers. I was told: "The regulars guard the place." After the 1989 earthquake, with building debris littering the sidewalks, the customers came by—not to eat— but to ask, "Are you OK?" Often, they bring in their grandchildren for a first visit to Tadich's, introducing them to their favorite servers.[1]

Professionalism prevails—none of the servers are in between casting calls; serving is how they make their living. For Michael Buich, owner and general manager, the show and performance are right here on that tile floor. White jacketed, the servers flash past in a nimble kitchen ballet, a *pas de quatre* for servers and busers. Service is snappy—as soon as I sit down, the sliced lemons, water, salt, pepper, freshly sliced sourdough bread, and butter land in front of me alongside the cloth napkin and stainless steel cutlery. The four-page menu on vellum-like paper slips into my hand. Printed daily, it is dark green ink on one side, black ink on the other. Shortly after the food arrives, the server checks in to make sure it is to my liking and my wine glass is full, along with a friendly word.

Late one summer night I lingered to visit with my server. I told him that the cioppino and garlic bread had been my favorite over the past dozen years, how much I enjoyed each visit. "Where's the boss?" I asked, in hopes of meeting the leader behind this restaurant's perennial excellence.

"I'm the boss." Then he pointed to another server down the bar and said, "He's the boss." Then gesturing toward the bartender he repeated, "He's the boss." I liked the sound of that and thought I knew what he meant, but was left wondering how it played out in the running of the organization.

Three years later I asked Mike Buich what he thought that server meant. He told me, "It's the server's taking responsibility; it speaks to his being a professional. When they say, 'I'm the boss,' they're expressing pride in how well they perform."

For the servers it means you're the boss of your section, you are in charge of that part of the dining room. It also means: "Let's do the job!" This "let's get on with it" attitude permeates the place. However, it is far less about getting more butts in seats than about doing the best job for the people who are dining at any moment. If each customer leaves feeling well served, more customers will follow.

Although Mike is the leader—and the servers are followers—both contribute the qualities needed for their restaurant to remain a success. By infusing the Tadich values, expecting staff to do their best, to be as professional and competent as they can be—and the staff's responding to this expectation—Mike enables what I call "leading from the middle."

That phrase, the title of this chapter, derives from a workshop activity in which a dozen or more participants line up single file, with a balloon in between each two people. Sort of like this: XOXOXOXOXOXOX, with people as Xs and balloons as Os. It's called the balloon trolley.

The challenge: overcome obstacles, navigate a hairpin turn, hop over a threshold, circle around a tree, or whatever the itinerary, without dropping a balloon. There are two rules: no hands on the balloons, and if you drop a balloon, you must start over.

The person in the front (the nominal leader, with a balloon in the back but none in the front) leads the group through the first leg of the obstacle course. Then another leader is appointed—this time someone from the middle. Typically, that person steps out of the line to make his or her way to the front—that's where the leader is, right?

Not always.

I place them back where they were—and they experience, literally, leading from the middle, remaining a follower while leading—pushing a balloon in front and not losing contact with the balloon behind.

Belying its simplicity, the balloon trolley taps into a mother lode of metaphors about leading, leadership, and being a follower. The more obvious insights are as follows:

- There's a literal link (the balloon) between follower and leader—without willing followers the line does not move, the balloons go nowhere.

- Because of the shape of this organization—a long line—not everyone will hear nor (literally) share the leader's vision.

- The smallest action, say, a change in tempo, has an ever-widening repercussion, just like those unintended consequences of any policy, especially one developed without consulting the people involved.

The most effective leader/follower in the balloon trolley is aware of those around him or her, in front, in back, at the tail, and at the head. She is the one most comfortable being in the midst of something and someone who has the ability to communicate ways to advance the organization.

Recently the scholarly field of leadership studies has made progress in explaining what leaders do and what leadership is.[2] Current theories emphasize the role of the follower. When leaders and followers take action, they are involved in leadership. Leadership is never a person; it is a process between leader and followers. Imagine two overlapping circles: the leader is one circle and follower is the other. The overlap is the leadership process. A few scholars describe leadership as an eclipsing relationship— the leader and follower are "two sides of the same coin," the "yin and the yang," the "eternal male and female"—but the balloon trolley example does a better job, for the way I think about leadership, in approximating a less occluding relationship.

Kelley (1988) adds to our understanding of followership through charting out types of followers.[3] Of the five I've observed in libraries, the effective follower benefits the leadership process. These followers manage themselves well; they are leaders in their own areas, similar to the servers at Tadich's. They require little supervision. And they are committed to the organization and to a purpose or person outside themselves. Following are some of the types in Kelley's chart:

- *Alienated or Entrenched*—independent thinkers but alienated and often actively passive, as in passive/aggressive. They are proactive in articulating reasons *not* to do something. They drain the organization's intellectual energy to protect the existing way of doing things. When a leader (or an effective follower) seeks to change the status quo, the entrenched follower resists.

- *Sheep*—passive thinkers. Submissive to any leader, but, depending on which way the wind is blowing, they can be stampeded by the entrenched.

- *Yes People, Nodders, or Accommodators*—dependent thinkers, and prone to be YES people for leaders, fearful of challenging a leader's premise and gaining his or her displeasure. Still, they do the leader's bidding, so they are active.

In the middle of Kelley's chart we find:

- *Survivors/Pragmatists*—somewhat independent, somewhat active—not exactly "deadwood"—these pragmatists keep a low profile, do their job, and often enjoy more rewarding interests outside the library. They are be-mused by the antics of ambitious librarians seeking the spotlight.

If you were to sort your fellow library staff members by type of follower, what would the distribution be? What does that breakout say about your organization? One subgroup of about forty staff for which I was the appointed leader had this distribution: an equal number of entrenched and effective (18 percent each), with more than a third as sheep and the balance either accommodators or survivors. Because the effective followers balanced out the entrenched, I think we were able to make progress. However, had there been more of the entrenched, little change would have occurred until the other categories rallied in support.

What kind of follower are you? What kind of follower is your boss? As you might guess, effective followers lead proactively and do not behave like the typecast follower—a servant in need of direction. A personal illustration follows.

I have long been committed to Ranganathan's Laws. "Save the time of the user" has been my mantra, a touchstone in every job. No one told me to adopt these tenets; I read them in library school and, intuitively, they appealed to me, made eminent sense. So some years later, I was delighted when my boss asked me to benefit library users by leading a complex streamlining effort. It felt good to be singled out, to be given the responsibility for making a genuine difference. Well, I was less happy to hear why he had chosen me. Although he believed me capable enough, the real reason was that I was the "least resistant reed to the wind of change" he was bringing to the organization!

In truth, I already had a good idea of what needed doing and was confident it could be done. My vision happened to align with the leader's; to me, he was a co-adventurer. What was unique about this leader was his strength and wisdom in fending off the political machinations of those opposed to his change agenda.

Kelley identifies a quality that sets effective followers apart from leaders: the follower's ability and desire to participate in a team effort for the accomplishment of some greater common purpose. We succeeded in my example because the several dozen staff and I collaborated. If I had chosen to direct the followers, to tell them what and where to change, the results would have been different—and negligible.

What percentage did you assign to the survivor category in your library? I sense this category includes some very good librarians, potentially effective followers and leaders. Unfortunately, many of the survivors I know are disenchanted with management roles. One told me that for her and her closest peers, "Management jobs are more stressful than satisfying. We don't have any happy, effective manager role models."

How can we create an environment that encourages effective followers? These tangible ideas require bold leaders, ones who want to create a more effective followership:

- **Value independent critical thinking.** Critical thinking is bountiful in libraries, but often it waits to be invited into the decision-making arena. A friend told me of a first job experience. He was a newly hired reference librarian, bright and earnest. One day he saw the director and offered him some ideas on how the library could improve. He was admonished when the director scowled: "You are not here to make suggestions."

- **Manage self.** Develop practical techniques for disagreeing agreeably and building credibility. This is an essential process for the effective follower who wants to bring others along with his vision rather than becoming isolated as the organization's knee-jerk cynic, its irrelevant contrarian.

- **Act responsibly toward the organization, leaders, coworkers, and oneself.** It can be as simple as adhering to a few guidelines, such as not talking about colleagues behind their backs.

- **Appoint leaderless task forces in which everyone is a leader.** Experiment with groups in which all members assume responsibility for achieving goals.

- **Use temporary or rotating leaders of departments, divisions, and units.** A six-month term should give incumbents experience and new perspectives. Why do this? Because followers need to understand what leading is, and leaders need to know what it means to be a follower. And when followers help out an ineffective temporary leader, they learn something of value about leadership.

Finally, it is important to know that effective followers are on a perilous path. Kelley claims that about half the time effective followers are punished for speaking up, articulating their own viewpoints, or threatening an organization's complacency.

If the boss is insecure, your taking a well-reasoned contrarian stand will frighten him or her, leading to envy and fault finding. Over time, your only recourse may be to leave, to find a secure leader who values the courageous follower.

While leaving is a drastic step—unquestionably one of the most difficult career choices—it is too rarely exercised by followers. Many, for economic and other pragmatic reasons, stay and endure with ever-diminishing returns, joining the ranks of the survivors or the entrenched. There are costs. Staying instead of leaving superficially validates a poor leader and lets the organization meander along. Far worse is the personal cost of suborning your vision, of giving up.

It does not have to be that way. Remember, "You're the boss."

CHAPTER 3

Teams: Theory and Practice

Teamwork is my preferred organizational model for accomplishing our library mission. There are, of course, other models that can liberate staff to do their best and achieve service improvements, but based on personal experience, I root for teams. Team structures appear to be gaining something like a toehold in our libraries. This may be an extension of the participatory management style that has had wide acceptance. Or libraries may be under pressure to reduce administrative costs—fewer managers, lower costs. Or the desire for teamwork in some libraries may be a rejection of the command and control style some library directors practice. I can actually point to a half dozen current team applications in the United States, including one at the medical library of New York University, that appear to be making good strides. In fact, the NYU staff told me that although there are problems with the team concept, no one wants to go back to the hierarchy.

I want this chapter to be more than bromides and fad phrases from a self-appointed expert. Therefore I have drawn from my several-year personal experiences in working with teams and learning about why teams can succeed and why teams can fail. Please note that I say teams *can* succeed, not that they always *will* succeed. The reader should have no illusions that effective teams are easily implemented or that teamwork is intuitive. Everything depends on the organization's commitment to and the value top leaders place on teamwork.

I hope what I have learned from my numerous *mistakes* in working with teams can lead to the reader's better understanding of team concepts.

Like Continuous Improvement and Management by Objective, and unlike fads like the One Minute Manager or the FISH Philosophy, teamwork has a solid base of proven theory and results to support its use. If applied well, teamwork will get better results than top-down decision making. If applied poorly, teamwork is less effective than command and control.

WHAT ARE TEAMS?

Katzenbach and Smith (2001) tell us: "A team is a small number of people with complementary skills who are committed to a common purpose, set of performance goals, and approach for which *they hold themselves accountable*" (emphasis added).

My team experiences include a decade of working with self-managing teams. We had some astonishing successes—with innovation and productivity sky-rocketing—but other so-called teams drifted along, really no better than the departments or committees they had been. There were teams that lived up to the highest expectations and teams that never crossed the finish line. A few never left the starting gate.

How well a team worked was distinctly related to the level of engagement by the participants, particularly the team leader. Some team leaders, almost always the former unit head in this case, went no further than changing the name from "department" to "team." Theirs was a passive acceptance of the new model with no intention to change—these "teams" were going to ride it out until the resurrection of the pecking order. Worse, these leaders were silent opponents of teamwork.

A large organization may have little choice but to live with this resistance at the start, but when training and coaching resources are limited—as they always are in libraries—it may be best to focus on those groups in the library that are truly interested.

Work with *them*, develop *them*. If any team leaders are slow to take part, but are doing an adequate job, put them on hold and see if you can persuade them to sign on later once some highly successful teams emerge.

Have you been part of a natural team? Often natural teams come about in times of crisis. The upside of a disaster includes these positives: *no time wasted on the trivial, no manuals of procedure, wide-open communication, no risk—it's already a disaster!*, and *there's no delaying decisions.*

We probably all have a favorite story to tell about how a small group of people took matters into their own hands and fixed some problem. Would it not be wonderful if that spontaneous creativity could illuminate our work?

Teams are not committees. There are observable differences between an effective team and a committee:

- Team members are equals, whereas committees may have an implicit pecking order or hierarchy.

- Conflict in teams is normal and addressed, whereas committees may labor under unresolved, often historic, conflict.

- Teams seek high trust, whereas committee members may have turf issues and hidden agendas.

- Teams strive for open communication, whereas committee members may be overly cautious in discussion.

- Team members are mutually supportive, whereas committee members may work independently and represent factions.

With a bit of imagination, these contrasts can be used to explain why most departments behave like committees and why pseudo-teams behave like committees or departments.

Why are some teams better than others? Consider this question and jot down what qualities or behaviors—the intangibles—made a team or a group of people you know work really well. Your example does not have to be a library.

What attributes, characteristics, and values did your best team and its members have?

TEAMWORK RESEARCH

There is much advice about teams. Like much of the management literature, it is often elliptical in presentation or confusing in meaning. But there is some excellent teamwork research, some of it quantitative:

According to 6,000 team members surveyed over two decades and reported on by LaFasto and Larson (2001), these are the five conditions effective teams need:

Collaborative team members

Positive team relationships

Productive group problem solving

Leaders who *encourage* collective achievements

An organization that *genuinely* promotes collaboration and teamwork

Compare these five to what qualities you think made for the success of your team. None of these five aspects is intuitive to any group of randomly selected people. Gaining these qualities requires skills that have to be learned, worked through, and developed. Conflicts of purpose have to be addressed. You cannot work effectively with people you do not trust, with hidden agendas, or who seek to dominate. Effective teams talk through these issues—they do not avoid them.

Another team researcher, Richard Hackman (2002a), espouses five necessary variables for successful teamwork:

The team must be a *real* team, rather than a team in name only.

It has *compelling* direction for its work.

The team has an *enabling structure* that facilitates teamwork.

It operates within a *supportive* organizational context.

The team has expert teamwork *coaching*.

Again, these attributes suggest team members must learn skills and make an extra effort for teams to succeed. A coach may be essential. In one traditional university library, all staff were taught facilitation skills. Those skills have made a positive difference in the work done by traditional departments.

The definitive study on teams is by Katzenbach and Smith (2001). Their research revealed that all *high performance* teams have certain elements in common (see figure 3.1):

- **Element 1.** The team's **purpose/mission** is clear and understood by each team member. Although the mission may be stated by the executive, the best statements of purpose/mission are done in collaboration between the team and the library's leadership. It is essential that team members understand the administration's commitment and support for the team's purpose/mission and that it is congruent with the overall mission of the library.

Purpose/mission

Team member roles

Real work

The *how*

Outcomes

Deadlines

Support

Accountable

Interdependent

Figure 3.1. Elements of Successful Teams. Adapted from Katzenbach and Smith (2001).

- **Element 2. Team member roles** are explicit, agreed upon, and understood. Team members are conversant with each of these roles and responsibilities in achieving the goal. To minimize misunderstandings about roles, the more clarity, the better for the team. People will have different roles, but all roles are essential to achieving objectives. Role confusion will inevitably interfere with the work of the team.

    In a few workshops I have noticed team members effectively working together and clarifying roles; when completing complex activities, people took on different roles, sometimes with discussion, sometimes just on intuition. The best teams were those who, within time constraints, were able to clarify everyone's role quickly and to move forward to completion.

- **Element 3.** All team members work an equal amount doing **real work.** One of the major concerns I hear about in my classroom with small group projects is that some students loaf and other students pick up their slack. In other words, some students do more than their fair share. I encourage my students to confront observed inequities. Only a few follow through, even though they have my express permission to do so. In workplace teams, any notion that workload is unfairly distributed needs to be addressed and worked out. Open and frank discussion is the only way to do this. Of course, to have that candid discussion demands a high level of trust and a voice more like a lion than a mouse.

  Team members in a few of my workshops had no difficulty with the concept of everyone doing real work. If anything, some were eager to do *more* than their fair share of real work. If this sort of enthusiasm could be transferred to the workplace, I expect that all realistic projects would be accomplished.

  The next Katzenbach and Smith element, the **how**, is about anticipating and answering questions about how the team will work.

- **Element 4.** Members of effective teams pay attention to the *how* of working together. This means team members reaching agreement, in an open discussion, on how they will make decisions, work through problems, and give each other feedback.

  Katzenbach and Smith observe: "Most of us enter a potential team situation cautiously because ingrained individualism and experience discourage us from putting our fates in the hands of others or accepting responsibility for others" (2001, 116).

  Instead of ignoring or avoiding the how of working together—Tuckman (1965) calls this phase *storming*—work groups need to spend extra time on this process.

  I once had an experience with storming that convinced me it was inevitable and unpredictable. I was at a multiday training-the-trainer session. We were twenty strangers split into two teams. The training curriculum was the same, and we were usually within sight of each other during the day. We shared meals.

  By the end of the first day, I was miserable. I'd alienated all but one of my teammates by not going along with guidelines the majority set up. I disagreed, and I told them so in strong terms. When my partner and I did our presentation to the group, their feedback was terse and unsupportive. That our presentation was not all that good made it even more humiliating.

  Across the way, the other team was always laughing, working together, clearly supportive. I was drawn to that happy team. When I asked the instructors to transfer me into the other team, the answer was no. That night I thought about leaving, catching the bus back to the airport.

The dawn, to coin a phrase, brought a new day. Slowly my teammates and I, with a little help from the instructors, worked at our differences, and by the end of day two things were not so grim. I'd explained my views, they'd listened and made a few concessions—things were lightening up. Importantly, my most vehement opponent helped me with one activity—it was done in a spirit of generosity, and I responded in kind. We were making good progress.

On day three, the other group stopped talking. Now they were the unhappy campers, sending envious glances our way. There'd been a falling out, cliques had formed, and the last hours were spent in conflict. There was little time to resolve the differences, but with the instructors intervening, progress was made. By the morning of day four, with a scheduled noon departure, things had pretty much calmed down. Storming was never featured in the curriculum, but I hope all learned as much as I did about it.

Ineffective teams often fail to take time to talk through "team issues"; for example, are members *in or out* of the team; is the team's purpose clear or ambiguous; is decision making based on opinion or fact; does the team work on conflict or avoid it; and do team members support each other or only themselves?

If the team can be open and trusting, a cycle of incremental improvement is put into play, enhancing the team's ability to come up with answers to complex issues and to get results.

Coaching and giving feedback is a team member and team leader responsibility and should not be minimized. Articulating the issues impeding the work of the team can be the most difficult part of teamwork, but with practice, a team member or a leader can gain proficiency at correcting a wayward team and helping the team achieve its potential.

Sometimes dysfunctional teams have blind luck—the mission is accomplished against all odds—but, in my experience that is rare, and the odds are stacked against any repetition of performance. That same team may implode on its next assignment.

In a recent workshop, I observed a considerable ability by role play participants to give blunt, candid, and *useful* feedback to team members impeding the work of the team. However, the idea of giving the oddball team member the silent treatment did surface. I cannot recommend it, because silence assumes a willful ignorance on the part of the problem team member. It may be that the offender actually lacks training or is completely unaware that his or her behavior impedes the work of the team. Clarification requires a verbal exchange done in an agreeable manner, and if necessary in a private setting.

- **Element 5. Outcomes** drive the team's purpose. Why? Because, according to Katzenbach and Smith, "Only when appropriate performance goals are set does the process of discussing the goals and the approaches to them give team members a clearer purpose and choice: they can disagree with a goal and opt out or they can become accountable" (2001, 116). One may question who sets the outcomes. Often managers believe it is their role to set team goals. In practice, teams who set their own goals often aspire higher than managers do.

That has been my experience in the library workplace, and I recall a women's basketball coach telling me that when she set team goals, they were fairly modest. When she turned goal setting over to the players, their unanimous goal (and fully invested commitment) was a national championship! Although some library teams do not have stated goals—out of a disdain for quantifying library work—it is a profound error, internal and external to the library, not to be accountable.

- **Element 6.** Job **deadlines** are stated and respected. A set time limit helps a team focus and deliver its product. A realistic deadline will help a team come up to speed and move from "storming" to the performing phase. Without deadlines, some teams, especially in the not-for-profit sector, regard time as an unlimited resource.

  My workshop activities have brief time limits. Although expecting a team to accomplish some task in ten minutes may not seem realistic, the teams do just that! This often leads to discussion about how so much work could get done in so little time when in the workplace, there seems to be never enough time.

- **Element 7.** Demonstrable **support** comes from the "top" leadership. Support includes the supervisor's being an active participant, maybe not a member, but an advisor, a coach, an interested and supportive listener. The team has to be open and honest with the administrative leader. If the relationship becomes uncollaborative—"us versus them"—then the team will not be effective as it could be. The team supervisor has a tricky job to do. While letting the team alone enough to develop to full capacity, the supervisor has to be close enough to guide team development.

  An example from a sports story ("800!" 2008): during a basketball game the coach (supervisor of the team) decided to step away from the huddle and turned the decision making over to the team. His rationale was that the players were not doing what he wanted. He made a conscious decision, at some risk, to get out of the way: "For a couple of late timeouts, I let anyone who would actually want to talk—and say something that somebody would listen to—run the huddle," the coach said. "Teams become really good when they talk to each other. What happens is, they take ownership."

- **Element 8.** The team is **accountable** to the organizational leadership. Team members are not free agents. Teams don't go off and do something that has nothing to do with the library's purpose. It is delusional for any team to think it has gotten a pass from being accountable to its supervisor. When the team believes itself independent from the organization, it may still do good work, but not necessarily in support of the organization's mission. Over time the unaccountable team begins to exclude administrative leaders from participating in the work of the team and begins to believe that the team has an absolute right to make unilateral decisions, even ones effecting the overall organization.

- **Element 9.** Finally, an element that I have added is the realization among team members that the team is **interdependent** with other teams in the organization. They are aware of not being alone and **never** blame other teams. Interdependent teams are supportive and will often selflessly help other teams achieve their goals. Because they understand their part in the organization, they know that an organization's success depends on more than their individual team. An emphasis on interdependence is especially important for libraries that at times suffer from an all too common jealousy among departments.

In my team research studies on a women's basketball team, the Orpheus Chamber Orchestra, and the Southwest Airlines ramp teams, I have found a full matchup between the Katzenbach and Smith elements and the success of those teams.

I can reach a similar conclusion from my work with library teams. The absence or presence of the required team elements made a difference in outcomes. Sometimes we were fortunate and the team simply emerged as effective—no matter what we might have done wrong, this team rose above it and performed excellent work. They became self-managing and self-achieving. Other times, the team failed. The team could have worked had we had the patience, courage, and will to make sure all the elements were in place.

Of course, if we do not have any team players—only captains—we will not have effective teams. No doubt you can suggest the essential characteristics of effective team members. Here is my job ad for the best kind of team member:

Wanted: Team member with a commitment to team goals, a nurturing nature to help others, assertive enough to make personal ideas known, an active listener, and a willing participant in decision making. Someone who openly shares own ideas and accepts other ideas, gives feedback, supports others, is diplomatic in working with other teams, knows his or her expert role, and is accountable for the work of the team.

Here is what I would emphasize in working with teams, based on what I now know and have learned in observing superior teams:

Do *not* underestimate the time it takes to implement team structures.

Consciously follow the cycle of Plan, Do, Check, and Act (PDCA), always seeking improvements.

Celebrate, regularly, team results. Having fun is the secret ingredient for successful team "chemistry."

Implement teams in phases, starting with those most interested. Realize there are many ways, but there is no *perfect* way, to move from an old model to a new one.

Be generous with time and resources to train and develop staff about teamwork.

Experiment with different kinds of teams and take turns in leading teams.

Recognize that some staff may not be team players but are productive in their solitary ways. Accept them as essential to getting the work out and design ways to make the best use of their skills outside of teams.

Commit to in-depth conversations with those for and those against teams. Take time to hear the issues and to respond in constructive ways.

Have a trusted outside observer talk with your teams and give the library's leader candid feedback on what is working well and what needs improving.

I would also look at the organizational structures and procedures (salary, appraisal, reward and recognition based on individual staff) that will need adjustment for instilling a team culture.

CHAPTER 4

Letting Go: A Reflection on Teams That Were [1]

As the reader is well aware, any reflection, any *memoir*, is colored by what occurs *after* the event. Since giving up administrative responsibility for technical services teams, I have explored highly effective teams, like the self-managing Orpheus Chamber Orchestra, a women's basketball team, and the ramp agent teams at Southwest Airlines. Their successful teamwork influences my assessment of the technical services teams I worked with. And, as a teacher of library management, I explore team concepts, followership, and organizational change.

My purpose in telling this story is to demonstrate the power of administratively letting go—of creating channels for staff to seek innovative and productive ways. And to display how teams, when adequately supported and protected, with high expectations and freedom for action, generally outperform traditional structures.

WHY TEAMS?

During the late 1970s and early 1980s at the university at which I worked, the library and the technical services group began to draw unwanted attention from the university administration. To some extent it was unavoidable—a large payroll, some vocal dissatisfaction among students and faculty about slow turnaround times, and a large, visible backlog. And there was a perception that the library was backwards, when compared to peer institutions, in automating.

Exacerbating the situation was the steady opposition by librarians to any called-for economies or simplification. That knee-jerk response pretty much kept the library under the administrative microscope. The librarians were not closed to change per se—it just had to be on their terms: more funding, more staff—and more time. The library leadership (especially the executive group of which I became a member) was seemingly unable to develop any approach other than to rationalize away criticism or to add complexity to an already overly complex process.

Prior to my appointment, the university administration had brought in time and motion consultants (with clipboards and stopwatches) to assess the efficiency of library work. The consultants' recommendations were resisted, termed "ignorant," and otherwise ridiculed by the library staff. The reader can imagine what the T&M consultants told the university administration!

However ignorant these scientific managers might have been about the nuances of technical services work, there was no escaping library user dissatisfaction and the perception that the library was hindering the progress of a recently deemed "hot" university. Our telling the university administration that the library simply knew better was, well, self-destructive. If the library is a growing, living organism, we were closer, in administrative eyes, to the image of a growing mausoleum.

Had we responded differently, this contretemps might have been only a passing administrative pique. Instead, the library's eschewing administrative guidance aggravated an atmosphere of mutual distrust. Technical services, the library group with the largest payroll ("a bottomless pit") and the most problems (glacial processing times and mountainous backlogs), became an obvious reform target.

When a newly installed university president echoed the prior administration's calls for reform, the library responded as usual. The resulting standoff led to the morale busting, premature departure of the university librarian. A new, highly recruited librarian—the provost flew to the librarian's home state to convince him to accept the job—was brought in with a specific change agenda.

After a few months on the job, the new librarian concluded that what was needed was not more, but less. Less complexity, less hierarchy, and less resistance to new ideas. His first action was to ensure staff participation in decision making throughout the library, including technical services. All staff were permitted, indeed expected, to have an opinion and a say in decision making about streamlining and the shifting of resources. He set up monthly forums for support staff, supervisors, department heads, and frontline librarians.

The new librarian asked me to head up the technical services (TS) reform effort. This was a surprise, because I was the Assistant University Librarian for Public Services. Shortly after accepting the challenge, I realized my lack of expertise in TS was more a plus than a delta.

Immediately after my first meeting with the TS staff, in which I told them I needed their help—I did not have the answers—the staff produced a multipage list of suggestions they had been making over several years.

This list was the first glimmer of the positive effects from uncorking years of pent-up ideas, suggestions, and improvements. Our mandated reform goals were met and exceeded and new challenges were taken on—all in the first year.

My strengths were a passionate commitment to saving the time of the user; an ability to question why we did what we did; and a strong belief that staff, given the opportunity, knew the best way to do their work.

And, thanks to strong leadership covering my back, I had the opportunity to corral some of the sacred cows roaming the academic library pasture.

Following our rapid improvements through participation, we moved, naturally enough, toward a team-based structure. This was helped along by the president's encouragement of total quality management (TQM) applications.

Ultimately, our success was about letting go, turning good people loose to do the job they were fully capable of doing once free of supervisory second guessing and control.

In hindsight, we were working toward the ideals and attributes that Katzenbach and Smith (K&S, 2001) identified in their research on highly effective teams. These teams demonstrate clarity about and seek positive behaviors around several team elements, including purpose, roles, deadlines, and accountability.

Our *actual* teamwork was a half-baked mix of borrowed concepts from the literature and our best thinking on what teams should be. There was no library guide to teamwork that we followed. We were only vaguely aware of the K&S research, so we did not instill or practice all of the elements, but we did, intuitively, practice enough of them to make a difference. We made use of Streibel's pragmatic *Team Handbook* (2003) from the Joiner Associates, but how many department heads opened their personal copies or followed Streibel's concepts is unknown.

Indeed, our teams *were* half baked. We meant well and we achieved much, but not fully engaging all that does go into the development of best teams did diminish our effectiveness.

We had little difficulty in gathering the abundance of low-hanging fruit—those internal-to-TS processes, some redundant, that were easily merged, eliminated, or simplified. But harvesting the *high* fruit—often outside of TS in walled-off orchards, surrounded by moats brimming with faculty crocodiles—would have required *all* the skills and attributes of high-achieving teams.

CHALLENGES

There is opposition to any change initiative. Jealousies and other organizational pathologies are easily aroused. They cannot be eliminated, but they can be contained. As long as there is strong leadership to protect change agents against those who wish to derail the change process, the naysayers have little influence. However, once the shield is lowered, the nit pickers, and those genetically averse to any organization other than the hierarchy—the pecking order—will have their day.

Our biggest challenges were not unique to my institution—they were inherent to the culture of research libraries. This culture was less concerned about productivity and access than it was about achieving bibliographic control. It was, and may still be, a culture in which the size of the collection—the biggest pile of books—is the one measure of best practice.

Perhaps this focus on bibliographic control was reactive. It may have been the best we could do to cope with the bookish arms race among research libraries to add annually tons of redundant and marginal materials. I am not referring to books that might have *some* use; I am talking about the wholesale acquisition of materials that predictably would have little use—if any, ever.

Another challenge was that most of my TS peers—in comparable libraries elsewhere—were queasy in talking about or applying any quantitative measures to workflow. We either did not know about the "Law of Least Diminishing Returns," or if we did, it made no difference to how we worked. Ignoring this law, we persisted in seeking to improve on nearly error free processing by making huge commitments of resources (time, people, and processes) in a vain attempt to achieve the last few percentage points of accuracy.

Comparable to ignoring the Law of Least Diminishing Returns was our failing to appreciate complexity theory. The notion behind complexity theory is that even the smallest add-on to an existing process has implications for the total system. The tiniest twist, loop, or wrinkle adds its weight and exponentially more as its ramifications work their way through the system.

In apparent opposition to common sense, we preferred to make complex systems more complex. In reality, the less complicated the system, the less resistance in the workflow, the fewer the bottlenecks.

For me, Robert Henri (1984), the painter, put it best: "The easiest thing is the hardest. It is harder to be simple than it is to be complex." Many of us in TS believed—perhaps still do—that simple is easy, complex is hard (and better.)

I recall a regular feature at semiannual national meetings of TS directors—the tradition of hearing the Library of Congress's report on their achievements in cataloging. The head of LC cataloging would recite the current year's statistics, but never gave comparative figures. Had they done more or less than in previous years? It did not seem to matter even though they had the world's biggest backlog.

It mattered to us a lot. Because we relied on LC records, I really did want to know what their productivity was and whether they were improving on it. The faster they were pumping out records, the faster we could catalog and get books to users.

I am not implying that research libraries are statistics averse. Our TS had mounds of statistics—the problem was what we did with them. For the most part, we kept track of numbers in order to give them to outside agencies and stick them into annual reports.

We made better use of our statistics once we began to compare how we were doing year to year and, eventually, over several years. We could take genuine pride in gains achieved and when productivity took a dive assess how we could improve our workflow. Although we rarely used TQM's advanced statistical analyses, we were not afraid to use numbers to track our progress.

One unintended consequence of a survey of workload statistics among the largest research libraries—about twenty took part—was gaining a baseline to compare ourselves to. The first survey had us at the bottom of our peer group. This was no surprise to me, but it flabbergasted those on the staff who believed our cataloging was the best. It may have been the best, but it put us at the bottom of this putative productivity index.

Several years later, at the apex of our team initiatives, we were at the top of the index. I was rightly proud of our achievement, but our comparison group was still *other libraries*, not organizations with a clear focus on productivity. This was somewhat akin to Southwest Airlines annually winning the best customer satisfaction rating when compared to other *airlines*. As anyone who has being flying in the last decade knows, customer service is less of a priority than is making a profit, at any cost.

Revision Mess

Mess finding is that piece of problem solving in which you think there is something wrong, but you are not sure what. Messes are not problems, but they generally indicate the lurking presence of a problem.

Revision qualified as a mess in my library. This business, à la Parkinson's Law, of checking someone else's work, debilitated staff independence and pride in work. The revision message was clear: Staff could not be trusted. And our dedication to revision and rework took away hours and hours from getting books to the shelves.

Many staff could indeed be trusted, and revising all of their work was not the answer to increased productivity. We stopped revising the work of experienced staff. New staff were trained well. Senior staff work was revised voluntarily or revised when team leaders had reason to believe revision was needed.

Layers of Convenience

As we streamlined TS, we began to peel away layers of imposed procedures. These layers of extra work, of extra steps, were added for the convenience of librarians outside TS. Often these extraordinary procedures involved double checking, hand copying details, and seeking and finding information so someone outside TS would feel more comfortable in making decisions. No doubt to the requestor these were insignificant demands, but when compounded, they delayed workflow.

Stopping these practices led to quicker turnaround times, but we had minimal success in getting buy-in for streamlining among people external to TS.

I recall an eye-opening meeting at which a TS support staff supervisor revealed his statistical findings about each bibliographer's workflow in book selection. His statistical charts exposed several book selectors who appeared oblivious to what happens to a system when a raft of book orders comes in the last day of the month or during one week at the end of the year.

That meeting helped more than a few bibliographers comprehend that this practice results in an uneven distribution of work, delayed acquisition, backlogs—and delays getting books to readers.

Who's in Charge Here?

When you move toward self-management, toward empowerment, some staff members will want to know who is in charge. This was a question we never quite resolved, and the resulting confusion about empowerment could have been lessened if we had taken the time to talk it through. A few staff members, perversely enough, thought empowerment freed them to make their own schedules and pick their own work without talking to team leaders.

Overall, support staff gained the most from the new levels of freedom—more elbow room. Support staff—including some who had been sidelined for years—were instrumental in helping us make progress, often bringing brilliant ideas and short cuts, ideas that revised how we did our work and gained us large savings in resources.

A few of the former library department heads were fearless in allowing staff to think about their work and were able to adjust their attitudes and free up those workers, to work with them more as colleagues and less as subordinates. Although we did not solve the puzzle of letting go, we glimpsed enough of the positive side to believe firmly that less control is better than too much.

The ultimate challenge was the library's being a team organization in a command and control culture, an academic bureaucracy. People outside the library humored us in our team culture, but looked askance at the possibility of applying a similar approach in their bailiwicks. Keeping what they had, the way they had always had it, was their preference. We discovered, as an island of teams in an ocean of bureaucracies, that we had to explain, repeatedly, what we were doing and request special exemption from hierarchical processes, like the university's performance appraisal system. While the parent organization persisted in its hierarchical ways, we increasingly became the odd man out.

ACCOMPLISHMENTS

Here is how we did on a few of the most important elements found in the K&S formula for highly effective teams.

In most of our TS teams, **purpose/mission** was clear and understood by each team member. For these teams, success depended on the team's achieving the performance goals explicit in their purpose and mission. Performance goals were measurable. They had substance, and they were achieved in a timely way. In other words, something the team "touched" literally was changed for the better. The goal, if clear and compelling, pulled a team forward; it drew the team toward figuring out the best way to achieve the goal. Invariably, problematic teams were weak in purpose and mission and in other of the K&S variables.

Although rarely explicit in our most successful teams, **member roles** were tacitly stated, agreed upon, and understood. However, we did not achieve enough clarity about the role of the team leader. Although I compressed my role into three major functions—coaching, consulting, and leading—the roles of other team leaders were never clearly defined. Mostly, titles changed but the work relationships remained the same, so that the head of the Serials/Acquisitions Department became the leader of the serials/acquisitions team.

I recall a chart from industry for self-managing work teams, which showed the progression of the supervisor from the center of the team circle to the rim, and then off adrift to the side. Eventually, still afloat, the supervisor appears to be responsible—with invisible links—for *several* work teams. With the exception of my own role, most team leaders remained stuck in the center of their teams, rarely becoming one of the team or moving out of that circle as a coach/consultant.

Theirs was a genuine dilemma. If not making hands-on workflow decisions or imposing an expert will on the system, what did former department heads, now team leaders, do? Understandably—given our lack of clarity and training in what team leaders were to do—most kept doing the job they had been doing, albeit less autocratically. Of course a few believed teams were great—as long as they got to be captain!

My situation was somewhat different because I was assiduously giving away authority and responsibility, all the while coaching and consulting the former department heads. My immediate peers behaved more like the AULs of old, rather than taking on any of the roles laid out below. And there were days when even I wondered about becoming superfluous.

A less-discerning and unsupportive boss might have concluded that my new job roles were not the essential drivers for what we achieved. These were my primary roles, although I retained a large amount of administrative responsibility, including monitoring the budget:

- *Coaching*

  Helping

Challenging

Encouraging

- *Consulting*

   Investigating new ways

   Intervening

   Walking about

- *Leading*

   Eliminating barriers

   Managing "handoffs"

   Recommending

   Translating the vision

No question about it, TS teams could have done a better job in paying attention to the *how* of working together. These questions were rarely asked: How will we make decisions? How will we work through problems? How will we give each other feedback? How much risk will we take?

Regrettably, our training was limited, so it never took us far enough in this essential area of team building. We focused on getting the job done and hoped for the best when it came to relationship building and effective communication, both central to building trust and confidence in performance.

Outcomes drove the team's purpose. Initially, the team leaders and I set what we regarded as achievable team goals and identified who would do what and what resources it would take. The staff delivered on our expectations. Later, in keeping with our interpretation of self-managing teams, we asked team members to set their own goals. Their goals were higher each year!

Job *deadlines* were stated and respected among TS teams. Most understood that time was inelastic—gone were the days when we looked upon it as unlimited. Action, even with mistakes, was always preferred to no action with lots of analysis.

Demonstrable *support* did come from the "top"—at least during our golden years. However, we did have difficulty with the concept that the team leader was an active participant in unit teams. Some teams thought they could go off and do their own thing without discussion with a team leader or with me. Although it was delusional for any team to think it had gotten a pass from being accountable to its team leader, a few did.

Some resisted the concept that teams were *accountable* to the organizational leadership. Effective teams do not set their own agendas—not even self-managing teams—but some believed they could, much to my dismay. I supported maximum creative freedom for each team. They could question the basic assumptions. They could harass the sacred cows. If money was an issue, they could petition for more money and suggest creative ways to save money. But I believe that every team needs outside guidance, objective feedback to keep it in sync with other teams.

Our early success was enabled by the promises made and kept by the library's leader: no layoffs, no loss of jobs, and we would get to keep any money saved through salary attrition to use for equipment and staffing in TS and other parts of the library.

We shared our sizable gains. We followed a policy of open budgets. Salary savings were tracked monthly and a percentage assigned to TS. Team leaders reviewed monthly budget printouts and talked with me about ways to use savings. The branch libraries and public service units benefited from our streamlining with staff transfers and the purchase of equipment. We were able to implement new technological applications and address long-delayed needs—for example, retrospective conversion was launched out of salary savings and reassigned staff.

Training and Development

We invested in staff training, with mixed results. Technical training for better use of the TS databases and better use of productivity software was generally helpful. The outcome of using university trainers for teamwork, TQM, participatory management, and organizational change was less satisfactory.

These consultants had rarely worked in teams and had only elementary ideas about TQM. External consultants were hardly better. My suspicion was that these experts were pretty thin when it came to real experience. They talked the game, but had never played it.

A scarcity of players was a problem overall—there was a lack of other team-based institutions with whom we could relate. One or two other libraries were professing team-based structures, but on closer inspection, they seemed to be working more at the emotional and attitudinal level (the how of group dynamics) than on improving the library and achieving higher productivity.

Although coming up empty in much of the out-of-the-box team training, we did develop one staff development program that helped us develop camaraderie, risk taking, and creativity: adventure learning.

We offered backpacking trips, rock climbs, ropes courses, orienteering, and several "days in the woods" full of team building and problem solving. Our program was built around metaphors and designed to show new juxtapositions and possibilities. Our point was that none of us was immutably fixed in place—we were all capable of new things and new ways of working. The circle was our most obvious metaphor—it surfaced in every post-adventure discussion to describe our community, of how we worked together and how we literally supported each other.

Over the course of our adventuring, about a fifth of the total library staff volunteered to take part, mostly support staff. In TS a much larger contingent took and met the challenge. That our facilitators were two former Outward Bound instructors raised the probability for success. Their background gave them an outstanding ability to challenge us, guide us toward teamwork, and help us extract relevant, sometimes profound, meaning from each experience.

Our days in the woods had much to do with the success of the TS change efforts. I doubt it was coincidence that several of the people driving change in TS were active and frequent participants in outdoor learning. And upon reflection, those days did address in candid ways the how of our working together, how we would support each other, and how we made decisions.

WHAT I WOULD DO DIFFERENTLY

Train all staff in team concepts and practices. Make that training hands on with opportunities to practice team leadership and teamwork situations. Emphasize feedback giving, question asking, and dealing with dysfunctional team leaders and members.

Experiment with different kinds of teams and with turn taking in leading teams. Swap out team leaders to avoid the trap of expert control.

Cross train team members to help other teams.

Adjust the salary infrastructure to better reflect equal levels of teamwork.

Identify the level of empowerment in teams. Make clear the roles of the team leader, the team sponsor or overseer, and other leaders.

Recognize that some staff members may be team averse *and* productive. Accept them as uncomfortable with the team concept but essential to getting the work out.

Jettison any system of performance appraisal—which we did. Replace it with a culture of regular and respectful feedback, well considered and timely. Annually, have a conversation with each staff member about goals and aspirations. *They* talk, you listen.

Teach critical thinking, problem recognition, and factual decision making.

Seek diplomatic solutions to conflict between TS and other teams or departments that regularly interact with TS. Build strong relationships with units outside of TS. Appoint TS ambassadors to work with other units to reach mutually beneficial arrangements.

Ensure fair and adequate recognition of accomplishments in TS. When gains in TS benefit other units, make sure there is recognition of the TS staff and the benefiting staff.

Confront the naysayers early on. It is a mistake to ignore negative rumors about team efforts in TS in hopes the rumor mongers will go away or become reasonable as you demonstrate success. Your success is more reason for opponents to fear teams. Ignore them, and they will become more audacious.

Teach how to disagree agreeably.

CONCLUSION

In the late 1990s TS teams began to gravitate toward the traditional hierarchy. The main reason was the same as why we had abandoned the hierarchy a decade before: a new university president. The incumbent president was known for loosely holding the administrative reins, for encouraging independence and an entrepreneurial sprit. His promotion of TQM applications provided a protective shield for the library.

When he stepped down, the trustees recruited his replacement from the command and control tradition. It appeared they were seeking to dispel the "Who's in charge here?" question they might have had about the prior president's style. Not long after the new president's arrival, she quickly made clear her preference for the traditional model of administrative oversight—the days of proactive exploration and work innovation, at least in the library, quickly came to an end.

The incumbent librarian, hired by the previous president, realized his preference for an innovative organization was not going to fit in a bureaucracy. He had been highly effective at "challenging the process and enabling others to act," but these were now less important attributes. He left.

Top-down decision making and bottom-up permission seeking were once again the preferred model. Looking back, during that period of four or five golden years, those "teams that were" achieved much—more than we dreamed, beyond everyone's expectations. We did *let go* and marveled at how well a TS organization of more than 100 people could climb what seemed an impossible mountain.

CHAPTER 5

Bridger and Me

This is a dog story. If you bear with me, you may gain some insights into how you lead and how you follow. Are you an assertive pack leader, or are you a submissive follower?

Bridger, my daughter's nine-month-old Labrador, recently spent some quality time with me. The dog needed a place to stay while my daughter was away for three weeks of training.

I've not had a dog for decades, but I had seen a few of Cesar Millan's *Dog Whisperer* shows, so I knew to be *au courant* with dog management I'd need to do more for Bridger than feed her and let her sleep.[1] Cesar's mantra for healthy dogs is exercise, discipline, and affection. This struck me as wise, so I steeled myself for an hour-long early morning walk and to behave in a way that the dog would not be confused about who the pack leader was: me. That was the plan.

It is tempting for anyone who followed the weekly adventures of those canine savants, Lassie and Rin Tin Tin, to think of dogs as more than dogs. We are drawn to dogs, and they to us. Jack London's *The Call of the Wild* is great adventure literature with universal insights, but to try to extract leadership concepts from my mundane daily walks and other routine dog/human interactions may be a stretch.[2] Of course, sometimes it is the ordinary that brings clarity to a concept.

Reservations aside, including Cesar's admonition in every televised episode that dogs are not children, it is easy to anthropomorphize our canine friends. For example, in my management class lecture on staff performance appraisal, I use an airline ad—an upward evaluation of a human by Baxter, a dog, suggesting his owner's performance would improve if he took Baxter to the dog park more often. And along this line, I can dream up the next best-selling management book: *Dog-ness: Instilling the Way of the Pack into GenX Work Teams.*

Well, how did it work out between Bridger and me?

According to Cesar, "In the animal world, there are two positions: the leader and the follower." Perhaps we humans are at more complicated, graduated levels, but now and then it seems our behaviors in the workplace throw us back into a kinship with the pack. Something very similar to the barnyard's pecking order is easily discernible in the workplace.

William Golding's *Lord of the Flies* (1962) went so far as to suggest man's inherent savagery was only kept under wraps by enforced societal norms. Remove the norms, we revert to a dog eat dog existence. That analogy is unfair to the canine clan, because once a top dog is established, dog followers pretty much line up. It is only we cunning humans, like Golding's boys and Shakespeare's villains, who, consumed with ambition, seek to undermine leaders.

Well, I may not agree with Mr. Golding's dismal assessment of the human condition, but I do know we need to make conscious efforts not to become like his wild boys. I also am certain that leading or following is not a fixed role. Although I wish I could say definitely that I was the pack leader to Bridger, on reflection I am not all that sure. There were times when the pack leader role was up for grabs, and there were times when it seemed nobody was in charge.

Was that bad? Cesar says not to confuse the dog about who's boss. "This can cause aggression, anxiety, fear, obsessions, or phobias . . . ." Hmmm, just like my last library job. Only kidding! (Sorta!)

I don't know how on target Cesar is about pack leader/submissive follower relationships. There's a bit of California-new-age-dog-psychology speak that creeps into his language. His voice is more certain about disciplining for specific behaviors, like Bridger's lunging on the leash.

Bridger about to take flight after a squirrel, devil take the hindmost.
Used with permission of John Lubans Jr.

That behavior made our initial walks high stress and less than pleasant. Other dog owners offered me advice, more than enough to confuse me. The least effective advice—a canine version of the "keep 'em guessing" workplace strategy —was for me to halt the dog, turn, and head the other way.

Then, after a few steps, I'd stop and turn around again, thereby confusing the dog about the goal toward which it was pulling me; hence the lunging would decrease. I tried it and it worked for several yards, and then Bridger would single-mindedly revert to rushing headlong.

The disciplinary tactic that worked was a mix of Cesar's prescription to be a calm and assertive leader (let your posture show you are in charge, shorten the leash, keep the dog alongside, etc.) and a friend's suggestion to reward Bridger for the walk behaviors I wanted. So, whenever Bridger walked alongside of me at a steady pace, she would get a pebble of dog food. Very quickly, she lunged less and accommodated my slower pace.

After my weeks with Bridger, I scored something like a B+ on the Dog Whisperer's leadership quiz. While declaring me "Pack Leader" and entitling me to buy Cesar's Pack Leader sweatshirt and cap, the virtual Dog Whisperer hedged: "Congratulations! You are well on your way to having a balanced, calmsubmissive dog, if you don't already have one. However, you may still have a few areas that could use improvement, or *you* may be lacking the *discipline* and *consistency* that your dog requires."

I italicize the terms—*you, discipline , consistency*—to remind me of some of my ambiguity about the leader/follower roles. As I tried to get Bridger to accommodate my tempo and my need to not be jerked around, I was often reminded of my way of leading. Or, as some would say, my way of non-leading. I have always preferred to let people do their best on their own with maximum support from me and minimum *discipline*. There were times when I probably should have disciplined staff more, to let them know they could do better. Cesar has insights relevant to how a manager's behavior on the job could influence others, sometimes not for the better: "[M]any owners assume it's their dog that is the problem. I try to help people understand that their *own* behavior has a powerful affect on their dog, and I offer them suggestions for 'retraining' themselves to be calm-assertive pack leaders."

Indeed, when I was working as a library administrator, a few did question whether my hands-off approach added value to the library leadership equation. Of course, anyone interested in end results would see the plus side in my method of letting go of the reins of power. However, some managers were so uncomfortable with this notion that they ignored our unprecedented productivity; for whatever reason these managers valued maintaining the pecking order above achieving our desired goals. That said, I have to admit there were a few situations in which my hands-off approach was not the right one. I recall one work group (the very antithesis of self-organizing) of seemingly incorrigible and self-destructive staff that never did improve. A hands-on approach was long overdue. By the time I applied it, it was too late.

**Bridger humoring me, playing the calm submissive role
(There's a cookie in that pocket, right?)**

Bridger did humor me and occasionally became the submissive follower in our walks. Left to her own devices, she would prefer much more freedom to do what she excels at: leaping over fallen logs, chasing squirrels, sniffing out dead frogs in mounds of leaves, dragging twigs and sticks with head held high, exploring unseen trails, and, when so moved, cavorting for the sheer joy of it! And there were some odors that took priority over walking down the trail. They had to be sniffed, lingered over, reflected upon. Dog-ness is about seizing the day. Understandably, I would get in her way, holding her back from doing what she was born to do: achieve dog-ness. Would Bridger have been happiest with me totally out of the way? Without discipline? I do not believe so. There is a bond between dog and master above the fundamental need for food and shelter. At times she would have preferred freedom to come and go, but after she learned the trick of backing out of her collar, she would always return to me.

Yes, leaders often interfere with what followers want to do. Sometimes we frustrate followers. Who is right? Bridger, for wanting to eradicate squirrels, or me, for not wanting to be yanked off my feet? I would guess we are both right and need to reach an accommodation, in which I get to stay on my feet and avoid a dislocated shoulder and Bridger gets to chase the occasional squirrel.

For the "my way or the highway" leader there is no room for such ambiguity. When I ran across the disciplinarian dog owner, Bridger would want to play, but this type of dog owner takes pride in the dog staying focused, murmuring "good dog, good dog" as master and dog ignored and ran wide of us. Bridger would look forlornly after them, one ear cocked.

Under this kind of leader Bridger would have to "heel" and forget those squirrels or suffer the consequences. That's sort of the way our dualistic theory of management works. There are two kinds of workers, the responsible and the irresponsible. The latter stereotype demands discipline, prodding, reminding, nagging, oversight, and corrective action by the manager. The other kind of worker is an intuitive self-starter, eager to work and do his or her best. The manager's job is help make that happen.

In my experience there are far more of the responsible group than the other. Yet most of our control systems, workplace "leashes," are designed for the irresponsible and take a vastly disproportionate amount of our time away from meaningful work. There are numerous other controls, often invisible, that make up library-ness, the customs and the mores, the do's and don'ts.

What happens when there is an absence of leash? What happens in the library workplace when supervisors lighten up? Do workers go wild? Do workers become indolent, willful, and self-destructive? In my experience, minimizing the organizational controls that inhibit creativity, impede freedom of expression, and require permission before doing, consistently result in greater productivity, greater service, and more staff who like their jobs.

The potential of what *can* happen with less control is captured in this statement from a member of the *conductor-less* Orpheus Chamber Orchestra, as videotaped in Hackman's *Nobody on the Podium* (2002b): "When you have an orchestra with a conductor, it is always leashed. . . . In Orpheus, the energy that's there doesn't get leashed. It's there, . . . and then it starts to go!" (Into a beautiful musical performance.)

Being unleashed in the workplace can be like that. I saw it happen in a major reform I led. All the controls put into place over years of idolizing the sacred cow of AACR2 had tied the hands of the staff. Many of my administrative peers regarded those layered rules as best practice. In short, we were suffering from a long-running tyranny of the experts. Good, thinking people were prohibited from using their common sense. We looked foolish to our users, who wanted books, not rationalizations as to why we could not work any faster. These staff members were more than leashed—they were chained to an iron stake in a fenced backyard.

As we undid the controls—releasing the energy that had always been there—using our collective intelligence to the best of our ability and blending leader and follower roles, we found the freedom to bring about the needed reforms.

LEADERS AND DOGS

Roland Huntford's book (1986) about the explorer Shackleton talks about how dogs were considered but rejected or misapplied for exploring the ice- and snow-covered regions. Horses were preferred in spite of evidence of the dogs' overall excellence for polar exploration.

As a result, the Norwegians on dogsleds flew by the British teams and their horses in pursuit of the South Pole. The horses fell through the thick snow cover, while the dogs padded calmly and smoothly over. There was no contest, except perhaps in who could suffer the greatest amount of self-induced hardship. Shackleton won that contest hands down, with courage and distinction, many would say. But much of the suffering could have been avoided had he used dogs instead of horses. And when he finally made a concession to use dogs, he could have used them better.

Huntford quotes Roald Amundsen, the Norwegian explorer who won the race to the South Pole—"Some misunderstanding must lie behind the English view of the use of the Eskimo dog in the polar regions. Could it be that the dog has not understood his master? Or is it the master who has not understood his dog?" (1986, 171)—a classic statement on the relationship between follower and leader, between servant and master. The more we understand each other, the better off our mutual endeavors will be.

THE WAY OF THE DOG

The way of the dog is doing what you were born to do. Bridger knows what that means. Humans may not. We may be dancers who pore over publisher catalogs to select books and never move to the music in our muscles , or we may be farmers who negotiate data access contracts, never seeing the sky, the hawk's shadow in the tall grass as it swoops overhead.

Because dogs are not willful creatures, it was difficult to be the disciplinarian with Bridger. A thing of beauty, she got away with much that left me frustrated. But in the way of the dog, infractions are quickly forgotten. A short memory has many advantages. Add other attributes like unstinting loyalty and ferocious friendliness to one and all, with no unseemly ambition, and you have an ideal companion, a gallant colleague with whom to conquer dragons.

Both of us learned about each other. I like to think we met somewhere in the middle. In my study, after our walks, she'd lay her head in my lap and look up at me with the most peaceful expression, as if saying "All's right with the world, mate." I'd turn to my work, and she would lie for hours in companionable silence next to my chair—content to be near. Now and then, I'd look away from the computer screen and catch a glimpse of dog-ness: Happily contented, Playful. Trusting.

Time for a cookie!

CHAPTER 6

The Invisible Leader: Lessons for Leaders from the Orpheus Chamber Orchestra

In its thirty-third year, the Orpheus Chamber Orchestra dazzles still. The "Wow!" of a first time listener and the polished accolades of international music critics— "One of the great marvels of the musical world"—confirm Orpheus's musical success.

Orpheus plays without a conductor, that nucleus of orchestral music. There's no podium, no one waving a baton, directing musicians what beat to keep or sound to make. That there's no boss runs contrary to accepted "best" practice in the autocratic music world and the corporate realm: *somebody* has to be in charge, otherwise it's anarchy, a cacophony going nowhere. Orpheus's contrarian approach consistently *proves* what leadership theorists (Marshall 1992), as far back as Lao Tzu, the sixth-century BC Taoist, *claim* is possible: self-management and high achievement.

Boss-lessness is hardly Orpheus's reason for being. Their main purpose is to make beautiful music, on their terms. It is *how* Orpheus moves idea to product, how these musicians work together toward a perfect performance, that offers much to the business world, particularly to groupings of professionals who want to keep their flat structures loosely knit, with high energy, participation, and fresh, creative output.

Orpheus is not leader*less*. The members are the first to tell you, "Every piece of music requires leadership." How Orpheus differs is that the leader (the concert master, the chief of the process, for *each* piece of music) and the follower roles are rotated frequently and deliberately to keep perspectives and music fresh. About a third of the orchestra regularly serves as concert masters. The concert master and the first chairs of the musical sections make up what is called a "core," usually six musicians, with as many as four cores for one concert.

Core players are responsible for the initial decisions about the shape and character of the music. They are to identify an orchestral "voice," agreeing on the interpretation of the composer's score. It is in the core that the process of *integration* first glimmers—where the best thinking of virtuoso musicians blends into something more than one person could envision.

A core is Orpheus's concession to efficiency—it takes less time in sorting out and shaping the music than would the entire orchestra. Prior to inventing the core, the full orchestra staged marathon rehearsals far into the night, which overburdened even the most energetically democratic of the Orpheus troupe.

Were famed management theorist Mary Parker Follett (1996b) living, she would regard the core as a splendid example of what best leadership is about: "Leader and followers are both following *the invisible leader*—the common purpose." This notion of leading has "penetrated" the organization.

There's a tacit commitment in the core to speak truthfully, to not settle for "good enough." That commitment carries over to the full rehearsal, at which musicians, besides those in a core, chime in with precise commentary economically stated, with much fine tuning of nuances and interpretations (see sidebar).

Following a composer's score is not "painting by the numbers." At best, the composer's score is an incomplete road map—numerous turnings and interpretations are possible—light, dark, tense, relaxed, dreamy, moody, exhilarated. Simone Young, a conductor, defines conducting: "I am an *advocate* for the composer—my place is to bring the will of the composer (in the most honest way that I can *interpret* it) to the minds of the musicians and on to the hearts of the audience." Hence conductors (and Orpheus) are hailed as geniuses or reviled as wannabes based on how well they interpret the composer's intent.

Any musician who believes the interpretation is wanting can stop the music to tell everyone what's bugging him or her. Based on observing several rehearsals, about half of the players (different in each rehearsal) actively engage in refining the piece being rehearsed. "Say it, sing it, play it" is the catchphrase for the communications skill set essential in an Orpheus rehearsal. The sidebar illustrates the several prevailing "norms"—tacit understandings that give players permission to critique. All of these norms apply to nonmusical groups, for example, "It's OK to say I don't know."

Rehearsal Norms: Overheard at Rehearsal

An Orpheus rehearsal is a collaboration of experts; disagreement happens within the bounds of mutual respect. Two or more clashing views are explored and merged, sometimes creating a superior third interpretation, other times settling on the best of the two ideas. All ideas get their turn, even bad ones. Strict time limits keep the discussion economical.

It's OK to say "I don't know":

"I can't figure it out, can you play it for me?"

If you don't agree, say so, and explain your thoughts:

"It needs more glue."

"We should do this a bit slower; some people are not getting it."

"Winds, answer our (strings') gesture. Rather than just being on time, answer our gesture."

Above all else, keep a sense of humor:

After a long discussion without agreement the player bemusedly tells the group: "I have to play it." The group responds: "We have to listen to it." (All laugh.)

Keep asking until you really understand:

"Is there any way to push up the tempo?" A wind speaks up to the group, "Do you want an organ sound or a chorale sound—what's the style you want?"

Criticize the music, not the player:

"We're trying to stay with you—points to ear—can't hear you."

"There's too much of a 'we're in the forest' [sound]."

"Let it happen, don't push it."

Orpheus's high level of engagement, its aspiration to excellence, exacts a personal cost. These musicians study the entire score, not just their instruments' segments; they listen to recordings of the entire piece and practice individually most days. For one player, gaining a 10 percent improvement in performance means working 30 percent harder than in a conductor-led rehearsal. Doing so takes sacrifice, and was, until recent years, largely uncompensated. That sacrifice represents the necessary involvement that leads to a better product. "At this level of participation, we own the company," says an Orphean.

"You must hate conductors" is an assumption some listeners make about Orpheus. One year the Orpheus marketing flier featured a snapped baton—an icon of what this orchestra is *not* about. Dispensing with the conductor, Orpheus confounds our accepted ways of working, of following, of being led. How Orpheus works questions the conventional definition of leader: to envision and direct.

Yet Orpheus members will tell you: "We don't hate conductors." What Orpheus does hate is abdicating personal responsibility. These musicians want a say in their music. They want elbow room, just like anyone else, to make the decisions that influence their work. And they want their expert voices to be heard. In fact, Orpheus is an unintended training ground for conductors, with two current players taking up the baton from time to time and three emeriti conducters, one full time!

Further proof of Orpheus's détente with the conducting kingdom is that the recently formed Orpheus Artistic Advisory Council features the maestro conductor James Levine of the Metropolitan Opera.

The contrast between a conductor-led rehearsal and an Orpheus rehearsal is immediately apparent. Under the baton, communication is almost always one way. Eric Bartlett, cellist, says that the ready give and take at Orpheus is never seen in a large orchestra. You simply, "cannot comment like [that] to a symphony conductor." Eric adds, "The large orchestra is built around the notion that the conductor's authority is absolute. If he/she were ever to accept advice or a suggestion from a member of the orchestra, it would have to be done in private . . . . Any other scenario would suggest weakness."

Jenny Douglass, a substitute viola player, says the "difference between playing with Orpheus and traditional conductors is that you are fully engaged, not just following the leader." If two people have different ideas, they try it both ways and then decide *together* how it will be done in the end. "They really try it both ways *without* not trying." The honest discussion of an Orpheus rehearsal is "riskier," yet for Douglass, all the "extra work and self-investment makes playing *more fulfilling*."

"I learned more about conducting by watching you rehearse, than I have in all my conducting classes." That is what a Juilliard School of Music conducting student had to say after sitting in on an Orpheus rehearsal. While this student one day will be a conductor, he now better understands there is a process for and value in soliciting ideas from the players—the people doing the work. And although that may sound obvious to most managers, it is a lesson worth restating and practicing.

ORPHEUS TAKE-AWAYS FOR THE NONMUSICAL BOSS

Take turns leading take turns following.

Encourage independent and articulate critical thinking.

Manage your self; disagree agreeably.

Listen with all your heart.

Be responsible toward the organization.

Demonstrate a philosophy of work that values followers and leaders.

Not everyone agrees that the Orpheus model of music making is best. One critic (Tommasini 2008) prefers the conductor model: "A conductor would make it better, but with a conductor it wouldn't be Orpheus." Paradoxically, the critic seems to believe a boss man would improve Orpheus's sound. He is not alone in what may be a genetic predisposition toward a pecking order, a social Darwinism. Some one *has* to be in charge for things to really work. For this same critic, Orpheus's sound is not as refined or precise as it could be because "of infinitesimal uncertainties natural to pure democracies. Pinpoint agreement of pitch and gesture is stretched to a kind of benign vagueness."

Some people just can't trust the process—there has to be a boss, and they are it! When the Teutonic chanteuse, Ute Lemper, guested with Orpheus, "Ms. Lemper made sure no one could miss any points, right down to the . . . orchestra, *which she kept conducting with her left arm.*"

There are imperfections and limitations in the Orphean model. At one rehearsal the timpanist never raised his head from the soccer magazine he was reading, and similarly, one of the horn players multitasked between the musical score and the *Daily News.* More significantly, a former executive director told me that at times Orpheus may choose to "not do things we don't like, like holding ourselves accountable to the highest standards of musicianship or confronting players no longer performing well enough." For example, Orpheans still talk about the violinist who turned into a tyrant whenever it was her turn as concert master. *Five or six years* passed before she was finally confronted. To everyone's relief, she quit the organization.

Of course the hierarchy may not do much better in dealing with those "things we don't like to do"—it may, at times, do worse.

Orpheus recognizes that orchestras exceeding forty or fifty musicians in size may be too complex for the Orpheus model: the distances between seats among 120 players interrupt the required intimacy and congest the sight lines.

So, although the Orpheus model will not fit all organizations or situations, elements of Orpheus are relevant to most organizations. Their ideas may be most applicable in keeping leadership fresh in organizations of the right size with an unchanging repertoire. Many nonprofits come to mind, including service agencies and educational enterprises.

Connie Steensma, now in her second term as chair of the Orpheus Board of Directors, testifies to Orpheus's relevance to the business world. She has been an avid fan of Orpheus since 1987. Initially Connie was drawn by the beauty of the music—"these are my rock stars." Then, in the early 1990s, as the president of a consulting firm (The Accel Group), she was drawn to the ways in which Orpheus worked: the sharing of leadership, the taking of individual responsibility, and the literal movement of players to fit the musical sound. It dawned on her that *how* Orpheus worked just might apply to the business world. When faced with facilitating a merger of two corporate information technology departments, she applied several Orpheus-inspired ideas. She rotated the IT leadership and mixed levels of leaders and followers to the maximum advantage. Because of the Orpheus influence and, importantly, the "consummate professionalism of the IT staff involved"—and their desire for success—the IT merger clicked.

All has not gone smoothly for Orpheus. Julian Fifer, the cellist founder of Orpheus, left in 1999. Since then there have been three executive leaders. In 2002, after a series of financial and leadership crises, Orpheus was "on the brink" of dissolution—the music just about died. The classic elements of "founder's syndrome" had sapped the players' confidence and left some "traumatized" by uncertainty and ambiguity.

Connie Steensma, during her first term as chair of the Orpheus Board, guided Orpheus through the refiner's fire of that tumultuous thirtieth year. Responding to the musicians' pleas, "You have to save Orpheus," she applied her consulting knowledge, helping the musicians not just get past the immediate crisis but decide *what* they wanted to be.

The orchestra regrouped and concluded it wanted to be a viable and *continuing* institution. While their music lingers in the hearts of the audience after each concert, Orpheus believes its way of working—the how—is a large part of their legacy. According to Connie and several musicians, Orpheus now has "a view of the future . . . a common view." It is a shared vision that seeks to perpetuate Orpheus's unique music making and *leadership*.

An essential task, after their near-musical-death experience, was to recast Orpheus's administrative infrastructure to help the organization achieve well-planned and -managed development. The musicians recalled how the dynamics changed not for the best when Julian, the cellist founder, stopped playing and became the full-time executive director. Nor did the two succeeding EDs play in the orchestra. The next-to-last executive was seen by many players, amid reports of shouting matches and bad feelings, as more boss than colleague, someone who was imposing his will on the business side and trespassing into musical decision making.

The organization opted for a higher risk model, a return to its roots, replacing the executive director position with a player/leader akin to the managing partner idea in some law firms. Ronnie Bauch, a longtime Orpheus violinist, was persuaded by Connie in 2002 to lead the organization *and* to keep playing. To help him balance the two roles, Ronnie negotiated for the *business* side of the organization to be as professional as the artistic. On the business side sits Graham Parker, general director, entrusted with much of the day-to-day operations. He, Ronnie, and three *elected* senior musician "coordinators" share in the running of the organization with its annual $4 million budget.

Unpretentious and unassuming—Ronnie dispensed with the "Executive Director" title and converted the former ED's office into a meeting room—he seems the perfect *unboss*. His understated, thoughtful approach is what Orpheus needed. Three years later, Orpheus is solvent and spirits are high. New initiatives include the Orpheus Institute at Juilliard, a platform for broadcasting the Orpheus approach to music. And there's a fascinating collaboration with the Manhattan School of Music in which Orpheus musicians coach the MSM student orchestra to play without a conductor.

As solicitous and protective as Ronnie is of his musician colleagues, so are they of him. Eric Bartlett, for one, is concerned about the potential burnout in Ronnie's two-headed role. He hopes that various initiatives to ensure Orpheus' long-term stability will thrive and lessen the financial stresses and anxieties to which Orpheus (and most art groups in this country) can often succumb. An endowment would help. Orpheans will tell you that in the not too distant past, "Our 'endowment' was Mr. ____'s (a Board member) American Express card!" This angel would annually (and most generously) pluck the organization out of its red ink. An endowment, of course, would steady Orpheus and lessen the predictable administrative angst over a deficit.

Another plus is that Ronnie shares willingly, with Graham and the artistic, program, and personnel coordinators, the load of running the organization—a semipermanent administrative version of an Orpheus musical core.

Legacy Unfolding

It is Orpheus's opening night at Carnegie Hall for the 2005/2006 season. To-night they're partnering with the legendary pianist Richard Goode in perform-ing pieces by Mozart and J. C. Bach. Orpheus also has two solo pieces. One is Luigi Cherubini's 1801 *Overture to Faniska*.

Harumi Rhodes, a twenty-three-year-old newcomer to Orpheus, is the concert master for the Cherubini. Her musical ambition, harking back to the mythical Orpheus, the orchestra's namesake, is to "create even just one magical moment for someone who is really listening." With an imperceptible gesture from her, the music starts quietly, an awakening, a blending of gentle and strong, then, a gathering of musical forces, stirring the audience. Heads lift and eyebrows raise. Cherubini's lyrical music soars to Carnegie's heights, magically permeates the hall's golden light, and touches the listener's heart.

Epilogue

At opening night at Carnegie Hall in October 2008 Ronnie Bauch was hon-ored with the first Orpheus Leadership Award and a new title: Senior Advisor and Managing Director Emeritus. He continues to play in the orchestra—he played that night—but has stepped away from the rigors of his directorial re-sponsibilities to focus on his music. Albeit assuming a different role, the Board of Trustees' chair said this about Mr. Bauch: "We look forward to working with him in his new capacity . . . certain that the same steady hand and clear mind will ensure the future of this vital and irreplaceable orchestra."

CHAPTER 7

Southwest: The Unstodgy Airline

In an industry where many falter and fail, how does an organization stay profitable and resilient?

One company appears to do this better than most: Southwest Airlines. What's the secret? Is it some locked-up algorithm of ticket price, available seat miles, and inventory allocations? Sure, Southwest's inventory is parked less than other airlines, but getting fully booked flights takes more than that. Visionary leaders? They help, yet those same leaders disavow any top-down, cause-and-effect relationship for success. How, after thirty-four years and with a workforce of more than 32,000, does Southwest make money and avoid enfeeblement, even while reeling from the economic body slam of September 11, 2001?

In search of an answer, I sampled a slice of life at Southwest: the ramp agent team—a group not dissimilar to the folks who work in our library circulation departments. During several days at the Raleigh Durham airport (RDU), I glimpsed some of the attributes that make Southwest a consistent winner (see sidebar). Those attributes offer clues for improving any business, including libraries.

Ramp agents are Southwest's muscle. Southwest's president, Colleen Barrett (2000), sums up what ramp agents do:

> They touch every aspect of your flight, from the time you check your bags until you leave the baggage claims area. Ramp agents collect and sort your outbound luggage . . . and transport these items to the aircraft. They marshal the inbound flight into the gate, chock the tires, service the lavatories, and in some cities, provision the aircraft. . . . After the aircraft is closed up, ramp agents push the aircraft off the gate, disconnect the tow bar, and confirm with the pilots that the flight is ready to taxi.

Doing all that in twenty minutes or less gets as intense as NASCAR's pit lane, where crews make or break a run for the checkered flag. Ramp agents, far from the limelight, have their own race to run—the industry's monthly and annual Triple Crown: baggage handling, on-time performance, and customer complaints. Each point on the crown depends on how well ramp agents do their jobs; lost bags and slow turns are guaranteed to trigger customer complaints and late arrivals and departures.

Southwest Attributes

Letting Go

"We Compete Against Ourselves"

A Desirable Future

"If the Plane Sits, It's Not Making Money"

The Unstodgy Airline

"Help Each Other Out"

"It's the People"

LETTING GO

Southwest has little difficulty letting go of the command-and-control functions (the holding on) observable in companies and libraries, large and small. Gary Barron, the former executive vice president of operations, said, "I suspect that if you left our people to their own devices, it would run pretty smoothly out there, without us messing with it. Maybe it runs *despite* us messing with it. . . . Maybe it would run *better* without us messing with it" (Freiberg and Freiberg 1998, 232).

A vulnerable admission? Not for Southwest, where a healthy self-deprecation is encouraged and practiced. That humility produces an empowering climate for the many who thrive where there is mutual support and respect.

There's a risk—letting go can be seen as weakness, especially in command-and-control, stodginess-prone organizations. Well, the letting go I saw at Southwest did *not* mean leaders abandoning responsibility or becoming superfluous. Nor did it mean workers getting to pick and choose what they do.

When Executive Chairman Herb Kelleher asserts his job is to liberate people, he means the people get to use all their skills and talents without fear of punishment for doing whatever it takes to get the job done. It's known and practiced throughout the organization that if you make a mistake leaning toward the customer, you'll be forgiven.

Tricia Smith, field support representative for the Southeast region, explains with an organizational maxim: "It's easier to seek forgiveness than to ask for permission [at Southwest]." She's encouraging staff to be proactive, to do what is right. If you err, you'll be supported.

Letting go strengthens the relationship between follower and leader: many decisions are best made in consultation, rather than in isolation in an executive suite, and many decisions can be made by the frontline worker—within guidelines—without asking permission. Letting go is akin to Mary Parker Follett's (1996b, 188) classic term "integration," in which leaders and followers both "take orders" from the situation, rather than expecting the leader to make all decisions.

Although "legacy"—a word we've heard applied to libraries—airlines may deploy four or six ramp agents for each incoming plane, Southwest generally works with two or three. Supervisors often are on the front line doing "real work," besides observing and monitoring performance data. Supervisors, including the station manager, may be unloading carts they've hauled to the baggage claim area—a quarter mile away from the gates—or on hands and knees in one of the four bins unloading crammed-in bags.

Southwest ramp agents don't stand around waiting to be told what to do; they make decisions and anticipate next moves while getting their immediate jobs done. Anyone claiming "It's not my job" gets an earful from his or her teammates. Southwest's policy of trusting staff to make decisions, improvise, and help out makes their ramp agents contenders for every Triple Crown.

"WE COMPETE AGAINST OURSELVES"

Who is Southwest's closest competitor? Bart Dockins, operations supervisor, knows: "We compete against ourselves."

Southwest has a tradition of getting better, of making the next turn better than the last. That may explain why this airline, according to Jerry Useem's *Fortune* 2005 listing, is the number one most-admired company in the industry and gets top scores in employee talent, use of corporate assets, long-term investment, and innovation.

John Voyles, station manager at Orlando, echoes Bart: "We focus on being on time, and on local performance." Voyles, who served in the Air Force, likens each day's work to a military mission—there's "a specific target in mind."

Southwest is not aloof to the competition. They have a healthy respect for competitors, but they are less reactive to what the competition does than they are motivated to get better. Southwest's dedication to getting better keeps it out of the obituary pages.

A DESIRABLE FUTURE

The job ad for a ramp agent is a challenge: "Must be strong and agile, with ability to climb, bend, kneel, crawl, and work out-of-doors in hot and cold weather." Handling hundreds of seventy-pound bags and clambering in and out of luggage bins is distinctly unglamorous, yet essential.

"This work wears you out," is how Lori Fletcher, a five-foot-two member of the RDU team, candidly put it. She hopes to qualify as a flight attendant. Hers is not a vain hope. Southwest promotes from within—a policy confirmed to me numerous times by the Southwest people I met. Many enter as ramp agents and then move on to other work, from flight attendant, to operations, to head of station. Along the way, you can count on your colleagues to help you pursue your dream. A RDU ramp agent was helped by coworkers in his quest for a new job at Southwest—his teammates swapped shifts so he could go to school to qualify for that job.

Voyles, a former operations agent in Oakland, now station manager at Orlando, commented on how Southwest was different from other airlines: there is a "sense of pride, an enjoyment of the job. It's a career, not just a job."

Scott Noseworthy, a ramp agent in his first week at RDU, told me he likes how everyone helps with his training—he even enjoys the good-natured kidding he gets: "It's a family." I agree with his assessment. By my third visit to the RDU station, I was getting friendly punches in the arm and being asked, "Are you ready to join up?"

New and old staff train extensively—often for weeks at RDU and at Love Field in Dallas. The training emphasis reflects Southwest's patent approach of "hire attitude, train for skills." Training is anchored in Southwest's tradition and purpose, with heavy doses of aggressive customer service. The opportunity to learn on the job, in combination with the promote-from-within policy, helps Southwest people realize what most workers want: a desirable future.

There is a downside. The combination of the grueling, repetitive nature of ramp agent work and the potential for good pay (the hourly rate tops out at $23, plus overtime and very good benefits) can result in disgruntled employees— "lifers" is what they're called in some libraries. A few (5 percent was one estimate) ramp agents want to do something else but cannot qualify. Quitting is undesirable because it probably means a radically slimmer wallet. So, even if you are well-paid, if your job is boring, "It is easy to find things wrong," as Glen English, RDU's station manager, told me.[1] There is no easy way out of this dilemma, even at Southwest.

Southwest does offer opportunities for frank discussion between staff and top leadership, particularly during the national programs, Leaders on Location and the Message to the Field. The Message to the Field is held six times a year, usually at the larger airports. The meeting draws as many as 3,000 employees from all over the country to hear candid assessments by leadership, to get straight from the hip answers to tough questions, and—this is Southwest—to party.

Leaders on Location is an annual event, with vice presidents and directors from Love Field visiting sixty-one locations. Each leader goes to two or three airports and spends time with frontline staff, then hosts a lunch for station managers and supervisors to talk about the industry.

Recognition and respect can be as simple as RDU shop steward Will Engleman's all-you-can-eat barbecue for the staff working the July 4 holiday. English explains: Some of the "BBQs are to raise money for charity, but many are 'just because'."

"If the Plane Sits, It's Not Making Money"

Ramp agents are impressively aware of the corporate big picture—maybe not at the detailed level of a station manager, who is conversant with revenue passenger miles and available seat miles—but they firmly grasp the connection between what they do and the airline's profitability.

The efficiency tracking sheets posted at RDU were behind by a month when I was there, but there was no shortage of understanding about performance and profit. Lori Fletcher tells it the way it is: "If the plane sits, it's not making money."

The Unstodgy Airline

Many frequent flyers can recite from memory the impersonal verbal drill used by flight attendants to greet and inform passengers: "pull on the plastic tubing until fully extended . . ." or the ominous "or wherever your *final* destination may be" farewell.

Cabin crews at Southwest follow the FAA safety rules, but in ways uniquely Southwest. On my flight to Orlando, the attendant joked during the welcome message: "If you press the attendant call button, you get to stay and clean up." There's more, "We are lowering the lights, so you get real sleepy and we don't have to do anything."

Now that's different. And although it may surprise the rule abiders among us, a sense of humor does not mean you are a slacker. This same attendant helped, more than once, an elderly passenger who had difficulty walking and seemed disoriented at times. The plane was full—with many claims on both attendants—yet she persisted in asking him about his needs, making sure he understood he could have something to drink whenever he wanted.

Southwest encourages each staff member to "feel free to be yourself." This lack of pretense contributes to mutually beneficial relationships. An example is Voyles's regarding the Orlando union shop stewards as *leadership* positions, and his meeting monthly with them to discuss issues.

Irreverence is OK at Southwest; it has a purpose in sustaining humility, in pricking inflated egos. If a staff member terms Executive Chairman Herb Kelleher a "gregarious St. Bernard puppy" romping and making friends, it's OK. In the ramp agent break room, I noticed a poster announcing the next Message to the Field event. At the top was the headline: I AM SOUTHWEST, I AM . . . with a blank space for the inventive to write in their attributes. At RDU, the ramp agents had scribbled in "hungry, tired, horny . . . ." Glen saw the graffiti, remarked on it, but had no intention of whitewashing it.

The prevalent humility seems to reduce workplace conflict. Freiberg and Freiberg (1998, 220) tells us: "You will rarely find SW employees engaged in the kind of backbiting gossip that puts people down. It's as though there were an unwritten rule or cultural norm in the company that says, 'We don't talk bad about family member and teammates'."

Though "seldom is heard a discouraging word," at Southwest, love is an often-heard word. LUV is not just Southwest's clever stock listing abbreviation. Glen English, e-mailing me that Gary Barron is no longer with Southwest, spontaneously added, "He is, of course, still very respected and LUVed."

"You got to love what you do or you're not livin' life!" is how Tricia Smith sums up her on-the-job philosophy. "If you are happy and love what you do, then you will be able to deliver the customer service people deserve."

Tricia's philosophy comes through in a retelling of a story in *Employee Customer Relationship Video* (Southwest Airlines 2008a) about a young woman (Katie) who was flying on Southwest to a hospital for open heart surgery. She was 2,000 miles away from family. The Southwest counter agent (Darvina) knew from the reservation notes that Katie was heading into surgery and went out of her way to help. "An angel," is how Katie describes Darvina. "I felt like I was the only person in that airport." Darvina assured her all would be well: "I really needed to hear that," Katie says. And then Darvina followed through, calling her family at the hospital and checking on her progress. For Darvina, it is people like Katie who make all the difference in doing *her* job. Imagine that!

In a Southwest recruiting film, an operations agent states what he likes most about working at Southwest is, "The love I get from all my co-workers."

Love does not mean a lack of discipline or accommodating bad performance. Quite the opposite—if you care about people, you confront issues; not doing so is a lack of concern, a lack of respect. It is unloving to avoid giving constructive criticism or termination when an employee repeatedly fails to measure up.

"HELP EACH OTHER OUT"

Southwest is resourceful. Ramp agents know to plan ahead, to anticipate. Doing that ensures that equipment is where it should be. And if there is a shortage of equipment—for example, when all four gates are taken at RDU, there are not enough belt loaders to go around—that means adapting rather than delaying the process while waiting for equipment to become free. "Our turnaround time is not the result of tricks," Kelleher says (Freiberg and Freiberg 1998, 57) "but the result of our dedicated employees, who have the willpower and pride to do whatever it takes." On an occasion, pilots have helped empty luggage bins.

In Orlando, while waiting for my connecting flight, I timed a competitor's turn. Thirty long minutes after passengers exited into the terminal, their offloaded bags were sitting in trucks on the tarmac. Finally a tractor appeared to haul off the luggage. During that thirty minutes, I saw six staff members in and around the plane. Two were unloading luggage. The four who were not helping never made eye contact with the two luggage handlers. No wonder the last few bags came flying out of the bins to crash, most emphatically, on the tarmac.

I asked if "whatever it takes" was indeed widely practiced at Southwest. Bart's answer: "Some people help so much they miss their lunch."

Bill McCray, the training coordinator at RDU, strives to make sure that every ramp agent has the working knowledge "to think ahead, to anticipate, what needs doing." It's common sense to "help each other out," he told me. "Not helping is rare; you know if you are helped, you help in return."

"It's the people"

James MacGregor Burns defines leadership as "leaders inducing followers to act for certain goals that represent the values and the motivations . . . of both leaders and followers" (1978, 100).

Paraphrasing Burns, Southwest's organizational genius is found in the ways smart leaders engage followers in an enterprise that builds on their own and their followers' values and motivations.

Bart Dockins told me about a competing airline's spying on Southwest. They were at a distant gate, using binoculars, no doubt looking for Southwest's secrets to its world-famous quick turns.

Bart phoned the other airline and told them to put away their binoculars and to come on over—there's no secret, "It's nothing we do, it's how we do it." Most of all, "It's the people."

A Day on the Tarmac

Glen English, station manager at RDU, is more upbeat than usual. It's the first day of spring break for the Raleigh-Durham–Chapel Hill schools and colleges: full planes, long boarding lines, and mega luggage loads. After a postholiday lull, today's the kickoff for what looks like a record-setting spring and summer travel season.

"An ibuprofen kind of day," is how Bart Dockins, operations supervisor, sees it. I'm tagging along with Bart.

We start out in the break room, an open space for viewing videos and TV, hanging out, and eating at a communal lunch table flanked by wall lockers. Operations agents and pilots flow through this space, often stopping to visit.

"Flight 132 is in range" breaks in on the idle chatter, an announcement giving advance notice to the ramp agents. They hear it and go back to their nachos and watching the ACC basketball finals—the Wolfpack is on.

Next comes, "Flight 132 is on the ground," the all-hands-on-deck signal, the call to get to the tarmac. On the tarmac's edge, the ramp agents circle up under the covered walkway. The marshaller is already out there, upright on top of the tow tractor, greeting and guiding flight 132 into gate 26. The weather has turned raw and wet, alternating from misty showers to drenching downpours. I question the wisdom of wearing only the top of the full set of rain gear considerately provided by Glen. A lashing of wet, cold wind convinces me to yank on the yellow rain slicker pants, put on an extra sweater, and clamp on my hat. Some ramp agents wear the yellow rain gear, but most prefer their own mix of hooded sweatshirts or hats and windbreakers. Kneepads and bright orange earplugs are de rigueur.

The terrain around Southwest's four gates is a confused obstacle course of glistening puddles; uncoiled hoses; and power, communication, and static lines, all potential hazards to the newbie.

The incoming plane, marshaled through the wind and drizzle, looks like a ship slipping into a fogged harbor. Chocked in place and connected to the jetway, the ship rests, its skin glistening under the gate lights.

Above, the portholes give me glimpses of arriving passengers—enviably dry and warm—slowly exiting, seemingly unaware of what's happening beneath their feet: the ramp agents unlatch the holds and pull themselves in. The luggage is held in place with cargo netting, separating the crammed-to-the-rafters luggage on each side of the bin door—a full load.

The ramp agent in the bin sends the first bags down the belt loader—as the bin empties the scraped and bruised metal walls of the hold are exposed. Soon the bin swallows up the ramp agent as he works further in. At the bottom of the belt loader, the ramp agent is steadily filling up the empty luggage trucks, ones he's pulled nearby.

One by one, each bag is scrutinized for its destination. The tag signals where it goes on the luggage cart—catching a misdirected bag means one more satisfied customer.

Nearby stand several top-heavy, tarp-covered baggage carts—the outgoing luggage and freight. The outgoing bags were sorted at the transfer-point, or T-point, a vast warehouse space behind where the ticket agent checks in your luggage.

On the side of the plane, Bart spots an off-loaded child's car seat—or an *assistive device* in airport talk. It's not necessarily *his* job, but without hesitation he scoops it up and hurries it up the outside stairwell into the jetway for the exiting passenger to pick up. A job like that is on everyone's to-do list. If you're in-between tasks, do it.

Southwest Ramp Agents ready for rain: from L to R: Lori Fletcher, Will Engleman, Trent Williams, James Witherspoon, and Jason Wiggins.

Marshalling in an arriving plane.

I sense a mood of "let's get on with it" among the ramp agents. The rain, wind, and a couple of late-arriving planes make the ramp agents all the more resolute to make up minutes, doing whatever it takes to empty each plane, gas it up, clean it, fill it with luggage and passengers, and send it on its way in under twenty minutes. The challenge is real—there are now four planes on the ground, all four gates full. The ramp agents work methodically and steadily, anticipating and helping each other out. Rushing about would only raise the risk level.

The four planes, the gas truck, the tractors, luggage carts, and jetways make the scene seem more traffic pileup than something choreographed. The ramp agents do triage on available resources. I glimpse Glen through the rain, in a fleece sweater and jeans, wearing earplugs, as he hops up into a hold to pass out luggage—there are not enough belt loaders to go around, so the ramp agent pulls the luggage cart up to the bin and with Glen handing down luggage, they fill up the cart.

Where else but Southwest? I glance up at the cockpit windows: there's a pilot waving at me—a nice gesture for my camera? He's waving something out of his bag of tricks— a dismembered hand left over from Halloween!

For a few minutes the plane sits empty, a peaceful eddy in the tidal flow of passengers. The tide turns and new passengers come on board, looking for seats and space in the overhead bins. Simultaneously down below, the empty holds are refilled. The ramp agent pulls the bags off the staged trucks and tosses them on the belt loader, sending them up to the ramp agent in the bin. Both scan the tags to make sure the luggage and bin match their destination. Helping out, Will Engleman, the provisioner, his job done for the moment, works a belt loader sending up luggage into one of the bins.

Bart and I roar off in an open tractor with a full load, 200 bags, probably over a ton of luggage on each truck. Leaving the gate lights, we snake our way out of the congestion into the dark, heading for luggage claim. Once through the locked chain link gate—a sign requires the driver to wait until the gate closes before driving on—we pull up at the backside of the claim area. The flapped door through which the outside conveyor belt passes gives me glimpses of passengers waiting for their luggage.

In a matter of minutes, Bart smoothly lifts and tosses all four trucks' worth of bags onto the conveyor belt. Trucks empty, we circle around and bump along to the security gate, back to the gates to stage the empty trucks and tractor for the next flight.

An outgoing plane, doors closed, passengers peering out of the portholes, is ready to go. The jet bridge moves away. A tow truck, connected with a bar to the front wheel and a line to the communication box, pushes back the plane, out into the open runway. Alongside, a wingman walks the plane out while the tractor driver talks with the pilot. Away from the congestion of the gates, all by itself at the top of the runway, the plane is a thing of symmetrical beauty, burgundy and sand in the reflected light. Telling the pilot, "You're good to go," the marshaller hand signals to the wing walker to unlock the tow bar and disconnect the communication link.

The plane, free of its tethering harness, like a mythological winged creature gathers speed and surges into the dark.

Back in the break room we hear: "Flight 455 is in range.*"*

CHAPTER 8

More Than a Game: A Season with a Women's Basketball Team

Although the metaphor is often trite, sports teams can give us insights into teamwork, into the essential dynamics of what it takes for a team to excel. What are these dynamics, and do they transfer to the workplace? This essay on a women's basketball team tries to provide answers.

It was love at first sight for me when I saw this team. I was intrigued by the Duke women's basketball team huddle—no coaches, just players—out on the court, circled up with arms around shoulders, heads up, eyes and words giving encouragement. The tight circle symbolized what's best about teams—mutual support, physical and verbal, and each participant fully engaged in the real work of the team—no holding back—in pursuit of clear and desirable goal. Satchel Page put it well: *Winning is not everything, wanting to is.* There's no shortage of wanting on the best teams.

After that game I asked Coach Gail Goestenkoers (Coach G) if she would let me observe the team during the next season of play. It is a long season, starting with drills in August and concluding with the women's own version of "March Madness" late in the spring. This would be a new team, several players would graduate, and five freshmen would arrive in the summer months: new relationships, new players, and new hopes.

Coach G said sure, and I went to numerous practices, sat in on coach and player individual meetings, observed the locker room ritual at half time, and got to know everyone. I saw the players develop and how they each dealt with the many ups and downs of the season.

Players huddle without coach. Left to right: Sheana Mosch, two unidentified, Rochelle Parent, Lauren Rice. Used with permission from Toni Tetterton.

This team was not supposed to play in the championship game. Early on sportswriters predicted a mediocre season. It was a rebuilding year, they proclaimed. The team's two leading scorers were gone, and five freshmen were new to the twelve-player roster. If they split wins and losses, they'd meet journalistic expectations. That was not how the team saw it.

The coach told me early on, "You cannot let the players think this is a rebuilding year. It's over if they do." This team never did think that. One player later told me, "We love to prove people wrong."

They built their success on the negative expectation of others. An interesting observation Gail made was about team goals. As coach she used to set out the team goals. After she learned that her goals, her expectations, for the team were always less than those the players aspired to, she let them set the goals. What was the goal for the freshmen players? The national championship, of course!

"*Whatever you need, whatever you want*, I'll be right here waiting. I'll be right here waiting"—lyrics from the season highlights videotape at the year-end banquet. Like one of the team's chants, "1, 2, 3, Together!," the song is about relationships and trust.

I relished the warm camaraderie of the team's practices. The players' support for each other was palpable, even in that great empty echoing hall, amid the din of a dozen basketballs pounding the floor. The good times among the players and coaches were manifestly welcoming to me. I *wanted* to be part of this team!

Fun preceded and followed every practice. There'd be Coach G, at five-foot-six, slam-dunking. Yes, the basket was lowered two feet from its usual ten-foot height. Sheana Mosch, a freshman, outdoes the coach, soars through the air, whirling the ball between her legs and overhead, then driving the ball through the basket. Cheers erupt as she dangles from the rim.

There's no need for an alarm clock for this job; everyone is early to practice—often fifteen minutes or more. Coaches take shots alongside their players, challenging each other to make impossible shots. It's also a time for coaches and captains to check in with individual players, to follow up on something they are working on, an injury, or something of concern in their family at home. Or to engage an anxious freshman player to help her loosen up and enjoy the fun before the workout begins.

Besides the horseplay, there's visiting among the players, among the assistants with frequent eye contact, a touching of hands in passing, a chanting of team goals: "In our Quest for a national championship" followed by a circling up of the entire team and coaches, with Coach G in the center, "*National Champs!*" Near the end of the season, with many of the team injured, "*We are warriors*" would rise into the air.

LaNedra Brown, a freshman, greatly homesick early in the season, told me her image of the team was "a family eating together, where everyone cuts loose." Like the coach told me at season's end, there was "more laughter than ever this year."

There's an early season locker room ritual. Each team member and coach gives a brief talk on a word of her choice. Assistant Coach Joanne Boyle spoke about the friendships the players will make. A former Duke player, she speaks about friendships that will last long after the end of their college careers. For Joanne, "Friends leave footprints in your heart." Sweet and heartfelt. A frame from the highlights tape that was shown at the end of season banquet stays with me: Sheana, at five-foot-six, hugging the six-foot-six Lello.

Bullshit is what I am seeing. Get your ass out of the grass.
—Coach G

On a rare occasion Coach G yells at the team. It is disconcerting—the blunt language and the angry voice seem opposite to team and trust building. The coach lets the players know in advance, she will yell—expect it. There's no yelling at the start, when physical conditioning is paramount. Errors are caused by exhaustion, not by lapses in judgment or intensity. New players, many of whom have never been yelled at in high school, are prepared and cautioned by Gail weeks ahead, "I will yell at you, but I am doing it to make you play better. Do not take it personally." The yelling starts before the first game, a time when players are less prone to make mistakes from fatigue than from a lack of intensity, from a lack of focus. When Lello calls out a pass to LaNedra and the ball hits her in the head, when Jamie surrenders a ball without a struggle to Michael, the male practice player, when six-foot-two-inch Rochelle stands flatfooted while five-foot-eight-inch Krista snags a rebound, a series of those mistakes will trigger a tirade.

Like a slap, the yelling snaps every player to attention. The court falls silent. All eyes on Coach G, she explains what she wants instead of what she is seeing. If she wants a player to be in one position on the court, she'll take that player in hand and place her where she is supposed to be. When defense is wanting, Coach G gives a demonstration of what exemplary defense is—ferocious, up close, arms windmilling, chanting "Ball! Ball! Ball!" in the opposing player's face.

Once, when the play did not improve, there was more yelling, followed by a break. The team captain, Lauren Rice, got all the players up before the thirty-second break was over. They circle up: "*Together!*" Play improves.

The coach plays the taskmaster to get results—the three assistant coaches stand silently by—if Coach G has to be the "bad cop," they'll be the "good cops." Coach G metes out her anger in doses sufficient to cure what's ailing the team. She makes no physical threats, throws no chairs, slams no doors, doesn't demean individual players—her anger is a tool (among several others) to get attention and to be heard. When Coach G tells the player, "Not the right shot, but it was pretty," that's just another way, like yelling, to fine tune performance.

Players told me they expect to be held accountable by the coaches. LaNedra was pragmatic about the yelling: "If the coach is doing her job she has to yell at you!" That requires trusting the coach is doing what is best for you and the team. When she blasts the team with "*Get your head out of your ass*," you forgive the vernacular but appreciate that you are not defending or passing the ball as you should. You will yourself to do better.

Nor are there any surprises in the yelling. The coaches make clear what is expected in practice. "When you get tired, you stop talking" is a state to be avoided. It's an explicit belief—silence leads to isolation, to miscues among the players and a drop-off in the quality of teamwork. In practice, you're expected to call out player names, make eye contact, and talk through stressful parts of a scrimmage. Coach Gale Valley once updated the other coaches with one player's positive progress: "Lello is talking more, even if it is nonsense."

Coach G's criticism is always meant to improve what the players do. She does not dwell on disappointment. Only once in the season did I observe her shaking her head over a player's simply not getting it—a rare concession that the player was not going to make it much beyond being a good practice player. Coach G demonstrates the best attributes for letting people know how they are doing: immediate, frequent, explicit, and specific. Players told me "There is a balance to the criticism." What I saw was far more positive recognition than negative, something like a ratio of 4:1, positive to negative. For every criticism of a bad play, three or four positive comments were made by Coach G and other players about that player.

Here are the comments I noted while Coach G reviewed a videotape of the previous day's practice. Coach stands by a monitor in the locker room, the dozen players seated on chairs in front of her, the assistants, trainer, and other coaches at the back:

> Peppi, best defense I've seen you play all year.
>
> Here's Ro's "triangle" cut to the basket (laughter—Ro, seated at the front, appears to squirm).
>
> You all are just going into areas and not setting screens.
>
> . . .
>
> You did not take care of the ball yesterday!
>
> Nice cut, Ro.
>
> Great drive, Ro.
>
> Same thing Georgia, set screen.
>
> Lello, you've got to see the ball and the player at the same time, not just the player.
>
> . . .
>
> Good hustle, Ro.
>
> When we get tired we stop talking.
>
> Lello you're doing a great job.
>
> Nedra, do not fade away (when shooting). We want to get fouled. We want to go to the free throw line.

A season-ending injury to one of the team's starting players was potentially devastating. It happened when least expected, at the end of a game already won, the season two-thirds over.

In a lightning quick move, Peppi Brown reaches in against her opponent and knocks the ball loose at mid court. Her long loping strides take her toward the other team's basket, it's steel rim 10 ft above the hardwood. Nearing the basket, she gathers the ball into both hands, launches herself upward, one knee above the other, and lays up the ball, gently pushing it alongside the hoop. The ball slides up the glass, onto and around the rim, disappears into the net. Soaring past the net, Peppi lands on one foot. Her knee gives, buckles. On her back, she hugs the injured knee. Cheers dwindle into silence. Peppi is helped off the floor by the team doctor and trainer, out of the bright lights, away from teammates, away from fans, into the deserted wood paneled lobby toward the locker room. A senior, she knows her playing days are over.

There were to be no more of Peppi's impossible, inspiring scores—in traffic, off balance, the ball flying through a tangle of arms, gently tapping the backboard and rolling in. She had speed enough to drive past much taller and wider opponents, getting around them, canceling their height advantage. How was the team going to compensate for Peppi? They lost the next two games.

Then the team adjusted. The coach screened a highlights tape of great plays and shots made while Peppi was off the court, out of the mix, resting on the sidelines. From that tape they began to believe they could be a very good team even with Peppi in street clothes on the bench, her support limited to being there.

Coach Gail explained to me that "when people feel really needed, they give a little bit more." She was not mindlessly implying—like so many sportscasters—that the team needed only to *play harder*, to give more effort, as if they had been holding back, some percentage less than 100 percent. When Peppi went out, each player had to adjust her role and responsibilities to create new opportunities. The players did not replace her with a Peppi-like player—as a team they devised new strategies. Peppi's injury was a turning point for the team, an adversity that increased team unity, ratcheted up their resolve of "us against them." And, Peppi's injury happening in front of their bench reminded each player of her own vulnerability. With that realization came a greater dependency on each other—a greater desire "to help each other get through" tough practices or tough games. "Just taking care of each other" and "Trusting one another" became paramount.

Junior Rochelle Parent summed it up: "There is a reason for rain. Sunny days are always desirable, but if there were no rain I would have no basis for comparing sunny days. Sunny days are so much brighter after it has rained. I have begun to love the rain."

I trust you.—player to Coach G

How players and coaches treat each other is made clear, in print, at the first team meeting: "Criticism of teammates and any form of prejudice is totally unacceptable."

If you have differences with another player, you are expected to work them out, one on one. A player told me: "We . . . need to make sure that everyone feels like they can approach anyone on the team so the two of them can deal with whatever problem that may arise."

Coach G told me about a conflict in which a junior player was annoyed by a veteran's yelling at the younger players in preseason pick up games. The younger player understood what the yelling was about, but knew that this way of motivating was not working. Coach G offered the younger player two options: deal with it one on one with the other player, or Coach G would intervene. The player chose the direct approach and settled the dispute.

The pursuit of clarity in what the team is about and who is doing what, Coach G told me, was a major difference maker for this team. "It is not easy [to tell half the team they will not be starting], but in the long run it is best to be clear." It is best because the less confusion about expectations and who does what, the greater the contribution a player can make. It is not easy because these are top recruits who want a fair share of playing time, who want to play on TV, and who have been told how good they are since before high school. When Gail asks a player what she wants her role to be, all twelve tell her they want to start, to play thirty minutes or more, and to average fifteen or more points.

After a player sets out her ideal role, Gail tells the majority of players their role will be to come off the bench, and their play will be in half-minute increments. She tells each: "If you work hard, and help the team, your role can change." And it will change if you do not.

Most players, who have always started in high school, struggle with accepting the expectation that, *"Scoring points is not the only way to help this team!"* Most players understand, but if they have any doubts, Gail will go over their statistics or watch a practice video with them to explain her decision.

Telling a starter she will no longer be the first on the floor is no less difficult. Two players who started as freshmen and sophomores became bench players in their junior year. In one case, the starter's defense was not productive. Her defense had to get better, and until it did, she would not be coming off the bench. Through tears, she accepted this tough decision, adding, "I trust you." Since losing the starting role, she plays off the bench with renewed intensity. She was the first to welcome and support her replacement—essentially giving her the "permission" to excel and to thrive.

It is not enough to make a decision and let the chips fall where they may. When Gail took a good player out of the starting line up, she told the players why. The new starter was not a better player, but she was better able to deal with the pressure of starting a game. Taking the starter out was a way to alleviate pressure that was leading to poor decisions and ball handling at the tip off.

On March 1, just before the conference tournament, the team is at center court, clustered around Coach G. She's holding the strands of a cut-down net. It's the net from last year's victory in a regional NCAA tournament at the Greensboro Coliseum. That venue is the same for the upcoming nine-team conference tournament, something the Duke women have never won.

Gail raises goose bumps with her story of the unforgettable thrill of cutting down the net. She passes the net to a player, asking each player to tell what she remembers from the experience:

> I remember Peppi's dancing with the Blue Devil [the team mascot]. Whole thing seems like yesterday, I can replay in my mind who tripped and fell, who was crying.

> What can you say? I can't explain the emotional feeling that we all came together and contributed.

> Out of body.

When the net gets to Krista she sums it up: "Everyone [on the team] knew we were going to win. Everyone [else] swore we could not."

Coach G brings them back from last year, pointing them to the conference tournament only four days away. She picks up on Krista's comment: "People feel like we won't win. You are a very special team. We deserve to have that feeling back [of cutting down the nets]. *It's our floor, it's our title. . . . All together!*"

Duke's opponent (University of North Carolina) in the conference championship game relies heavily on a star player, Nikki Teasley. When she plays well, the team wins. If she has a bad day, they tend to lose. Teasley intimidates opponents with her physical play and in-your-face attitude. In the conference game the day before, loud booing ensued when Nikki, disputing a held ball, lifted her opponent and swung her offside, ignoring the referees' whistles. The anti-UNC fans were further incensed when the referee did not call a technical foul—a tacit approval of overly aggressive play.

UNC has the reputation. Krista, a sophomore, matter of factly told me about a first-year experience: a UNC player punched her during a game. It happened away from the ball. The game videotape caught the incident, and the UNC player was punished and warned by the ACC—Do it again, you'll never play collegiate ball.

This UNC team appears more an autocracy than a team; Nikki, a queen with her minions. The other players depend on Nikki to lead, to score, to make the difference—they've pretty much relinquished any say. In contrast, Lello told me, "[Duke] didn't have five all-Americans in our starting line up, but we had five women who knew their roles and were willing to work hard to execute them as best they can."

Lauren's shot from the corner ties the game, but the game is still to be decided. The lead goes back and forth. An impossible shot by Teasley arcs in from far away. The high fives and yells from the UNC fans send a message: it's over, UNC will prevail again, and Carolina blue balloons will cascade down on the court.

Give up? Duke's unheralded senior, Missy West, matches Teasley with a distant three, pumping her fists, sprints back to defend her basket. Then Duke's suffocating team defense takes over. Whenever Teasley's off the floor, the UNC team falters. Duke traps the less-confident UNC players, forcing turnovers from double dribbles and held balls. And whenever a shooting foul is called against UNC, Duke does not miss the free throw.

UNC makes a two-point shot, reducing the lead. When Duke misses its next shot, UNC rebounds the ball and stands to tie the game. But, intensely defended, Teasley hurries the shot; the ball clangs off the rim. Duke's last play of the game leaves the Tar Heels hapless. From under the Duke basket, Lauren Rice hurls the ball high up. Down court, Georgia Schweitzer gathers in the pass, then hands it off to freshman Michele Matyasovsky. Her lay up rolls in, the buzzer sounds. Final score: 79–76. With five players scoring in double digits, Duke claims its first conference championship.

This was now *my* team, as good as any I have worked or played with.

TRANSFERS FROM THE HARDWOOD TO THE WORKPLACE

- **Overcome adversity**: Injuries, losing, scholastic problems, loneliness, all can undermine an entire team or an individual player. But anticipating and dealing with adversity in a realistic and open way has surprisingly positive outcomes. Adversity can add clarity about the team's purpose. Focus on goal, purpose. I saw the team enduring hardship and adversity, but it was the mutual support and trust, on and off the court, that mattered—that helped them become a very good team.

- **Give feedback (getting toward positive relationships):**These players welcomed feedback when it was given fairly and meant to improve their play. They also gave feedback to each other. They knew that if they could not look each other in the eye off the court, then they would not look at each other on the court.

- **Have a clear purpose and role:** Shared clarity about roles was *the* difference maker for this team. If something needs to be said, say it! Don't avoid.

- **Never forget time matters**: "You don't know when your minutes will run out" is how a player put it. Time is finite for effective teams. Honor deadlines. Because players cherish their minutes of play, they choose action over talk.

- **Build trust and develop relationships:** "These are my sisters" to quote a player. This is developed through hours of practice, days of travel, and socializing in the off season. Their success did not just happen; much more than luck, there was time spent on trust building.

- **Have fun**: Fun was this team's secret ingredient for team "chemistry." Fun facilitated close relationships, essential for the best team play. The playfulness among players and coaches led to "team closeness and mutual support." This team had fun and got results because the fun was part of the hard work, the daily regimen.

- **Understand there are no magic bullets:** "You cannot control everything," a player said. Nor are there magic leadership or coaching techniques that work for everyone, all the time. Some games will be lost, but the best teams will win more games.

Epilogue

The best of times come to an end; a new season starts, roles change, some starters now sit on the bench waiting. Three of the freshmen bench players transferred out and waited for a year to play again: LaNedra opted for a team with which she was promised a starting position. Lello went back to her home state and played, with her sister, for the state university. Lello had huge potential but was gentle as a giraffe, never putting on her game face to push and shove back under the basket. Unassertive, she was outhustled and outplayed by more aggressive players.

LaNedra did start for her new team, but remained erratic, with runs of great playing, tripped up by mistakes.

A third player (Olga) gave up basketball for tennis. It seemed she never fully trusted her knee after she recovered from an ACL injury. Another member of the team (Jamie) married and left the team. Two seniors (Lauren and Peppi) graduated. Another player—whose jersey is now one of two hanging from the Cameron Indoor stadium rafters—would be suspended for a year for an undisclosed violation of team rules.

In two years' time, the team would be down to eight players ("Eight is enough!" was their mantra) versus the normal dozen, yet those eight exceeded all expectations once again, going to the national tournament and its championship game.

Teams change, decisions get made, starters become bench players replaced by new players more athletic and talented. Under Coach G's tutelage the team—while changing and enduring the inevitable adversity—got better year after year.

It is now 2009, and Coach G is the head coach and fully focused on rebuilding the basketball program at the University of Texas at Austin.

PART 2

Leaders, Bosses, Challenges, Values

CHAPTER 9

"I Can't Find You Anywhere But Gone" Revisited

Several years ago, I did a series of Internet use studies among library users.[1]

Why did I do that? Plummeting reference statistics. As a library administrator, I was tracking the precipitous drop-off in reference questions. The decline, starting in 1992, was akin to an S-shaped curve on which we had passed the happy upward years of long lines and never-ending demand. Now we were slipping downward into a quaint inutility unless we reversed the trend with other, upward curves.

At the same time, I observed large numbers of library users migrating to the CD-ROM reference tools and the OPAC, avoiding ye olde card catalog at all costs. Also, the unstaffed "computer lab" with its thirty or more word processing computers was crowded day and night. Then, first with Gopher, Mosaic, and Netscape, and the World Wide Web concept, users moved to Yahoo and to Google. Instead of lining up at the reference desk, our users were lining up to use library computers. These computers had high-speed connections to the Internet, including e-mail, and free printing. More users became *nonusers* of the library. The Internet has "moved library resources to my desktop," a student observed.

My research hypothesis, in mid-1997, was that the Internet was causing different use patterns and that the library would be marginalized if we ignored what was happening.

This chapter has two parts. First, I review why users love the Internet and how that affinity is relevant to today's library. Student users, from middle schoolers to graduate students, were my focus, but what they had to say applies in many ways to public libraries. Also, because these studies were highly predictive of information-seeking behavior, the findings are still relevant, especially when augmented with post-study observations and experiences. Second, I want to explore library leadership's response. How effective have we been? What are some of the program initiatives that leaders can claim as new upward curves?

73

USERS LOVE THE INTERNET

Why? Some reasons are obvious; a few more subtle:

- First, it's *everywhere*. Because the Internet is ubiquitous, we can access digital information from any location as long as we have the equipment and the connection.

- *Anytime*. Users are drawn to the Internet because we can use electronic information 24/7. Connectivity has reached such a point that we need to ask ourselves, how much do we want?

- *Time savings*. Internet use can save time. Using e-resources can mean spending less time finding what we are looking for and can give us more time using what we find. Of course, not all Internet use is time efficient or economical. Nor are all searches successful in finding the desired information.

- *Learning*. For students there is something about the Internet that helps them learn, that satisfies their need to know. Learning does not happen every time we use the Net, but often enough to make us want to come back. At the same time, many users state that the Internet can be distracting and that it is easy to lose your way and become frustrated.

- *Recycling information*. Because electronic information can be manipulated easily, we can copy someone's work and paste it into our own. While we can more easily attribute others' ideas in our papers, this process can also make plagiarism as easy as click and drag. We can move e-info everywhere, from e-note pad to cell phone to Blackberry to Facebook.com, to anywhere a digital connection exists and accepts the data stream. OCR— taking text on paper and making it digital—is now available on personal fax/copy/scan devices.

- I've saved the most important reason for last: *disintermediation*. The Internet's self-service feeds the user's desire to be independent. As it turns out, it's not information that "wants to be free," as we used to enthuse in the pre-dot.com Web era; it's the user who wants to be free! User-driven blogs and Web 2 initiatives suggest just how strongly many users seek independence.

Many students told me that the Internet allows *less* dependence on libraries. According to them, that was a plus. Students, like the rest of us, value anything that saves steps in way finding. It is why when we can access journals online and print out articles, we stop going to the stacks or microfilm machines. Economists probably would call this last item the law of least effort.

What library users want:

- They want *high-speed connectivity* and do not want to lug around a laptop; they want computer hardware available for their use.

- *Digital resources.* If it is in print, users want it digital. Google, Yahoo, Microsoft, and the Open Content Alliance's efforts to convert print to digital resonate with users. If publishers and librarians are unhappy about that, the users still want it. A student: "[The library] should try to have more books, etc., available online so that students can access it *without need[ing] to actually go to the library.*"

    Users also expect libraries to provide them with access to the *best* e-resources. They trust and rely on our selection and organization role. "If it is in the library, it is OK."

- *Print resources.* Perhaps surprisingly, many users know that print resources are essential to a complete understanding of a topic. They know that "Internet only" or "Print only" is no longer sufficient. Students know that if they are to understand a subject really well, both electronic and print have to be used, but their preference is clearly digital.

- *Navigation help.* "Internet use can be problematic" was one student's understatement.

    Users want a simplified way to get to the best sources. They believe the library should streamline access without referring students to a help desk or having to scroll down multiple pages on the library's site. While Google aspires to be the "World's Answer Desk"—the WAD—many students know googling is not enough. Currently, a thorough search on a topic results in a patchwork mix of sources from Google or Yahoo; local databases, including OPACs and consortial access portals; subscription databases; and Web 2 databases, including blogs and Wikis.

- *Our help* is needed in weaving these resources into something useful. This may be difficult for librarians to accept, and it may be even more difficult to implement, but users do not want tutorials on information literacy any more than they wanted instruction in pre-Internet library use. Many endure(d) our well-intentioned efforts at user education, but given this powerful new tool—the Internet—the users believe they can get to resources they need without our intervention, unless *they* ask for our assistance.

- *A single search box.* Users want a transparent, easy to use, and organized approach to information. Organizing information is what we do best. It is what we have done better than anyone else for the print collections, and users would like this service in the electronic format—they want to find what they need and with minimal effort.

Impossible! Utopian! we may exclaim; it is still what the users want. That is the direction our planning and design should be taking.

- *Trustworthy Internet resources.* Users would like libraries to rate the accuracy/authoritativeness of information sites. They want a "seal of approval"—implicit will do—on links provided by the library. To make this happen, according to Jensen (2007, B6) we need to collaborate with others who are exploring ways to help users discover the best and most reputable information.

Unlike some critics, I look forward to Google's applying their search algorithms to the use of their digitized books. One aspect of quality is how many people are using a particular item. This is the principle behind the *New York Times* best-seller lists and on many disintermediated reputation sites, like Trip Advisor. If I am looking for a good translation of *Don Quixote*, I will be very happy to see which translation is linked most often. Unless I am looking for a particular translation for some erudite purpose, the first few that come up on the Google page will likely include one I want to read. And, no, I do not need the AACR2 cataloging entry.

Creating a New Curve or "Jumping the Shark?" Challenges for Leaders

This unprecedented shift in how people find and use information—how they use libraries—cannot be addressed by doing business as usual. As dropping reference statistics demonstrate, our traditional services may not be as effective as they once were. Our users, our customers, have changed their behavior. Have we kept up with them? Have we anticipated what they want and need? Are we behind or out in front of our users?

It is precisely in ambiguous times like these—in the midst of transformational change—that leaders get to lead the development of new services, to implement new upward curves. If we want to *reintermediate* ourselves, to integrate the library's many good services and facilitate the "virtual" user's finding and using information while *outside* the building, what can we do?

Remember, users prefer independence. They flock to sites that permit disintermediation: the elimination of the middleman. The user is in charge and decides when and what he or she wants. If we are to have a presence, the more seamless the better.

Take a moment and consider where your library is on the S-shaped curve. What actions have leaders taken? What new upward curves are in place?

Do some library shape-shifting initiatives suggest we are "jumping the shark?" This term comes from the entertainment realm and describes the desperate measures some take to revive a failing television series. Instead of exiting gracefully, producers flog writers to come up with new episodes even if the muse is unwilling and unable. The shark phrase comes from a *Happy Days* segment in which the Fonz character literally jumps, on water skis, over a shark in San Francisco bay! This outlandish measure failed to revive viewer interest. If anything, jumping the shark confirmed it was time for the curtain to come down.

LEADERSHIP RESPONSES

A colleague recently told me: "It seems like all we do [at my library] is react to whatever comes our way." My colleague yearns for action by his leaders. Leaders are presumed to have a vision for their enterprise. Actions are to flow from that vision. The best leaders are blessed with an inner compass, a sense of true north, that guides them through uncertainty. I have met a few visionary leaders who demonstrate this capacity. When confronted with a situation needing resolution, they do not delay. Convinced, they act. A few might be accused of foolhardy haste, but at least they are taking action, not standing on the sidelines like spectators. They step into the fray without waiting to be asked, without seeking permission or being prodded. If their efforts stumble and fail, they and their organizations learn and are better for the experience.

I can appreciate what my colleague is missing by his library's lack of action. He's losing out on the joy of having a mission, of setting after purposeful goals. I'm reminded of a joyful summer spent building a tree house. My friends and I had no plan to speak of, but we had time and desire to build something high up in that tree—the joy was in the doing. I am not sure what we built, but we sure had a great time, from sunrise onward until our mothers summoned us home for supper. We did not need alarm clocks to go to the tree house job.

There have been some positive responses to the ongoing challenges.

Librarians have added impressively beautiful spaces. These renovations/ additions have repopulated some parts of library buildings. One architect enthused about an increase of 700 percent in the door count! Another academic observer drolly noted that new library furnishings were so comfortable that there were more students sleeping in the library than in the dormitories.

Users are drawn to these new spaces in part because they are a merged design of upscale retail bookstore and sports bar. In colleges, they feature group study rooms, flat screen TVs, and coffee bars, and, less obviously, they may appeal to more than a few users seeking a quiet "sanctuary." Another change: no ban on food and drink. One library, desperate to increase its door count, permits pizza and chicken wing deliveries to anywhere in its twenty-story building!

But all that aside, the real magnet is dozens, in some cases hundreds, of computer workstations, often located in an "information commons." Although we do not have a firm grasp of what is happening in the information commons, we point with proprietary pride to the hordes of users, day and night. Absent computers, it is unlikely the new coffee shop, the "eat and drink anywhere" policy, the "games and gamers" nights and dance bands, the plush furnishings and calming or, in some cases, frenzied color schemes would alone account for the numbers.

Users are the first to admit that there are times when they are stumped and need our help. They want us to mediate. How can we "be there" when they need us without our nagging the user or staffing little-used service desks? How can we help connect users to information when they need our help, inside or outside the library building?

If you go to many academic library Web sites and click on Reference, up pop "virtual reference" services: chat, instant messaging, phone, and e-mail. In-person reference service is still available, supplemented by these other formats. All are *mediated* services.

Are these reference services being used? John Hubbard's (2007) study statistics are unimpressive. There are steady annual increases, but in 2006 fewer than 2,000 questions were asked, half via chat and half by e-mail. On a 300-day schedule, that is 6.6 queries per day. Am I alone in finding Second Life's virtual reference desks, staffed by buff and buxom information attendants in a Walter-Mitty-on-LSD landscape, as forlorn as some real reference desks?

Library as Internet portal. Where do library Web pages fit into what people do on the Internet? If library leaders claim increased library use through the information commons, do these leaders have a strategy for drawing more people to the library Web page and the OPAC? An OCLC study (2006) found that 89 percent of college student information searches start with search engines. How often did they start with the library Web page? Two percent of the time.

How can library Web pages gain market share?

We know users would do better if they consulted us, but if we do not save their time, if we do not add enough value, if we make e-resources and printed material difficult to locate and use, then users will not return to our Web sites.

Let me illustrate. I had forgotten the title of an article I needed to cite, so I put NCLive (the North Carolina state library network) to the test against Google. It took me twenty minutes to drill down to the actual article in EBSCO Host. I got what I wanted from Google in twenty seconds. Which source would I return to? Which source would a user give up on?

Our most obvious success is the information commons, arguably a new upward curve. Although architects may claim the IC as their innovation, it represents an upgraded service that was already evident in the standing-room-only popularity of drably functional computer labs, some of which were located in libraries. A question that needs an answer is whether ICs result in increased use of library materials, print and electronic.

Could we do better in developing new upward curves? No question. Consider the two examples I've discussed in this essay: seamless navigation assistance and increasing library Web page use.

Unlike the compromises often seen in library strategic plans, sometimes a new curve means literally abandoning the old ways. This is high risk and probably accounts for why many new curves are flat, imitative, and overly cautious.

One student's sweeping statement—unhindered by pragmatism—should embolden us to look beyond our present practices:

> The library could really be an *electronic* window into the wider world. In some respects it already is, but it could expand its opening onto the world much more . . . . The library shouldn't just concentrate on putting its own resources online—it should bring more information in from the outside. Bring the world in, make it accessible to students and fun to study.

CHAPTER 10

"It's in the DNA": Infusing Organizational Values at Southwest

Since writing my first Southwest paper (see chapter 7), I have flown on SWA several times a year. Doing so, I've gotten up close to the SWA culture in practice: how it treats people, how it delivers its services, how it deals with crises.

I continue to marvel at how SWA stays ahead of its competition, how it keeps fares affordable and still makes a profit, how most of its flight attendants respond to full planes with good cheer and obvious interest in passengers.

Whenever I read "Colleen's Corner," Colleen Barrett's in-flight magazine presidential column, I was impressed by her uncluttered, undefensive style, and Employee focus. Yes, the word is capitalized at SWA.

Some readers may be wondering, why bother to read about an airline's values in a library management magazine?

Fair enough. For me there is much to gain in getting a close look at how any organization effectively infuses values so that staff translate them into action and the highest levels of customer service. Southwest happens to be one of the few companies that walks the talk about its values.

A look at the concrete steps SWA employs to maintain the SWA Spirit might offer up insights for our libraries. If not, at least the reader will have a better understanding of what infusing values is all about. It is more than professing what we think the people want to hear.

Business experts told Southwest's cofounder, Herb Kelleher, that the airline could not continue its unique culture beyond a workforce of 1,000. Above that number, the airline would need to become like the larger airlines; in other words, to survive SWA would need to get stodgy.

Now at 34,000 and growing, the airline still is the maverick of the industry, making money, innovating, and providing the best customer service among the surviving airlines—seemingly always a step ahead of the competition. Other businesses, including airlines, have sought to emulate the SWA model, but a successful replication of the SWA way remains elusive. Why not simply hand out Southwest's core values and, voila!, there you have it? Or is it more complicated than that?

One clue is that for Southwest's top leadership, the SWA way is "a matter of the heart" rather than something formulaic. Herb tells about an executive who wanted to adopt the SWA way for his company, but discovered to his dismay that his new open door policy had a downside. He told Herb: "*People were tracking mud on my carpet!*" For him, emulating SWA was "too big a burden; he had more important things to do."[1]

We've all been encouraged to enumerate our library values; to produce a library mission statement that tells everyone who we are, what we do, and why we do it; and to plan strategically for the future. Many of us have done all three. But if those iterations inspire greater creativity, productivity, and staff morale, I have yet to see or read about it.

The values and mission statements I've helped develop appear, in hindsight, more obligatory than essential to our work. We did them because if we didn't do them, we'd be labeled bad managers. An example of the obligatory type of strategic planning is how one highly regarded library would go about, ever-so-tentatively, empowering its staff: they would "further empower Department Heads to take central, ongoing, responsibility for designated projects once they have been discussed and evaluated by appropriate staff and approved in principle by the Library Administration."

What does it take for an organization's core values to drive how an organization behaves? Somehow, SWA inspires a great many people to go beyond their job descriptions and apply stated organizational values.

How does SWA keep fresh and relevant what in other industries quickly become clichés and triggers for cynicism and suspicion? How does a core value like having a "Servant's Heart" or a "Warrior spirit" retain meaning for SWA's 34,000 workers?

Is SWA's success mainly due to the charismatic Herb Kelleher and Colleen Barrett leading the way? When I asked them about what would happen to the SWA way after they stepped down this year, Herb was not worried, "It's in the DNA."

ORGANIZATIONAL CULTURE

In my library school management class, I use a self-scoring test for students to identify the work values with which they would be most comfortable (Litwin and Stringer 1968). The quiz defines three types of workplace culture: *systematized*, *supportive*, and *innovative*. Each has distinct values that sustain the culture.

Most organizations have one dominant style, with touches of the other two. In my experience, most libraries are a blend of the systematized (hierarchical/bureaucratic) and the supportive.

The hierarchical culture is largely self-explanatory: top down, with rules and regulations in place. Work is done systematically, everyone—for the most part—knows his or her role, and that role rarely changes. One day is like another.

A supportive culture allows people to feel welcome at work and fairly confident in getting their fair share of whatever benefits the workplace may offer: salary, furniture, space, etc. Competition is not encouraged, and decision making is by compromise and consensus.

The innovative culture is fluid, quick paced, and loosely structured, and offers the highest risks and the most rewards. It's entrepreneurial, with lots of ambiguity and a scarcity of routine decision making.

Each of the three has a downside:

- Excessive rigidity can be found in the systematized culture, along with a stifling reliance on methods, techniques, and procedures over soft human skills. Limiting variation in processes appears central to the systematized culture. For example, a library director once contacted me, in desperation, about helping his library streamline workflow because the institution was mandating staff reductions. When I explained my success in this area came from involving staff in idea generation and decision making, the director lost interest. Rather than a way of treating and trusting people to engage in problem solving, I suspect he was looking for a quick fix, maybe a time and motion study with productivity quotas.

- The supportive culture has its own problems Ineffective employees—even entire ineffective departments—may find sanctuary in the supportive culture. I have worked with very good librarians who shied at telling an underachiever to improve or leave. They avoided, signing off on satisfactory performance appraisals when the employee deserved a "fails to meet expectations" ranking. Often these supervisors rationalized that they were doing the problem employee a favor—"Emily needs the job to support her family"—but really what they did was self-serving. It was easier to see no problem than to confront the employee. Indeed, in the supportive culture one might earn the enmity of one's peers by challenging poor performance.

- In the high-risk innovative culture, people can burn out and fail. After a span of eighty plus hour weeks, eating at your desk and maybe even sleeping in the office, being "pumped" about your cool job might start to fizzle out. The innovative culture's loose-knit organization may rush shoddy work to market. Also, without time for reflection or coaching to help a struggling coworker along, that coworker might get run over.

Most of my library school students want to work in the supportive culture with an equal dose of the systematized. While my *outstanding* students also desire a supportive workplace, they differ in that they want the opportunity to innovate on the job and have freedom in how they do their jobs. Theirs is a higher risk tolerance. Their choice of workplace culture puts supportive first, followed by innovative and just enough of the systematized to give the day to day work its structure.

I tell the students who want more of the innovative culture that some libraries do offer what they want—often in departments, rarely in the library at large—and it will take some looking to find what they want. For all the talk about enlightened leaders, staff empowerment, learning organizations, and teamwork, libraries—or is it librarians?—tend more toward the systematized and supportive cultures and keep a safe distance from the innovative.

What about Southwest's culture? SWA functions in a highly regulated industry (systematized). The record $10.2 million FAA fine in 2008 for SWA's failure to make mandatory fuselage inspections suggests just how regulated the industry can be. Yet Southwest demonstrates a remarkably supportive culture and expects everyone to be resourceful and willing to innovate. More important, Southwest achieves what it sets out to do. It is supportive. It is innovative. It is systematized. The balance of the three has not gotten in the way of SWA's success. If anything, it is this balance that gives the company its success.

STEPS FOR INFUSING VALUES

First, you need to have positive values worth infusing. It appears to me that many of SWA's values were in place thirty years ago at its founding. Since then, new values have been added and others refined. All have been tested and have a basis in the tradition of the company; they appear again and again in the company's folklore. No value, as far as I can tell, is there because it's merely good for the corporate image.

I looked up a few library values statements; these are notable because the values are more about the library institution than about the people working in the library. One proclaims "truth" and "universal accessibility," another, "communication" and "diversity." And often we mention the *Library Bill of Rights* as the foundation for our values.

Although "civility" is expected in our interactions, there is not much guidance on what it means to behave in a civil way. One library claims "collaboration/teamwork" as a value. Another holds forth that a "positive attitude" is expected of all employees.

A major step for infusing values is hiring people comfortable with your culture, who embrace your values. SWA invests heavily in selection and training of staff—did you know SWA does group interviews? This is quite deliberate to observe how candidates get along with other people. Up front, SWA is clear about the qualities it desires in new staff. In short, it hires for attitude, less for certification. SWA knows it can improve technical knowledge through training; it is far more difficult, perhaps impossible, to change personality.

Also, SWA's consistent "promote from within" practice helps retain good people and keeps the SWA message on point. Once a new hire is on board, there is continual reference to the SWA way, the SWA spirit, and its importance in the airline's success. All orientation and leadership classes at the University of People discuss the Southwest way and that discussion, among peers, broadens understanding of the culture.

That said, SWA is aware that it has to constantly fight to stop regression. With year after year of success, it's easy to fall into a rut. I've experienced it on a rare occasion, from unhelpful counter staff to flight attendants who've lost their customer focus. However, because these service lapses are unusual, I give SWA the benefit of the doubt.

SWA lists five basic principles for how staff members are to work. The five summarize and help organize the values. The principles are listed below, along with examples of actions that illuminate the principles' application. The "core values," in the appendix, flow from these principles.

1. **Focus on the situation, issue, or behavior, not on the person.** One example enabling this principle is an "Admit Your Bloopers" exercise during leadership classes, in which trainees talk about errors they have made. By being unafraid to talk about what normally would be embarrassing for managers or staff in other organizations, SWA moves from blaming others to openly talking about how things could be done better

    Colleen views her role as empowering staff to think. After some mistake, "I may call you in and suggest ways to handle a situation differently. I won't be upset with you if you used judgment, and were leaning to the customer."

2. **Maintain the self-confidence and self-esteem of others.** SWA regularly recognizes individual, team, and corporate accomplishment. To get to the brick fronted University of People at the back of the headquarters building, I went down a hall, 150 yards long and Texas-wide, lined with framed memorabilia, from floor to ceiling: photographs, T-shirts, programs, objects, proclamations, declarations, and celebrations. It's palpable: We're Southwest and we're proud. (Having FUN is a core value—right along with Working Hard—and the photographs along the wall show thousands of people doing just that.) There's a joke told at SWA: How many Southwest staff does it take to change a lightbulb? Four—one to screw in the lightbulb and three to design the T-shirt to commemorate the event.

SWA leaders are convinced that if you treat your staff in a compassionate and caring way with generous amounts of humor, that good feeling will extend to customers in all their contacts with the airline.

3. **Maintain constructive relationships with customers and coworkers.** Yes, you can be fired at SWA. If it turns out you are incompatible with the SWA values, then there will be a parting of the ways. However, if you are asked to leave, you will not be surprised. Performance appraisals are respectful, very frank, and face to face. Tough love is the generic phrase for how SWA supervises.

Following 9/11, when other airlines declined to refund tickets for people afraid to fly, Southwest never hesitated. When a customer asked for a refund, he or she got it. Some sent the refund checks *back to SWA* to help it get past the downturn in business (Southwest Airlines 2008b).

4. **Take the initiative to make things better.** The company encourages people to think like mavericks—*to think service before adherence to rules*.

When the events of September 11, 2001, forced all airlines to stop flying, one of the SWA planes was forced to land at Grand Rapids, an airport not served by Southwest. Grand Rapids told the pilot that he would have to wait on the tarmac four hours for a gate. Spotting an idle belt luggage loader, the crew improvised. They pulled it up and led the passengers off the plane down the belt carrier. From there they bussed them to Amtrak and paid for their tickets (Southwest Airlines 2008b).

5. **Lead by example.** To quote the sage Herb Kelleher (n.d.): "Most things in life are easy to envision. It's easy to conceptualize something. The really difficult part is executing it. I mean, we can sit around and talk about (infusing values) and both of us walk out of this room and never do another thing . . . and we would enjoy, perhaps, a stimulating conversation, but the point is that when you leave the room you have to go do it!"

Obviously Herb Kelleher's and Colleen Barrett's personal values have indelibly defined the Southwest culture. Herb's personal philosophy is that, *"Since we are all going to die* [someday]," instead of seeing who can lie or steal the most, "it is important in all of our dealings to exhibit good ethical values, to demonstrate the importance of the well being of other people, including the customer."

Values are not something you acquire out of thin air or from a library workshop handout. Values that produce desired outcomes are ones you believe—they guide you, instinctively and intuitively, how to relate to staff and to library users.

Colleen Barrett, known affectionately as the Queen of Heart, told me three short stories about how her values were formed. She recalled that when she was a legal secretary, in one law office a long-term secretary was let go without explanation. The boss was not satisfied with her performance but never spoke to her about what he wanted. Colleen vowed that no employees would be surprised about where they stood in her organization. If there are problems, they have to be talked through and resolved. If problems continue, you may need to move on, but you will know full well why. And that is how SWA works.

When Colleen was Herb's legal secretary prior to SWA's founding, she noted that he was always wanting to help new clients and then having to delay on promises made to existing clients. This was not good for Herb or the law office. Her advice to Herb gave rise to the underlying customer service philosophy at SWA: underpromise, overdeliver!

What influenced Colleen's way of leading? As a young girl in Vermont she realized, "I was born to serve." She explained that her servant leader attitude "comes from wanting to please and being an over achiever."

Finally, another contrarian story explains why windows are scarce at SWA's headquarters. There are plenty of windows in the public areas, a vast lobby, and a rooftop cafeteria; just not in offices, including those of the executive staff. The windowless philosophy, as told at the University of People, is all Herb, at his quintessentially egalitarian best. It is his stand against the in-fighting for the corner office and the rug on the floor, and other so called "perks of position" that get in the way of real work.

Epilogue

In mid-2008 SWA held an organizationwide recognition ceremony honoring the transfer of the leadership responsibility from Herb and Colleen to Gary Kelly, a longtime Southwest leader. Herb Kelleher was named Chairman Emeritus and Colleen Barrett became President Emeritus. They'll keep their offices and staff through 2013.

Just prior to her "departure," Colleen produced a DVD, a "parting gift," on the customer/employee relationship, with approximately twenty customers and twenty Southwest staff speaking about what Southwest means to them. When she first proposed the idea of the DVD to her ad agency, they wanted her to script what the people were to say. Scripting, Colleen wrote me, "would have defeated the entire purpose. . . . I didn't want to have any influence on those stories and I didn't want to tell them what stories to tell." So she gave the ad agency names and telephone numbers along with a simple request: Would the forty staff and customers be willing to spend a couple of days talking about Southwest?

Seventy-two hours of videotaped statements were distilled into a thirteen-minute DVD. It is a remarkable result of honest and heartfelt thoughts and reflects Colleen's values and her trust in the SWA tradition. In her July 7, 2008, internal staff memo that accompanied the launch of the DVD, she wrote: "When we know each other as real People with actual names and familiar faces, we tend to forgive human foibles, and we treat each other with respect, trust, and understanding of the frustrations and stresses of the day. The Golden Rule becomes real. . . . We say 'thank you' more; we apologize and mean it; and, most importantly, we treat each other like neighbors."

APPENDIX: CORE VALUES AT SOUTHWEST

Warrior Spirit: Work Hard
> Desire to be the best
> Be courageous
> Display a sense of urgency
> Persevere
> Innovate

Servant's Heart: Follow the Golden Rule
> Adhere to the Basic Principles
> Treat others with respect
> Put others first
> Be egalitarian
> Demonstrate Proactive Customer Service
> Embrace the SWA Family

Fun-LUVing Attitude
> Have FUN
> Don't take yourself too seriously
> Maintain perspective (balance)
> Celebrate successes
> Enjoy your work

Be a passionate Team player

Chapter 11

"She Took Everything But the Blame": The Bad Boss Is Back

The following reports of egregiously bad bosses, coming in three consecutive months, gave me pause. Was the much-reviled bad boss of yore now getting more respect than deserved? Was Mary Parker Follett's wisdom from the 1920s about the folly of ordering people about now a relic of another era?[1] Maybe, or was bad bossism developing into an accepted leadership style?

- Miss a shot, take off an item of clothing—that's the novel twist the Rutgers men's basketball coach added to foul-shooting drills. Nude losers did wind sprints. Humiliated, three team members transferred to other schools. As reported in a story by Alex Kellogg (2001), the New Jersey Court of Appeals ruled the players can sue for this ridicule, terming it a violation of their civil rights.

- African explorer J. Michael Fay's exploits are celebrated in David Quammen's cover article in the August 2001 issue of *National Geographic Magazine*. The story documents Fay's propensity for temper tantrums, sulking, and name-calling. The author is convinced that Fay's abusive ways toward native bearers drove the expedition to success.

- A June 2001 article by Abigail Pogrebin in *Brill's Content,* "Cult of Bloomberg," features the bad bossism of the editor-in-chief of *Bloomberg News*. Editorial staff members endure a brutal, daily grilling by their boss about the mistakes they've made or are sure to make. Former Bloomberg staffers claim they've had to go into therapy to cope with the residual effects of public debasement.

There's little doubt that workplace bullies have been encouraged by our national economic swoon. Many corporations believe their survival depends on reducing costs and becoming "lean and mean"—who better than bad-to-the-core bosses to lead that effort? The irony is that a few years ago Deming, of TQM fame, was advising this same corporate leadership to "drive out fear" from their workplaces.[2] Fear as corporate fashion is back, with a vengeance.

BAD BOSSES IN LIBRARIES

Thinking back on the good and bad bosses I've worked with in libraries, I wonder why I viewed them that way. Were they inherently good or bad people? Was a boss's goodness or badness in the eye of the beholder, or was it a personal trait? For that matter, what about my own leadership? For a few colleagues, because of differing beliefs on the end-purpose of our work, I was a boss from hell. For others, I was more than okay. This mixed review suggests some of the complexity in the good boss versus bad boss dialogue.

No one arrives on the job immutably set in his or her ways of leading. A combination of personal experience, work environment, and circumstances contributes to leadership behavior *and* to how one is rated, good or bad. If a manager makes necessary but unpopular changes, some of the affected staff will say they've got a real SOB for a boss. A manager who dawdles on change and stays out of the staff's way may be seen by some as a good boss. In truth, the one who brings about positive change is a good boss; the one who accommodates staff resistance is ineffective.

Some incompetent-appearing leaders may not understand what they are supposed to be doing—they've never been told what their role is or, if they've been told, that's not how it works in practice. Some are caught up in negative administrations—try as one might, the negative administration foils every positive idea. Another contributor to a good boss looking bad is tenured staff who balk at any change that threatens their comfort zone.

In one of my workshops I give participants a self-test on theory X and theory Y. (In brief, theory X managers supervise closely, theory Y managers are more hands-off.) Participants take the test twice, once for how they supervise others and once for how they want to be supervised. Then the participants arrange themselves around the room by their scores for how they *supervise*. There's usually a wide distribution from extreme X to extreme Y.

They then rearrange themselves, this time by the score for how they want to be *supervised*. There's usually a total shift to the theory Y side of the room. Those with a strong theory X inclination in supervising others find themselves wondering, "Why am I the boss that I would not want?"

According to one anonymous library leadership workshop handout, effective leaders practice their leadership by

- inspiring shared vision,

- enabling others to act,

- modeling the way,

- encouraging the heart, and

- challenging the process.

These are lofty, yet attainable, goals. They are well worth the requisite effort, because leaders who achieve these levels will inspire staff to do their very best. Leaders who do not aspire to these levels will impede their organizations.

Paradoxically, depending on where we work, not all of us will be permitted to reach these goals. Your boss may mark down a supervisor who challenges the process. Or there may not be a vision to share. In my experience, there are numerous library leaders without a glimmer of a vision, certainly not one of their own invention. Rather, they excel at rehearsing and maintaining a *tradition*.

If your library is part of a command-and-control organization, you will have little opportunity to enable others to act. A middle manager is in an uphill battle when

- decision making is hierarchical,

- organizational structure is rigid,

- information flow is filtered,

- supervisors micromanage workers,

- work process is by the rules,

- external feedback is met defensively, and

- budget is secret.

Lest you think I am suggesting that all bad bosses are products of their environment and personally blameless, I can assure you there are bosses who are atonal in their leadership style: all bad.

I've seen a few library peers who profess a Dr. Jekyll–type participatory management style who, once they get the key to the executive suite, turn into Mr. Hydes. Closing down decision making and filtering information is their personal preference. It is also symptomatic of the fear-driven illusion about being in control. A parent organization often encourages a library director to pursue this fantasy. The boss's boss wants clarity about who is in charge. Anything that suggests groups other than designated leaders are making decisions can make upper-level bosses nervous.

Good Bosses in Action

It's remarkable that micromanagement survives after decades of workplace research. The research conclusions are clear: When you involve staff in making decisions about their work, you get the best results. No one responds well to being ordered to do something. If you want the best results, you will give people the greatest freedom permissible to figure out ways to do their work. This is how organizations become productive and creative and are able to move past the status quo.

A profound inhibitor to best leadership practices is a manager's inability to address conflict in effective ways. Like the above X and Y test, I give my workshop participants a test on how they resolve conflict. The vast majority prefer and practice these strategies: compromising, avoiding, and accommodating. These can be legitimate strategies, but if they are used to excess, a library's progress will grind to a halt. The two least-used strategies, competing and collaborating, hold the most promise for moving an organization forward.

You, the boss in conflict, have choices to make: give in (become a weak boss) or fight (become a bad boss). Many directors, all too understandably, compromise on some version of the former, and the organization meanders along. A few library leaders hunker down and fight for their vision and principles. They win, but pay an extraordinary price.

My recommended option follows the premise that entrenched staff and enbunkered administrators are fearful of something. Both groups are articulate in laying blame and resisting change but are inarticulate about what is really driving their attitude—fear. Real reasons for resistance are never explicit.

I was working in an organization with serious conflict between staff and an embattled administration. In a town meeting, one of our best support staff members encouraged us to establish a trust committee. Well-intentioned, this committee labored at ways to build trust in an environment of mistrust. After several months of effort, the committee's enthusiasm waned and it stopped meeting.

Looking back, I am convinced the trust committee was a lost opportunity. I would now clarify and expand the group's purpose: to increase trust *and* to decrease fear. And I would provide ground rules for its work, with the explicit hope that they become organizational norms:

- no topic is off limits

- no retaliation for topics introduced

- respectful behavior at all times

- zero tolerance for vilification of past or current employees

- zero tolerance for talking about others behind their backs

- confidentiality in all matters

- everyone has the same information

- all share responsibility for finding and implementing solutions

It is easy to blame organizational ills on bad bosses—there's no shortage of bad boss stories. (Tenured faculty and long-term staff, too, are the legitimate subject of horror stories.) The term "bad boss" returns more than 800,000 Internet hits. What's more difficult, but rewarding, is exploring the underlying drivers to good boss versus bad boss behavior. Start with yourself. The more we know about why we are the way we are, the better we can be the leaders we want to be, either as bosses or colleagues.

CHAPTER 12

"I'll Ask the Questions": The Insecure Boss

There I was, all spiffy in coat and tie, nervously anticipating my first library job interview at the Placement Service during a Detroit ALA meeting. In the last semester of library school, I was looking for a job. Times were good: more vacancies than applicants, a ratio of 4:1. I forget the name of my interviewer—an academic library director—but I have not forgotten his admonishment to me shortly after shaking hands and getting the other pleasantries out of the way: "I'll ask the questions."

I'd been making polite conversation and expressing interest in the job and the college. I never have figured out what triggered his insecurity gene. Maybe he wasn't looking for someone to think; maybe he just needed someone to do as told. Job seeker or not, his "I'll ask the questions" scratched my entry in the race for that job.

After graduation, I wound up at Rensselaer Polytechnic Institute working for Edward A. Chapman, who encouraged me to ask questions and find answers. He was a mentor to me for many years, long after I moved on from RPI.

Library colleagues tell me I've had an exceptional run of luck in working with several of the genuine leaders in library land. Overall, only one of my bosses has been unsupportive; I would term that boss, though competent, insecure. What do I mean by insecure? To me, it's the often irrational dread of being found somehow wanting. A fear of our weaknesses being exposed, for all to see, like the Wizard in the Land of Oz, revealed as a charlatan. Most of us have some inner angst, like the cartoonish, "Honey, do these pants make me look fat?" But when our anxieties control us, we may develop a malevolent envy worthy of an Iago.

93

THE INSECURE BOSS DESCRIBED

Are insecure bosses a mirror image of good leaders? Where one group goes right, the other group goes left? If good leaders *inspire,* do insecure leaders *un-inspire*? Or is it more complicated than that?

Are insecure boss traits unique to the insecure, or do these traits stray over into the realm of the good boss?

Here are terms that describe the insecure boss: *aggressive, bully, control freak, deceitful, delusional, envious, indecisive, isolated, jealous, mean-spirited, micromanager, paranoid, petty, prissy, radioactive, reactive, rude, sneaky, sociopath, tidy, untrustworthy, vengeful.*

As you can see from this roll call, the generic insecure boss ranges from the prissy fuss budget to the vengeful tyrant. Some insecure bosses are disasters, whereas others hardly create a negative ripple. Insecurity, then, is a matter of degree.

Most of us can identify an insecure boss; we may be one. Insecurity does not always signal incapacity. Like childhood nightmares, we've learned to keep our insecurities at bay, holding back our petty responses, irrational fears, and impulses. And we've probably grown out of some of our inadequacies so they no longer impede our competence. Supporting others is a positive part of the library work culture; it's safe to say most of us genuinely care about and wish the best for our fellow workers.

Some highly insecure bosses can be decisive and seemingly effective; they are successful at masking the most visible of their insecurities. And if they are in a tradition-bound business with low expectations for innovation, they can be seen as "successful." However, over time the less secure boss tends to develop a largely reactive organization because, in my experience, he or she employs acquiescent people and avoids independent thinkers.

The insecure boss in the quadrant below is influenced by two conditions, competence and insecurity.[1]

The *radioactive boss* (high insecurity and high competence) has the capacity to be effective, but because of self-doubt has great difficulty letting go and sharing power. He fears independent followers and may punish an effective subordinate just because she thinks for herself. Externally, the radioactive boss may appear fully in charge and highly visible—indeed his *radioactivity* is invisible, unless you happen to carry a metaphorical Geiger counter. The RB is almost always the first on the job and the last to leave. Depending on the type of organization, the radioactive boss may be able to chase off, with impunity, any people who question the status quo. The organizational overseers may regard this action—"getting rid of troublemakers"—as decisive and good for the organization.

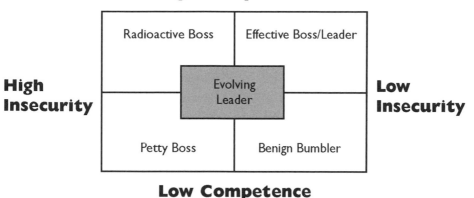

High Competence

Radioactive Boss	Effective Boss/Leader
Evolving Leader	
Petty Boss	Benign Bumbler

High Insecurity ← → Low Insecurity

Low Competence

Quadrant: Insecure Boss

The *effective leader* (low insecurity and high competence) capitalizes on the talents her subordinates bring to the organization. Because her personal confidence is high, letting others excel is genuinely satisfying, not envy inducing. The effective leader takes great pride in recruiting, promoting, staunchly defending, and mentoring independent subordinates. Subordinate mistakes are accepted as part of getting better. The resulting organizational climate permits staff to do their best without fear of punishment for excelling. It is only under this rare type of library leader that an organization can be proactive throughout.

The *petty boss* (low competence and high insecurity) does a poor job of masking his self-doubts and borders on incompetence. While resenting independent followers, he does not have the administrative support to run them off. The PB inevitably runs into trouble with staff and his bosses—unless they are equally or more inept. Even if his boss is competent and likely to abbreviate the petty boss's tenure, the PB can do significant damage. An accumulation of delayed decisions, poor hiring, and other pettifogging actions may take years to overcome.

The *benign bumbler* (low competence and low insecurity), beloved by subordinates, values effective followers. And because they are not threatened, these subordinates may excel; all the while, of course, enabling an incompetent boss. However, if no one steps in to help her out, internecine strife can lead to disarray among the staff. In exasperation, effective followers will abandon the field, leaving behind a largely ineffective staff, muddling along.

Evolving leaders—many of us—are found in the center of the quadrant. Our location is largely influenced by circumstances and experience, for better or for worse. We often have a hand or a foot in all four corners, as situations arise and circumstances impose. Through real work life experiences, hopefully, our self-doubts lessen, our competencies develop, and we become more effective over time.

We learn from our mistakes. If we were bullied once, we may learn how to respond the next time in a different, more positive way. Or if we are embarrassed by a hard-to-defend decision based on inadequate information, we may realize the essential need to know our job. By knowing our job, we will lessen the anxiety around a challenged, gut-level decision. If we work for a radioactive boss, we may learn from his or her competencies—for application elsewhere—while discounting his inadequacies.

On the down side, a long-term abusive relationship between boss and subordinate can lead to a permanently insecure subordinate. A junior staff member, regularly abused by a radioactive boss, may one day emulate the radioactive boss.

IN THE CROSS HAIRS

What should you do when several of those insecure boss "meta-tags" (like vengeful, radioactive, deceitful, paranoid) can be pinned on your boss? Worse, what do you do when your insecure boss wants you gone?

We can try to understand what is behind the behavior. We can look for clues that might help us with our well-being. Remember, an insecure boss wants it to be *your* fault the relationship did not work. He cannot admit to himself, except in those loathing glimpses in the mirror, that he, the boss, is the problem. A hallmark of RBs, and the organizations in which they flourish, is a profound inability to admit errors. If the organization stands behind the boss, as it often does, the targeted individual is on her own.

What follows is contrarian advice: Do not talk with the boss about the situation; get ready to move. I know, in this Oprah/Dr. Phil era, we want to have that heart-to-heart chat, no doubt ending in a hug. Well, doing that may only aggravate an already bad situation. The insecure boss does not want to talk about it. She does not want to have that quintessential conversation. A highly effective library leader told me how his radioactive university president—as expert as Lady Macbeth at wielding the "perfumed dagger"—reassured him when he questioned her level of support and asked her how he could do better. "You are doing a great job!" she exclaimed. Afterward she tacitly doubled her efforts to undermine him. That she now knew that *he knew* had made him even more of a threat.

Retaliation is a reason not to have that conversation. In one large metropolitan library system, anyone questioning a policy's rationale would receive one of two capricious punishments: banishment to the branch library farthest from the critic's home or two weeks' suspension without pay. The supervising board's apparent acquiescence shut off any avenue for staff to pursue grievances.

Having that conversation might earn you the "silent treatment," a favored tool of some insecure bosses to remove anyone no longer wanted. You become invisible. This shunning tactic works because many of us do not bear up well under ostracism (our own insecurities are heightened, along with our blood pressure), and ultimately we figure out what's happening and get while the going is good.

Of course, there are no absolutes. Do talk with the nontoxic boss. If your boss is more Austin Powers than Doctor Evil, you might have a shot at helping each other by calmly and openly offering her your support. If she is amenable—and has the competence to accept your offer—you may forge a productive relationship.

Well, a young manager might ask, what can I do to get past my anxieties and build my competencies? Here are some ideas I've picked up from reading Barbara Kellerman's book on bad leaders (2004, 233–35). Although her advice is meant to help the ethically challenged, these ideas can help anyone wanting to get the upper hand over job-related anxieties, whether self-induced or inflicted by a bad boss.

- *Get real and stay real*—If you work with others, understand that you cannot go it alone. You need everyone alongside and pulling in the same direction. To think that success is up to you alone is delusional. Listen to what library users are saying. Never dismiss them as uninformed; they often have the answer, years in advance of the profession. To reduce self-importance, use humor. A self-deprecating humor helps us not get carried away with our importance and remain anchored in reality. Practice getting outside yourself and seeing if you have become the butt of a joke. If you have, have a good chuckle, and learn from it. Herb Kelleher at Southwest Airlines says, "While I take my job very seriously, I don't take myself seriously."

- *Stay balanced*—Besides humor, maintain other interests, spend time with your family/friends, and do not dwell overly on work. Outside interests can lead to unexpected insights and give you anchoring ideas and the ability to gain some objectivity. Tuning out work can result in unexpected solutions.

- *Remember the mission*—It's not about you. It's about the purpose of the organization. When it starts to be about you, you're well on your way to a swollen-to-the-bursting-point insecurity. Think apoplexy. Think hubris.

  Focus on the long view. You will not get all you would like, but with patience, you will get much if your vision serves the best interests of the organization. Besides, ours is a noble profession.

- *Stay healthy*—If we fixate on work at the expense of our health, no one is well served. Healthiness can do much to maintain our psychological well-being. Work comes with stress; don't aggravate the stress with excess in diet or toiling, week in and week out, long hours on the job.

- ***Develop a personal support system***—Establish and maintain personal and professional friendships that you can trust for real conversations, ones in which you share your doubts and dreams, and that will give you insights and ideas for improving how you work with others. "Never eat lunch alone" is a useful adage to help you establish your personal support network.

- ***Be creative***—Although being creative, or proactive, can be a stress inducer because of organizational opposition to change, the creative process can lead to a glowing sense of accomplishment. That comes from enduring and overcoming adversity. Proactive endeavors will spotlight colleagues who have similar aspirations. They may be people to rely on during the next challenge. Plug them into your personal support system.

- ***Be reflective***—Think about what you do and why you are doing it. What would happen if you stopped doing what you are doing? From time to time, list goals and approximate where you are. Reflect on things that did not work out. Without blaming anyone, think of how things could have worked out. Learn from it. Include others in these reflections when doing so makes sense. Spend time alone—we are too rarely ever by ourselves. One colleague went to the desert and spent a night alone—with several gallons of water—considering his life and career. A few hours alone, say, off-trail in the woods, can lead to life-changing insights. With a little reflection, even the "I'll ask the questions" boss at the Detroit ALA might have quizzed himself, "*Why* do I need to ask all the questions?"

CHAPTER 13

The Spark Plug: A Leader's Catalyst for Change

"Spark plug" is my term for someone who, because of a can-do attitude, high energy, good humor, and people skills, helps leaders realize important objectives. The spark plug is the catalyst that triggers good team chemistry. Without a spark plug's support, many of my leadership efforts might have faltered.

So who are these people? What is a spark plug person? How do spark plugs contribute so much? Why are they essential to leaders? And what can leaders do to encourage them?

In my career, spark plugs are those who act on good ideas, initiate ideas, and need no more than a little encouragement. They'd consider a project and tell me, "I've been thinking . . . " followed by an improved idea. They do not seek permission to do something, nor do they wait to be told what to do. And in the doing—which is key—they inspire others to ramp up their involvement, to go that extra step, to do more than just enough.

They are often selfless individuals—an unusual quality in our competitive workplaces. Spark plugs seem content to be the fourth or fifth violin without envying the first chair. They have little administrative ambition and rarely would consider taking on supervisory work, because administration would remove them from doing the work; their satisfaction is in the doing, in the giving. They do not need a star (or title) on their doors; they appear to derive considerable satisfaction from getting results outside the limelight. And after enjoying the passing pleasure in the accomplishment, they're ready to move on to whatever's next.

When in a group, spark plugs do not order others around; it's simply not their style. Rather, they help break the ice and get discussion underway; they value other ideas and often build on them, candidly opening up their thought processes to others. Instead of succumbing to impatience when the group dithers, and telling others what to do, the spark plug collaborates for the best ideas and then follows through. Their energy and input spark ideas in the group. Spark plugs are vital to idea survival; they help free up the logjams and open the flow of ideas to lead the group to solutions. Through their own willingness to take risks, they encourage others to experiment.

Although a take-charge person may get the task done in half the time, the result may not be the best. And if this is a group that will be together for some time, being told what to do—and however nuanced the bossing, we know we've been bossed!—may result in little relationship building and even resentment among participants.

Much more than cheerleaders, spark plugs are immersed in the work. In group effort the spark plug counters the wet blanket, the participant who does not want to do the task. With enough wet blankets, nothing gets done beyond complaining about lack of support, the unreasonableness of the task, the ambiguity and complexity, and a dozen other reasons for inaction. The spark plug, undeterred by these inertial forces, suggests, "What if we do this?" and does it. Often this small step can trigger a group to act, to try out things.

A paper by Casciaro and Lobo (2005) is relevant to my discussion. They studied likeability versus competence in work teams and identified four stereotypical group members: the lovable fool, the incompetent jerk, the competent jerk, and the lovable star. Their paper, an assigned reading in my management class, resonates more than most for the students. Students *know* these four characters from personal experience! Although my spark plug does not quite fit into Casciaro and Lobo's model—only perhaps as a mixed persona of lovable star and lovable fool—their study makes clear the influence of personality on group success or failure.

The spark plugs' talk and enthusiasm prompts others to be more friendly, enthusiastic, or energetic. Casciaro and Lobo's competent jerk is less of a jerk when the spark plug is around. The spark plug's ability to bring out the best in people may well lead others to rethink their assumptions about the competent jerk.

I can envision a line graph that illustrates how spark plugs add value to a group. The spark plug's behavior influences others to a higher level of *commitment* (a long x axis) to getting the job done, which can lead to higher *productivity* (a long y axis) and accomplishment by the group. If the spark plug is absent, then the group may tend toward lower commitment (a truncated x axis) with lower outcome or productivity (a shortened y axis).

A spark plug example comes from a study I did several years ago of a women's basketball team. Lauren Rice, as I think about her, was a spark plug, a team catalyst. A senior and starter, she was not a star, nor was she the most accomplished athlete. This team had no stars; it was a "rebuilding year," and the team was predicted to finish somewhere in the middle of the league. The team's strengths were its coaching, chemistry, and players like Lauren who would not settle for mediocrity. Here's my evocative impression of how Lauren sparked this team to its first ever league championship:

It is the championship game: The Duke women against the University of North Carolina. With 2:29 left on the clock, Duke is down by three. Every basket has made a difference, tying the score or reclaiming the lead. Lauren Rice, Duke's six-foot-two-inch tall center, is visibly spent from the shoving and pushing under the nets. UNCs players have the height and heft advantage, with two over six-foot-two. Scrambling for a rebound, Lauren is knocked down in the corner, left in a daze, struggling to get up. UNC sends the ball down the court and puts a shot up on the run. It's intercepted. The long pass to Lauren finds her still in the corner, slightly swaying, but on her feet. Flatfooted, she pushes the ball in a straight line toward the distant basket. It swishes through, dropping from the net, bouncing once, before a chagrined UNC defender grabs it. Tied again.

Lauren had prepared for this game-changing moment—I'd seen her in grueling, all out practices, shooting foul shots through the thirty-second sit-down breaks, denying herself the respite, transcending the aching fatigue. And, in the process, modeling for the freshmen players (two of whom were starters) the anticipated level of grit.[1]

A story from professional basketball helps illustrate the value of the spark plug player. Shane Battier is not a star with impressive points per game, nor does he "snag many rebounds, block many shots, steal many balls or dish out many assists." What he does better than most is not counted. Although "he may not grab a huge numbers of rebounds," he has an uncanny ability to improve his teammates' rebounding. "He also has a knack for getting the ball to teammates who are in a position to [shoot]." On defense, although he routinely guards the "most prolific scorers, he significantly reduces their shooting percentages. At the same time he somehow improves the defensive efficiency of his teammates" (Lewis 2009, 3).

Another example comes from my management class. Because I use an array of teaching techniques—mystifying and challenging some students—the spark plug student is an essential ally. My most recent ally inspires the rest of the class through her eagerness to engage the activities, her question asking and relevant observations. She takes assignments to the next level of inquiry, often linking the current learning with previously discussed concepts and sharing what she finds. She's not showing off; hers is a genuine wanting to share what she has learned. That this comes from her, not the teacher, appears to help the students ratchet up their own efforts. Like Lauren the basketball player, this student raises the bar for the entire class and, because of her outgoing and inclusive personality—just like Lauren—brings other students along on her learning journey.

THE SPARK PLUG'S VALUE TO THE ORGANIZATION

Our profession, like many mature enterprises, seems to err on the side of passive reaction rather than proactive activity. Because much of a leader's power to implement change is granted by subordinates—they decide how far to go along—the spark plug assures the upward flow of that power. Although spark plugs are not the deal makers, they are essential to the leader in gaining commitment.

When the spark plug is absent, group dynamics change, rarely for the better. True, others ought to "step up," but that is hard to do—it may happen, but most groups revert to form. It's as if they need someone to take the lead, to accept the risk in leading.

Probably because spark plugs are selfless, their egos are in good shape; they do not fear coming off looking foolish. Action oriented, they learn from mistakes, adjust, and try again. Others join in and excel, because they don't have to take the initial responsibility, that much-dreaded first step off the cliff—even if the "drop" is less than a few feet. Spark plugs do what common sense urges them to do, swerving past what tradition maintains and cutting through to the essentials. In so doing, they may help lift the lethargy lowering like a dark cloud over those who have lost the pleasures of striving and accomplishing.

Also, as your ally the spark plug compensates for *your* personality differences. A low-key leader is complemented by the spark plug's exuberance. A loquacious leader benefits from the spark plug's good humor in letting the leader know it is time to act. A reluctant leader is emboldened by the spark plug's confidence and willingness to try out ideas.

There's another way in which the spark plug helps the organization. Because the spark plug has less of a career agenda than other staff, his or her observations and insights about the overall organization or some particular policy may be particularly of value. If a spark plug sees something that does not seem right and lets you know about it, I suggest you follow up. The spark plug is more likely to rock the boat because he or she is not an "organization man"—it is not part of his or her nature. When spark plugs see an unfair practice, they'll speak up. Pay attention.

Interestingly, much of spark plugs' effectiveness comes from an innate sensitivity to what is happening around them. Pardon the cliché, but their emotional IQ is at a higher level than most. They bring others along by intuiting anxieties and hesitations and working from that tacit awareness. A good friend from years ago at the University of Colorado perfectly demonstrated this ability. On social occasions she'd do palm readings—just for fun—with amazing insights into people. As far as I know, she didn't read palms at the circulation desk where she worked, but used her fine-tuned gift of insight to get outstanding results from her colleagues and in resolving customer grievances.

ENCOURAGING THE SPARK PLUG

Some of our organizational policies and practices may be unwelcoming to the spark plug. Remember, the spark plug wants what we all want when it comes to the workplace: the freedom to achieve. If a spark plug encounters repeated administrative inflexibility, more than most, he or she will have less patience and may well leave.

As a leader, give spark plugs the freedom to experiment and not be tied down by creativity-hobbling rules and regulations. Also, be aware that the spark plug's lack of conformity may cause resentment from those content in their comfort zone. The spark plug's quiet confidence and energetic achievement probably will be disconcerting to those settled in for the long haul, the "lifers." Similarly, a spark plug from the ranks of the support staff may rub the professional staff the wrong way. The entrenched professional may care less about the spark plug's accomplishments than about the spark plug's obliviousness to status— *their* status!

Because spark plugs tend to be productive individuals, they often achieve at a higher level than other staff. This puts them at risk of being treated like a "rate buster," someone who exceeds the tacit productivity standards. The worst thing you can do is to ask the spark plug to slow down, to do less!

Even if spark plugs are not star performers, their personalities and social skills make them invaluable to group process. So if it is a choice between hiring the competent class clown or the socially clueless techie, give the class clown a second look for his or her people skills. I would err on the side of attitude over certification, because a new person's positive attitude will contribute more to the organization than a colorless someone who meets the job's educational or experience requirements.

In large part, I've written this chapter as a reflection about the many spark plugs I've known—this is a composite portrait. They greatly benefited my career and the libraries in which we worked. Several are long-lasting friends.

Because I was aware of some of my weaknesses as a leader, I naturally gravitated to these people for help—they never threatened me, and from our easy interactions it appears I never threatened them. I also knew that although I didn't endow the spark plug's qualities, I could help set them free, and whenever I could, I did.

Finally, I've learned that the human spark plug is a seeking, learning, inquiring sort— destined to go on to other adventures, often outside of libraries. So appreciate and recognize spark plugs for their contributions while they are around.

CHAPTER 14

A Zabarian Experience

This chapter on Zabar's, "the world's best food store," joins the several stories I've written about enterprises and their leaders outside of libraries. These studies offer a comparative perspective on the library realm and are meant to help us understand leadership across organizations. Saul Zabar's hands-on leadership of a staff of over 250 speaks, in these economic times when loyalty is judged an ill-afforded foolishness, to all leaders. When I charted out the similarities between a retail operation like Zabar's and libraries, I found that we match up across eighteen aspects such as staffing, service desks, inventory, and uncertainty about the future. Apart from our not making a profit or paying taxes, we are alike in most ways. Like a library, Zabar's provides food for the soul, food for the spirit. And as a New York friend once told me: "If major corporations could organize themselves as well as Zabar's runs their fish department, American business would benefit greatly."

New Yorkers and out of towners are drawn to Zabar's for its vast selection, consistent good quality, and reasonable (a cup of premium coffee in 2009 for 80 cents!) price—35,000 people a week. Even the most assertive New Yorker tolerates the occasional shopping cart bump or unintentional elbow in the narrow aisles—paths really—through a fantasyland of culinary delight. On Saturdays, the Zagat guide says, "you can't see your feet." Overt aggression is left at the door—the smells and sights of olives, balsamic vinegars, cheese, salmon, bagels, croissants, coffee, and mountains of chocolate soothe us. It seems everyone is caught up in the pleasure of being there, of being in what may well qualify as a *great good place*.[1]

For years, I've noticed the same faces behind the service counters. Zabar's retains many staff members in spite of a highly competitive environment in a notoriously expensive place to live and raise a family—most people who start at Zabar's, stay. All the managers came in at lower level positions. Often their first job was as a temporary cashier during the holiday season. Olga Dominguez, the head of the cheese department, worked as a cashier while a tenth grader, and Scott Goldshine, the forty-year-old general manager, joined the business "as a kid."[2]

Zabar's lives up to its pledge of good food at a reasonable price. Throughout the store, many prices are below those of other New York specialty food stores. Saul Zabar's younger brother Eli (the "Napoleon of the East Side" food merchant) confirmed that Saul sells Eli's baked goods for less than Eli's gourmet stores. In a business with alleged microscopic margins, Zabar's currently increases its payroll 3.5–4.0 percent per year (in 2000, the increase was 8 percent) and pays staff bonuses, along with benefits, including some extraordinary ones like paying a third of college tuition and home down payment loans. And when the managers heard that loan sharks were getting at entry level staff—often first generation immigrants—a note about interest free loans went into each pay envelope. In 2001, there was $70,000 out on loan.

I first met Saul Zabar in late 2001 at the first floor customer service desk. It's the command post, battered by an unceasing flow of vendors, customers, job applicants, deliverymen, and maintenance people. Saul was dressed, as always, in khaki slacks and a sweatshirt with a small Zabar's logo. He was then in his early seventies, a fine-featured and silver-haired man.

During our tour of the store (actually five separate stores cobbled together with narrow passageways), I got a sense of who Saul is: Zabar's is his life. He knows everything about the store, from the cellar to the rooftops. Every backroom cranny is coveted and crammed—holding spare parts for electrical repairs, towers of paper, and canned goods—tomatoes dangle above chocolate and caviar. A conveyor belt takes up half a staircase. During the holidays, the overflow spills through the roof—blue tarps cover heaps of cheese under lowering winter skies.

Saul, brimming with ideas, routinely calls the store at 4:00 a.m. and leaves each manager detailed messages about what needs changing, fixing, or fine tuning. He is indefatigable in exploring and looking for the different and the unusual, from new food products to ways to display food. He experiments with food combinations even though he admits, "I almost never come up with a success." His explanation for why he experiments is worth putting up in Broadway lights: "Anyone can do it right. Guess what would happen when something you are not supposed to do comes out good?"

Saul runs interference throughout the store—some areas receive more attention, others less, depending on the ability and experience of the manager in charge of that department. When our tour took us into the food preparation area, Boris Bassin, the executive chef, told me Saul is hands-off in *his* kitchen. But that did not stop Boris from a gentle dig at Saul about his leadership: "I'll take what I can get. You've got your faults, but I can live with them."

Although declaring himself "too anal at times," Saul avoids most of the pit-falls of the micromanager. He is neither a bottleneck in decision making nor a mistrusting morale buster. I'd term him an *involved* leader; the staff regard him as the head of the family. Involved leaders do not just provide the big picture, the vision from afar; they are pointillists when they have to be to make sure everyone understands their interpretation. Still, Ann Zabar, daughter and under-study, wishes "he would let go more, so others can learn. He has a tough time doing that, [but] what if he disappears? No one would know [all he knows]."

Saul's involvement includes more than oversight of managers: with Ann by his side, he makes the fish and coffee decisions, personally tasting and selecting. This responsibility for fish links Saul to his father, Louis Zabar, who in 1936 rented space in a Daitsch's Dairy store to offer smoked fish and herring—the be-ginning. Louis died in 1950 and Saul, the eldest son, put aside his premed stud-ies at the University of Kansas to run the store. His brother Stanley joined Saul as a co-owner but continued his studies, earning a law degree. Eli, the youngest brother, worked as Zabar's night manager for a few years, then ventured forth on the city's upscale East Side with EAT, Eli's, the Vinegar Factory, and more, including several artisan bakeries.

Every Wednesday Ann drives herself and Saul—"She doesn't like my driv-ing"—to ACME Smoked Fish on Gem Street in Brooklyn's Williamsburg neighborhood. From it, the Empire State Building spikes up across the East River. ACME, an incongruously named family business (the founder wanted to be first in the yellow pages) has supplied fish to Zabar's for thirty years. This is but one of the long-term relationships between suppliers and Zabar's. Globe Pa-per, the paper goods supplier, was another family business with a long-standing connection with Zabar's. Now part of Imperial, Globe's principals have been working with Zabar's for over fifty years.

Saul and Ann will sample a selection of the 1,200 pounds of salmon Zabar's buys weekly. A measure of Zabar's clout in the smoked fish market: ACME cus-tom soaks Zabar's salmon in a 3 percent salt brine, producing a sweeter tasting salmon, unique to Zabar's. The lower level of salt is to Saul's direction. Self-taught in matters of taste, he explains you have to "do what you think is best" and hope it works out—that what you believe tastes good will find customers. The company employs over 200 staff in a block-long facility, with its own rabbi on site, ensuring kosher quality. There are vast spaces for freezing, thawing, cutting, curing, smoking, and packing. The doors to their two-story-tall freezer open onto an alien land. The freezer's arctic pale light and swirling cold va-por had me scanning for snowshoe hares and caribou. Barn-sized, computer-controlled convection ovens, behind sliding steel doors, can bake and smoke to perfection twenty rolled-in racks of salmon.

Wearing a white lab coat, plastic gloves, and Zabar's cap, Saul maneuvers among the six-foot-high carts, each with four racks of salmon, hooked and dan-gling. Saul likens each tasting to the intensity and concentration of a violinist in performance. "This is my performance!" he lets me know, lest I interrupt him.

He expertly digs out a morsel of flesh, savors it, and spits it into a wax-paper-lined cardboard box. Augustyn Silak, an ACME's manager, confides to me that Saul can be "very picky. I can count on one hand those [buyers] who care about quality."

When it comes to upholding standards, Saul can be a curmudgeon. Well before I knew Saul, I was distracted one morning from my shopping by his loudly and angrily declaring to David Tait, the floor manager, "This is not acceptable!"

Saul explains that his outbursts only happen after fair warning. It's not a lack of respect—rather it is impatience with something not going right. Saul's focus is always on what needs fixing, what needs improving. And sometimes, for Saul, the words have to be said with anger. On occasion there are volatile results. Scott Goldshine, the general manager, has quit over differences with Saul. Each time, after reconciliation initiated by Saul, he returns to the job he loves.

A MANAGER'S PERSPECTIVE

Harold Horowytz welcomes me to his "office": the end of the deli case near shelves filled with freshly baked knishes, empanadas, and strudels hot from the proofing ovens around the corner. At seventy-five, he looks a robust sixty-five beneath his tan baseball cap.

Harold was once the full-time deli counter manager. Ann Zabar says "he never said a final good-bye," but he left the job a decade ago, after twenty-eight years.

But he's not really retired—from Thanksgiving to New Year's he leaves his coastal retirement home in North Carolina and returns to manage the deli counter. He takes over, seamlessly, from Frankie Cabrera, the deli manager for the rest of the year. They work together, tasting and making decisions—"the highest quality at a good price"—about products from fifteen companies, all long-term relationships. The purchasing decision is theirs to make—"If I like, we order," says Frankie. The deli department offers salamis, knishes, and 220 freshly prepared entrees ranging from turkey meatloaf and garlic shrimp to Sicilian seafood salad and cold summer borscht.

The workings of the two separate deli and fish counters are worth study: customers take a number and wait in a crowd for their number to come up. Savvy customers, with their number clutched in hand, keep shopping, ears tuned for their turn. The aproned and deli-capped countermen (no women) prepare individual orders, slicing, weighing, pricing, and packaging. What stands out is their unwavering attention to the customer. Regardless of crowding, when it is your turn, you have the counterman's unhurried attention. The regular customer has his well-practiced repartee, while the first-timer asks for a recommendation, samples, and decides. There's camaraderie behind the counter, a quiet understanding and mutual support. It's most noticeable with the shared knowing looks when a demanding repeat customer kvetches. Howie (Howard Somers), a forty-five-year veteran and the resident jokester—told me Lauren Bacall was his favorite customer, "She asks for me by name." Another of Howie's favorites, a bathing suit model, is on display in a magazine he's handing around to his counter mates.

The deli workweek used to be 72–84 hours. Harold still calls it "a grind," at 60 hours a week, explaining "it's a *retail* business" (Harold underscores the word, *retail*). That said, he loves the work: "It's a good store, with lots of action."

Under Saul, the workweek for most staff now is five days, 9–12 hours per day, with the managers tending to work any marathon sessions.

When it comes to the consistent high quality of what they serve, Harold is not the first to tell me about the legendary Mr. Klein (always *Mister*), a former partner and daily operations manager with Saul and Stanley Zabar. His legend includes the celebrated caviar price war with Macy's and his riding roughshod over sales reps during the Wild West era of kitchenware surpluses. More important was Mr. Klein's being a stickler for quality—something never to be taken for granted, it was everyone's job. He helped instill high standards—the same ones Saul's father valued. Although now deceased, his name is the organization's shorthand for keeping high standards alive. When Saul and Stanley recently refused to sell lobster salad for four days because it did not taste right, that was like Mr. Klein. Scott Goldshine admiringly describes Mr. Klein as "one tough s.o.b" in demanding and getting the best quality and price from suppliers.

Ann Zabar grew up with Mr. Klein. She told me, "If you think my Dad can be bad [about expressing dissatisfaction], Mr. Klein was much worse." For example, while working behind the cheese counter Ann cut her hand, and Mr. Klein sent her home—his no-exceptions rule: you cut yourself, you go home. Yet, "you respected him and you were afraid of him." Another staffer told me: "He made us all cry at one time or another." Mr. Klein had a straightforward sick leave policy: "Don't get sick." David Tait related to me that when Mr. Klein gave you a job to do, he'd always follow up with: "Don't make it a *project!*"

Prior to his death, whenever the retired Mr. Klein visited the store the cashiers would "hug him and squeeze his ass," according to Scott. Even with staff adulation and a highly successful career, Ann told me, Mr. Klein worried that his cancer was "God getting even with me."

Another quality enhancer for Harold: "You buy the best" and freshest products. And it helps that Chef Bassin is "fussy," checking with a military precision for taste and freshness. Those 220 deli items behind the gleaming glass display cases come from the army of cooks and food preparers under Boris's command. Platoons of workers slice and dice at cutting boards in narrow aisles, flanked by steaming sinks and glowing ovens. Everyone has his or her daily orders—"to do" lists—personally prepared by Boris. Those lists include daily training on procedures so that "we never stop getting better."

Inspecting a cart of baked salmon, he takes the temperature of *each* fillet. Indeed, Boris sets the bar high: "I compare myself to good French and Italian chefs. I have different concerns, not how the sauce looks fifteen minutes from now but how it looks tomorrow and a few days after. I want my food to be as close to restaurant food as it can be."

As Harold and I talk, a deliveryman rolls in several boxes from a New York manufacturer. Before signing off on the invoice, Harold checks the shipment, opening each box, rifling through the wrapped tongues and pastramis. Frankie joins him and they feel the tongues (shaped like pink five-pound sacks of sugar), one by one, holding each in both hands, probing with gentle thumb pressure for consistency and texture. One is undercooked; the others are OK, but not as good as they could be. "This is shit," Harold says to the deliveryman. The delivery-man bears up fairly well, then makes excuses about how the ovens were not working like they should. Harold acknowledges the excuse but crosses off the undercooked tongues on the invoice—no sale.

Pastrami is next. Frankie and Harold scrutinize each, but spend less time, telling me, "It's hard to kill a pastrami!" Still, you can cheat by adding water. Some manufacturers do pump up the meat or add water to the wrapping. They don't get Zabar's business.

Harold ends what's been a lesson in quality control: "Take your tongue and get your ass out of here." Harold's crustiness is well intentioned, half jest, half reprimand. It's tough guy talk that makes the point to the young man and the manufacturer. Afterward, Harold tells me, "Usually this company makes a nice product."

How well you do at Zabar's is up to you, Harold believes. "A lot of people who work here care about what they do, they care about the store." It's one reason Harold comes back every year. "You can make a living working at Zabar's. The pay scale is a lot better than supermarkets. If you want overtime, you can get it. You can make money. In fact, managers can do nicely." Harold's simple business rules: you get customers in your store, treat them nicely, bend over backwards if you have to, and *get the money*. Regular customers are knowledge-able and demanding. Everyone wants the best cut—from the middle. But if you berate a customer, forget the money. Harold tells me there is no pleasing some customers. You cannot do enough to satisfy them, but you have to overlook that—it's a *retail* business!

"Calling all hungry shoppers. . . . Come to the fish counter . . . " a New York–accented voice calls out over the in-store loud speakers. On a cold January morning, it is the first of many announcements, interrupting the Mozart symphony. The words trigger in me a better understanding about what Zabar's is and how Saul derives joy from what he does. "There's a romance about what we do—we have a modern guise but we really do things the way they were done forty, fifty, seventy-five years ago." And Saul's leadership is driven by his belief that Zabar's is a repository for a tradition that may not exist much longer.

Zabar's offers up the charm of a rustic village market with something of "all the world's a stage." The vaudevillian font for the Zabar's logos is more than effective graphic design—the appeal is visceral, and we are drawn in. A visit fills us with the familiar and nostalgic. We know the script, but if not, we can improvise on the tradition.

The good feeling extends beyond the store. I'm standing on a crammed bus going up Broadway, laden with a couple of Zabar bags, when a seat comes open. The lady standing nearby urges me, "Take it." She smiles and wants to know what the wonderful smell is wafting up from the bags. Coffee, four pounds, freshly ground. We talk about Zabar's. The kids in her family have a different word for Zabar's salmon, they call it "delicious." The word comes from when they were little; when salmon was offered everyone called it *delicious,* so that is how they still ask for it; "I'll have a slice of the delicious."

One regular customer offers more insight into the feel-good, "third place" experience: "I think more community goes on inside Zabar's than in a lot of places," she said. "There are people you know and people that want to help you."[3]

An ever-present concern for Saul is "running out of programs"—ways to augment cash flow to support the enterprise and its people. And he is aware of the risks faced by what he calls "remnant" businesses, family concerns that appear near the end of their run. Some are targets for takeover by corporate chains. Others are petering out, with no one in the wings.

WILL ZABAR'S RUN OUT OF PROGRAMS?

Implicitly linked to any consideration of the future is Ann Zabar, age thirty-one. She's "been in the business full time for eight years, part time all my life." I visited Ann in 2001, on the third floor from where, on top of fish and coffee tasting, she oversees Internet and catalog sales. Jessie, her chocolate lab, was curled up under the desk, and her PC featured a screen saver of her smiling one-year-old.

Although her relaxed style—more Colorado than Upper West Side—is different from Saul's, she wants the store to remain the same—like a family. It's the word I've heard most often from staff to describe the organization—a big family. For Ann, family is more than metaphor: her brother, uncle, cousin, and father are in the store. She is confident they can avoid the downward curve that many long-term businesses experience, but she is more certain about what Zabar's must not do: "Go corporate—no procedure manuals! To keep it right, it must be in the family."

Epilogue

The last time I saw Saul was in spring 2007, his eightieth year. He told me that Ann was no longer with the store. If Zabar's future was uncertain, Ann's departure complicates it more.

In the meantime, at this writing and from a visit in early March 2009, Zabar's appears unchanged—the same counter staff, wonderful food, and coffee, the same crowds of customers. And the store is promoting a newly developed product, a freshly baked Jewish rye bread, which Saul claims is possibly the best in the city, selling at a more than reasonable price ($2.99). He may well be right.

CHAPTER 15

Orchestrating Success: A Profile of Simone Young, Conductor

> This is a very democratic organization, so let's take a vote.
> All those who disagree with me, raise their hands.
> —Eugene Ormandy, conductor, Philadelphia Orchestra

The 1930s film *Fantasia* contains one of the most enduring images of the all-powerful conductor. The towering Leopold Stokowsky fills the screen. *Without* a baton or a musical score, the conductor summons up Bach's *Toccata* and simultaneously brings forth light! Of course in real life, Mr. Stokowsky was less wizardlike. He did refer to the composer's score and used a baton to beat time while leading the Philadelphia Symphony.

Conductors, although celebrities, are real people. Nor are any two conductors alike: each displays a different leadership style just as leaders do in any organization—a diversity of approaches, from hands-on to hands-off, from autocratic to participatory. On one exasperation-inducing occasion Toscanini claimed his incontrovertible authority over the orchestra: "God lets me hear the music, but you get in the way." Eugene Ormandy jollied his players with a ditzy humor, at one rehearsal telling them: "I guess you thought I was conducting, but I wasn't."

What's most remarkable is a conductor's routinely inspiring an organization of over 100 independent professionals to engage in a collaborative enterprise, *under a spotlight*—with the customers in the room. The conductor is singularly responsible for the whole product. And a conductor must be accountable to the score—the composer's vision—in much the same way that a business leader must be responsible to a corporation's values and mission. For the best music, the orchestra has to move beyond individual needs and perspectives, beyond rivalries and personality conflicts. When that happens, the music can be magical—a unanimity of sound that transforms and exhilarates musicians and listeners. How a conductor develops an orchestra into a high-performing musical team speaks to us about the skillful blending of differences of talent and ability—in other words, how to lead, regardless of setting.

SIMONE YOUNG, OPERA AUSTRALIA

At forty, Simone Young is but an adolescent on the age scale for conductors. At around age seventy a few conductors may be termed *maestros*. Although she has thirty years to go, Simone is heralded as one of the music world's rising stars. In January 2001, following acclaim for her musical interpretations in European opera houses, she returned to her native Australia as musical director and conductor at Opera Australia. Her place of work—the architectural icon of the twentieth century—is the Sydney Opera House.

Simone Young leads the musical line at the Sydney Opera House.
Used with permission of Opera Australia.[1]

Ironically, although Simone Young is a pioneer among female conductors—the first woman to conduct in Berlin, Paris, and Vienna—many journalists (especially female writers) comment extensively on her hair color and her dress, down to the stilettos she favors while conducting. Once she was asked if her baton was different from those of her male peers. After a moment of silent consternation, she replied, that, indeed, her baton "sported a fetching pink bow."

This trivializing is not limited to the press. Franco de Carlos, a violinist, was miffed about the glitter butterfly on Simone's bare shoulder at the New Year's Eve Verdi Gala, "Some of us," he told me, "do not approve. She has let her hair down." What's understated in the media coverage is her leadership, that she gets excellent results from singers and instrumentalists. Nary a report concludes that these good results come by way of her incandescent intelligence and the collaborative way she works with musicians.

She could impose an iron-fisted will, but that could leave her with musicians who play without heart or understanding—a form of making music by the numbers. To inspire musicians to join her in momentous music making, Simone Young speaks from the heart and mind, with clarity and conviction. There's risk—like any leader who tells it like it is, she becomes vulnerable to those who differ with her interpretation. Tread on enough toes, and your rising star may fizz out.

Throughout a two-hour rehearsal at the Opera's workshop facility in Surry Hills, a Sydney neighborhood, many of the seventy or so musicians are vigorously erasing old instructions on their musical scores and penciling in the new. They're replacing the previous conductor's interpretation with those of their new boss. These jottings are tangible reminders of how the new leader wants the music played—tempo, tone, and emotional emphasis. The musicians do question and make comments, but for the most part what's written in is a record of *her* vision, as musical architect. "I am an *advocate* for the composer—my place is to bring the will of the composer (in the most honest way that I can interpret it) to the minds of the musicians and on to the hearts of the audience," she says.

Although there are a variety of interpretations of any musical composition, it is essential that the conductor's interpretation be one she believes best serves the composer. "I become . . . the medium through which the composer speaks to the orchestra," says Young. To do that means knowing and expressing what you, as leader, want the sound to be and why you want it. Even with her enhanced ability to hear the music because of her perfect pitch, Young understands she may lead the orchestra astray. Yet she must do what she believes. "I don't have all the answers, but I have to be sure that the answers I am giving the orchestra are the right ones for me now—are the rights ones for them now." Were she not to speak with conviction, she "would not be able to demand the musical and emotional honesty from my performers that is essential to realize the composer's intention."

A decade ago a musician in a German orchestra for which she was guest conducting demanded of her, "Tell us what you actually want the music to do." Clarity is what musicians most want from conductors, just as workers want clarity from bosses. When Simone took on the task of answering her musician's challenge, she recognized she'd been given sage advice. She considers that a pivotal moment in becoming a leader.

But clarity is not achieved by speaking your mind at someone. Mutual understanding is what successful communication is about. Success in telling "us what you actually want" requires convincing communication. If you've prepared thoroughly enough, you will have the knowledge to articulate the "why" of your decisions. Admittedly this describes a competent and confident leader. And to her credit, Simone also happens to be a leader who can be influenced by her fourteen-year-old daughter's declaration that a production "is boring."

Telling a large group of people what you want done so they can play it back, *improved*, requires an array of communication techniques.

Characteristically, Simone Young mixes humor with constructive criticism. When the Gypsy singer languishes on the stage floor directly in front of the conductor's space, she quips: "It's lovely to see you, but I'd appreciate some distance."

Telling What You Actually Want: Simone's Words

To Explain:

> *There's a power struggle between mother and son—put the struggle in the sound, a pungent, sobbing, vibrato to it; there's a pleading quality.*

> *This part needs a buoyancy, otherwise it is dull . . . . Very nice!*

To Direct:

> *A little more from basses, a little less from everyone else.*

> *Play it like someone's pulse, a bit feverish.*

> *I want a* long *short note. (*This gets a laugh *and* the improvement*).*

> *Your playing needs much more "line": I'm hearing separate notes.*

To Encourage:

> *Good! Very nice, when dark tones are brought out.*

> *Sure you can, you guys can do anything! (*To an all-male orchestra).

Saving Face

"The worse the conductor the more the confrontations," is how Tobias Foskett, a Young Artist conductor apprenticed to Ms. Young, explained to me why some conductors may be in a perpetually prickly state. The tyrannical conductor is music's counterpart to the cartoon world's worst boss, Dagwood's Mr. Dithers, whose atonal leadership is kicking people in the pants. Simone Young deliberately eschews personal attack, browbeating, or other fear-inducing tactics. When she has personal criticism for a singer, she climbs out of the conductor's space and gets up on the stage to talk with the singer. Or she moves the discussion into the deserted Opera House hallway. She keeps individual criticism one on one, "to save [the performer's] face"—rather than shouting it out from the conductor's box for all to hear. Tearing someone down destroys trust. The more trust in the Opera Company, the better the music.

The opera's director, Talya Masel, is more in the theatrical tradition of letting it all hang out. Sitting several rows back during a dress rehearsal, she lambasted the acrobat extras, shouting: "Do you know how long that took? Fifteen seconds more than it should! Come on guys, count the beat!"

Simone Young embraces the concept that we all "get better by making mistakes." She makes clear that rehearsals are for trying out different sound textures, tempos, and variations to find the best one—rehearsals are for *re-hearing*. If nothing else, she wants the musicians to play up! Timidly done music undercuts everyone's ability to learn from mistakes on their way to an improved process. Young gives permission to mess up: "Just try it."

"Time, Ladies and Gentlemen"

In today's opera, there are remarkably few full dress rehearsals at which singers, orchestra, chorus, conductor, and directors come together. Much of the opera is rehearsed in seemingly unrelated segments in different locations at different times, starting early in the day and going up to ten o'clock at night. Invariably two to three other operas, each with its own rehearsal needs, overlap. In the Green Room, far beneath the soaring sails of the Opera House, *Il Trovatore's* exotically costumed nuns mix with the amazingly costumed chorus members of the *Gypsy Princess*.

Rehearsals stop and go. Unless you are "on," it is easy to stop paying attention. The conductor's task is to be alert to what is going on and somehow be able to sort out the few significant details from among the irrelevant dozens, while grabbing a dinner of fries and a diet coke. For example, does the forty-eight-member chorus wear or carry its hats? That decision is an easy one—there's too little space in the wings for them *not* to wear their hats. Or at what speed should the curtain come down during a concluding and dramatic aria? It matters because the faster the curtain comes down, the more noise the motor makes, breaking the moment's aesthetic spell.

Rehearsals are highly efficient, calibrated to within a few minutes. Union rules about length of rehearsals apply to musicians and stagehands. To get a sense of labor's power, recall that strikes, stop-work meetings, "go slows," and other types of militant industrial unrest delayed the completion of the Sydney Opera House for thousands of hours from the start of construction in 1959 to its completion in 1966. When the stage manager calls, "Time, ladies and gentle-men," that's a full stop. Only an extraordinary appeal will prolong a rehearsal: the opera director's raising her skirt and flashing the stage manager gained a few more minutes.

Simone Young is not one to "muck around," musicians told me. That's un-derstandable given the time constraints, but it is another facet of who Simone Young is, regardless of the time available. During a rehearsal in the Opera House, Simone Young halts the action: "Quiet, please." The house grows quiet except backstage, where the technicians are working. Her polite request is now an imperious "I must have quiet!"

She is hearing a ping-like noise directly overhead. Only her ears pick up the noise at first, but then a few others hear it. No one knows the source or quite what to do about it. After the stage manager assures her that the ping will be eliminated, the rehearsal continues.

Some minutes later the company takes a break. As the stage empties, the electricians, carpenters, and other stage crew—eleven all—cluster together, no doubt about tracing the ping. One of the crew makes the unmistakably *cojones grandes* gesture, admitting a begrudging respect for Simone Young's resolve. (The intermittent ping was finally located in an elevator. When going up more than two floors with two people, there would be a ping. It took two days of back-and-forth work among the stage manager, the Opera House facilities staff, and the elevator vendor to silence the ping!)

The stage manager, Roger Press, whom I saw struggling to accommodate Young's certainty about what she wants, amid praising her good leadership would like a little recognition. "She does not appreciate the limitations I work with. Instead of listening to me, it's a command, 'You must do this!' " He feels unappreciated. The Sydney Opera stage is notoriously tiny, with only four to five feet from wall to fly in the wings. He'd like to hear more of what she says to the orchestra: "Let's meet in the middle."

When I asked Anne Frankenberg, the orchestra manager, to describe her re-lationship to Simone, she said it was staff to boss. She and other support staff spend time nurturing Simone and supplying her with endless diet cokes; "she is high maintenance."

Perhaps because she is now more attuned to bruised feelings or simply more aware that everyone has a stake in the opera's success, Simone Young is quick to build bridges among all participants—after one of the performances, she con-gratulated the stage crew for their good work.

As well, one player told me Simone Young's early-on temper tantrums have matured into a greater patience and willingness to listen to and consider other views. She can make the hard decisions—some singers are not back—and she can change her mind. The chorus master's job was on the chopping block, but after consideration, Simone relented.

The stories catch Simone Young's "narky" side. (Australian for what can be an ill-tempered perseverance). When her standards fail to be met, she'll explain what needs fixing (no ping!) and won't go on until she is satisfied.

When Simone Young pushes her viewpoint, she is prepared to "walk the walk," to take responsibility for a required action. If the conflict cannot be settled in a collaborative way, she may ultimately walk out, as she has twice in her career, with no intention of returning. Simone Young takes responsibility for pushing.

David Whyte, the poet and business consultant, has a phrase for it, putting "fire in one's voice" (1996, 117). He finds too few people in boardrooms willing to speak up about what they believe, especially when in conflict with powerful people. It's as if we play our corporate music all too timidly. Our timorous voices offer little resistance to the table-thumping executive bully, demanding buy-in to the latest scheme.

Simone Young achieves a seeming paradox: she convinces players they are free to innovate and express themselves, while getting them to accept her vision for the music and follow her direction. How does she do it? By encouraging everyone to feel they have the power to express themselves, without ever surrendering *her* power, *her* vision, or *her* responsibility. "If I can *inspire* the musicians to actually play the music the way I want to hear it, then everyone is happy!" Does this merely gloss over a fear-driven relationship between a strong leader and her subordinates? Not really. What I saw was collaboration among highly skilled people. Simone is confident in her musical interpretation but genuinely open to better ideas.

It's a manifestation of the Taoist adage: "The more power you give away, the more powerful you become." Bernadette Cullen, mezzo soprano, told me: "One does not feel like there's a cage around [Simone Young] or that there is a heavy creative borderline. You can put your stamp on [what you do]; there's freedom. It's like she's saying, 'Show me what you can do'."

Simone Young's genuine awareness and concern for people, her ability to "talk to you as another human," help gain trust, the must-have for creative freedom. A few musicians I interviewed used the same phrase, a "nurturing quality," to describe Simone Young's support. It's this nurturing quality that invites performers to place themselves in her hands. Musicians told me they regard her as "being with you," that "she is fighting for you." Unlike some conductors who prefer distance, Simone Young overtly develops trust relationships through, for example, post-rehearsal drinks with a few musicians, separate rehearsals with the brass (one of many orchestras' "benignly neglected" groups), and individual talks with musicians.

After a two-hour rehearsal she surprised me with: : "Not sure you saw much leadership." I asked her, "Do you always have this much fun?" Simone looked at me for a moment, then agreed. "They're a fun group to work with."

Her humanness was illustrated to me one hot February day in Sydney. One of the conductor's perks is a cab from the Surry Hills studios to the Opera House on the water. Simone Young's cab sat curbside, waiting for her. Mine was no-where in sight. While getting into the cab, she called out, "Let's share!"

We talked of cricket (one of her passions) and women's basketball (one of mine), how her dad volunteered during the 2000 Olympics to greet visitors at St. James' Church, and of a cabby who recognized her from a picture in the paper. "You're the Manly girl!" he exclaimed (to her genuine delight), referring to her hometown of Manly Beach, across the harbor.

Those touched by her camaraderie desire to excel: "I'm willing to do the best I can for her," Tony Gault, the concertmaster, told me.

Show Time

Milou de Castellane (OA's publicist) asked me, casually enough: "If we could arrange it, would you like to sit in the orchestra pit tomorrow night? You'd have to wear black."

Would I? I rushed out to the department store and instantly acquired the requisite black. The next day's e-mail brought the good news, "All arranged."

And there I was, ensconced among the horns, the tympani behind me in their own pit. The stage floor is suspended over all but three of the seven rows of musicians—the music has a ways to travel. It's an awful pit, everyone tells me, including Simone, but I have the best seat in the house.

Gazing out, I sense and share a growing anticipation among the audience. To-night is this season's last performance of Verdi's *Il Trovatore*. The house lights dim. The spotlight beams down on Simone Young's entry to swelling applause. All eyes in the orchestra pit are fixed on her. Now, with the curtain about to rise, she adds another ingredient to the magic of the evening—*her* style.

Simone Young conducts, literally, from the toes to the tip of her baton, with a dynamic, infectious energy and enthusiasm. Her commitment is "boots and all," leading at a *prestissimo* pace—no one has worked harder, studied longer, or understands better the composer's intention. Her eyes at key moments become hypnotic—summoning a unanimity of sound. Her love for the music and pas-sion for the sound elicit and command the best from the musicians. She shushes the strings, encourages the brass, smiles. She gestures for more, for less, with a slight frown followed by another frown with a touch to her ear or a smile, a thumbs up, "Good on you, mate!"

When Simone Young conducts, the music sings within you and through you. I find myself gladly swept along by this gathering of musical forces. Quintes-sentially Simone, during a nonmusical moment in the opera, she jokes with the first violin and gives the musicians two thumbs up. *This is fun!* Perhaps that is the one most transformational quality of a great leader—expressing joy in what she does.

Epilogue: "The Only Thing We'll Argue about Is Money"

That's what Adrian Colette, her Opera Australia boss, told Simone when he hired her for the Sydney job. And so it was.

In September 2002, while guest conducting in Los Angeles, Opera Australia's board chose not to renew Simone's contract, in a disagreement over the high cost of opera production. Simone had put her budget on the table—with little room for negotiation. If Opera Australia wanted to become a major player in the opera world, this is what it would cost. The board balked.

Not long after completing her contract in Sydney—and after much public furor over her departure—Ms. Young returned to Hamburg, Germany, as the triple-headed manager and artistic director, principal musical director of the Staatsoper, with its 300 years of tradition, including Otto Klemperer and Gustav Mahler. Another glass ceiling smashed, it was a bigger job, with nearly absolute control and a generous budget. The tenured musicians would nearly double, from 68 in Sydney to 125 in Hamburg. And unlike in Sydney, the orchestra pit is open, allowing the music to sail forth, with only the tympani floored over.

A Different Leader?

Not really. In December 2006, I spoke with Simone in the Hamburg opera house and observed her in rehearsal. I did so with a little trepidation, because several newspaper interviews cast her in the role of the iron-fisted orchestral leader—a tyrannical female Toscanini. Jana Wendt (2006), in her interview with Simone, termed her a "steely defender of the conductor as autocrat."

My anxiety was boosted a notch when, just before Ms. Young and her entourage of a half dozen brushed past us into the opera house, Ms. Sabine Rosenberg, assistant to Simone, cautioned me: "Frau Young does not wish to be spoken to prior to the rehearsal."

Well, my anxiety was soon alleviated. The rehearsal started with a long explanation by Simone, in German, about her interpretation of the piece. From there the rehearsal was open and collaborative, all the more remarkable since this was the Hamburg debut of John Neumeier's "creation," *Parsifal—Episoden und Echo*, a partial dress rehearsal with dancers and a full orchestra. Simone admitted mistakes ("Sorry, sorry." she said on one mess up). She asked for ideas from the musicians; she coached a singer ("Use more voice; otherwise you come across fantastically.") She listened ("My ears are two feet wide") and joked with the musicians and the singers.

After two hours of intense work, many in the orchestra tapped their bows on the music stands in tribute to the conductor, a job well done. Of course these are German musicians, and as Simone would explain to me during our interview, there is a self-imposed formality in Hamburg not to be found in Sydney. The German "language with its *Herrs und Fraus*, and social structure" tend toward formal, autocratic relationships. In Australia, "Egalitarianism is demanded, expected, daily."

Wendt quotes her: "Most good conductors inspire a certain amount of terror. . . . It's a very child-parent thing. And there is an element of that relationship between an orchestral player and the conductor, that if the player respects the conductor, they don't want to disappoint them."

What separates Ms. Young from the egotistical conductor is that she recognizes the reality of the relationship between musicians and conductors and uses it to achieve her goals. She does so in a pragmatic way, using her *earned* and *deserved* conductor mystique while remaining who she is throughout it all, "the Manly girl!"

PART 3

Coaching, Self-Management, Collaboration, Communication

CHAPTER 16

Coaching for Results

I define coaching as *the interactive* process through which a leader offers sound advice, speaks the *truth*, *challenges*, and encourages a *willing* colleague or group to *become better* at what they do. We'll find out in the next few pages how well this definition covers the coaching concept. Also, this chapter looks at

a few sports transfers to the workplace,

something I call genuine coaching, and

the five principles of coaching.

Sports coaching analogies rarely apply to the library workplace, such as "When the going gets tough, the tough get going!" or "Win one for the Gipper!" Also, many sports coaches are obsessed with winning. If we did in the office what some extreme coaches do on the practice field, we'd be arrested for abuse, if not assault! Yet how the best coaches work with their teams can help us better understand the coaching role. I especially listen to the coach who, when her team *loses*, says "I could have done a better job." Also, there's something to be gained by hearing player insights into how some coaches actually work.

The following quotes from two basketball players (Strickland 2005) suggest a level of coaching rarely found on the playing field or in the office:

"Coach is always going to tell you the truth, no matter what it is. And just to know where you stand is good—whether it's good or bad."

"[I]t's always good when he can tell you things that you're not seeing."

"It's always that he's real . . . , so after you leave you know where you stand, on and off the court."

These players are talking about their private meetings with Coach Mike Krzyzewski (Coach K), a distinguished basketball coach. He calls himself a leader and a teacher. For these players, based on their words, a good coach is consistent, truthful, pragmatic, clear, and an effective observer and communicator.

One day I got to observe the intensity with which Coach K] watches practice. He somehow makes sense from the blurred images of ten players going full speed, and he excels in communicating what he sees. Calmly spoken or tersely expressed, the truth, "no matter what it is," is shared fully and openly in ways that help the player. The truth is not bottled up or avoided. It helps, of course, that these players *want* their coach to tell them the truth.

Giving feedback is much of what a good coach does. When I lecture in library school about annual performance appraisals—a formal process in which supervisors get to coach their subordinates—I ask students to reflect on a time when someone gave them feedback, gave them advice that really made a difference, that changed them for the better. I start the exercise with an example of my own, about how a boss and colleague gave me some very valuable advice. He let me know that I was coming to him with problems in need of solutions—and he expected more: "Sure, bring me problems and questions. *And*, tell me what you think we should do. Tell me what suggestions *you* have for a solution." Why was I receptive to his advice when I might ignore the same advice from someone else? What made me *hear* his suggestion?

I ask the students to consider these questions, on paper, about what led to the feedback's effectiveness:

- What were your thoughts and mindset?

- How did the feedback giver relate to you?

- How did you feel about him or her?

- What did you hear?

Then I ask them to complete this statement: "I really heard what that person was saying because . . . ." These are the reasons they give for the feedback's making a difference:

- I saw the information could benefit me.

- The giver had my best interests at heart.

- I respected the person giving the feedback.

- I trusted the person giving me the feedback.

- It was important to me; I had a desire to change.

- We were one-on-one in private; the person had my full attention.

In other words, you hear feedback only when:

- The feedback comes from a credible source. The giver has expertise, is a valid source.

- The feedback giver is trustworthy. What he or she says is sincere.

- The feedback is well intended. The giver has the receiver's best interests at heart, or it's otherwise apparent that the feedback is to serve a worthy purpose.

- The feedback's timing and circumstances are conducive to learning. The receiver *wants* to hear what you have to say. I have italicized "wants" because the person may not always anticipate with pleasure what you have to say but is resolute in hearing the news, maybe good or maybe bad, just like Coach K's players.

- The feedback is given face to face, preferably in private. The receiver and giver can hear and observe facial expression and body language. There's opportunity to ask questions and clarify meanings.

- The message is clear. It adds clarity to what the receiver has done, not done, or needs to do.

- The feedback is helpful to the receiver. The message contains good information or new insights that are useful or enlightening.

This exercise is useful in showing that if the *conditions* for meaningful feedback are absent, performance appraisal becomes a futile exercise. And our coaching during the evaluation, however well intended, will make little difference to the person we are evaluating.[1]

It's been popular among organizational consultants to suggest that supervisors should *coach more, supervise less*. Indeed, there's a historical aspect to this all the way back to 500 BC, as suggested in Lao-Tzu's *The Book of the Way*. The Taoist offered up the image of leader as midwife, the leader as coach:

> If you do not trust a person's process, that person will not trust you.
>
> Imagine you are a midwife; you are assisting at someone else's birth.
>
> Do good without show or fuss.
>
> Facilitate what is happening rather than what you think ought to be happening.
>
> If you must take the lead, lead so that the mother is helped, yet still free and in charge.
>
> When the baby is born the mother will rightly say, *"We did it ourselves."*

Those last four words have puzzled management theorists for several decades. Some, without a real understanding of Taoism, have promoted that the best kind of leader is indeed one about whom when the work is done, the followers will say, "We did it ourselves!" There's a warm fuzziness about that; certainly something to aspire to in a humane and participatory organization with trust and respect abounding. Yet while it may be intuitively appealing, implementing the Taoist philosophy is less than intuitive. Our efforts to do more coaching and less supervising may result in our becoming absentee bosses.

"You Can't Coach a Pumpkin!"

That's the phrase that pretty much sums up my experience with coaching the unwilling and the uncertain. What happens when we try to coach staff who think they are doing fine and that their current level of performance is good enough? Our suggestion that they need coaching might lead them to ask us about when to find the time in an already impossible schedule. Writers who blithely advocate coaching more—I was using the term in my management articles as early as 1992—rarely tell us the *how* or the *when*. Nor do the experts talk about the changed expectations for those to be coached—what does it mean to be coached?

In my experience, unlike those admirable athletes under Coach K and Coach Gail and the student musicians coached by Orpheus, few library staff *want* to be coached, many are uncertain, and some *won't* be coached. The last are as unyielding as a November pumpkin. Anyone suggesting that managers should coach usually fails to address the special relationship demanded for genuine coaching.

A personal learning experience: When I led a large library's experiment with self-managing teams, my administrative job description changed—largely to reflect my desire (and assignment) to implement team and self-management concepts in our reinvented organization. I boiled down my two-page-long, single-spaced job description for Associate University Librarian into one sparsely populated piece of paper with three headers: coaching, consulting, and leading, with each followed by a few qualifying words.

Naturally, as part of my coaching I wanted to see how the self-managing teams and their team leaders were doing and how I could *help, challenge*, and *encourage*—the modifiers in my job description. So I invited myself to sit in on team meetings and promised to be little more than a fly on the wall, to observe unobtrusively. And after observing, I'd give feedback to the team leader about what I saw.

Most of the meetings were conducted in a formal way, seemingly rehearsed, with participants on their best behavior and no controversial items on any agenda. My fly-on-the-wall role felt like that of the jumbo fly in the classic sci-fi horror flick. Still, I did learn. These team meetings were little different from the department meetings I had sat through in previous years. During project reports, there were few offers of help or ideas for improvement coming from the team members. Complaints still abounded—always about issues external to their team, including the administration. Nor had the team leaders adopted new ways of engaging team members, of evoking ideas and opinions.

Another lesson: the hierarchy was clearly still in control, and we were far from achieving the highly effective teams we wanted. Our team development was stuck in phase one, immature. To put it euphemistically, most of our teams were developmentally delayed. However disappointed I felt personally, the meetings were not a total waste. What I saw underscored the difficulties of changing an organization—most team leaders, while saluting the team flag, were rooted in the familiar world of the department head. Another inhibitor was the organization not being clear about what was expected of team leaders and team members. Nor had the library done enough in the way of training teams.

I think many of us—team leaders and administrators—meant well. We acted in good, if naïve, faith in moving toward a team-based organization. But hoping for an intuitive, spontaneous, positive response to the new way—however much endorsed and practiced by the director of the library—was unrealistic.

Reflecting on that time dredges up mixed feelings: an amused embarrassment at my coaching naiveté; irritated bemusement at a few of the team leaders' intractability; and ultimately, puzzlement over why few wanted to do anything different, why there was so little receptivity to trying out new roles. I like to think a few could have humored me, borne with me, and given the situation the benefit of the doubt if only for learning's sake. I did persist in giving each team leader some feedback about what I had observed. That superficial feedback was expressed and accepted with a mutual sigh of relief—or so it seemed.

WHAT IS GENUINE COACHING?

A philosophically profound book, James Flaherty's *Coaching: Evoking Excellence in Others* (1999), offers insights into genuine coaching. For Mr. Flaherty the ends of coaching are self-correction, self-generation, and long-term excellent performance. Flaherty's five principles of coaching relate to my team observation experience:

1. **Relationship.** For the most part, I enjoyed good relationships with the team leaders. Not surprisingly, those most beholden to the boss-worker paradigm were the least willing to be observed. For Flaherty, the relationship has to be "mutually satisfying" and based on "mutual respect, mutual trust, and freedom of expression." This level of relationship may be difficult to achieve in the workplace. Supervising

has an explicit power imbalance between superior/subordinate, based in part on the supervisor's power to reward and punish, and that may impede coaching. Mary Parker Follett (1978) put it well: "Supervision is necessary, supervision is resented."

Still, if strong trust exists, I think it is possible for a supervisor to coach a subordinate, certainly in the Venn diagram–like zone where their job interests and responsibilities overlap. The coach's learning commitment and the client's learning commitment overlap into a shared, two-way wanting to learn. For example, in the situations listed below, coaching is more desirable than it was in my obtrusively sitting in on a team's meeting:

> *Performance assessment:* Where do you want to be next year? What do you want to work on? What's the most important area in which for you to grow?

> *Breakdown in a system:* The manager is in over his or her head and wants/needs help.

> *Request for advice:* "I need help disciplining a staff person."

> *Realization that new skills might result in promotion:* Help a person learn to be a supervisor, a better listener.

> *Library need:* How will we achieve higher quality, lower cost, higher speed, quicker turnaround?

> *Project milestones:* An opportunity to reflect and consider what went well and what might be done differently.

2. **Pragmatic.** According to Flaherty, coaching is outcome-based, with relentless correction based on feedback loops, similar to what's been termed the Deming cycle: plan an improvement, do the improvement, check on the improvement, act on the improvement (adopt it, abandon it, revise it, and so forth).

   My attempts to observe group dynamics were superficial, more information-seeking than outcome-based, nor was there "relentless correction." One observation of a team was hardly enough to get my foot in the door. To begin a relationship or create a series of feedback loops would need a greater time investment. Had I dedicated my limited time to those few teams that were open to improvement, I probably would have had more success.

3. **Two tracks.** Flaherty contends that coaching happens only when "both client and coach are engaged in learning." Good coaches question their own assumptions, vigilantly correct from outcomes, and abandon prescriptive techniques. My observing team meetings was a sort of learning. However, that "learning," as minimal as it was, was barely reciprocated by the team leaders—it certainly was not mutual!

Keith Lockhart, Boston Pops Orchestra conductor, is quoted in the video *The Art of Coaching in Business:* "The teachers who are very limited as conducting teachers are the ones who say, 'Do it exactly as I do and you'll get the same result that I get.' That's a big mistake. [If] you force your students to toe the line in a mimicry sort of way, you end up with a lot of *bad imitations of yourself.*" So the teacher who has nothing to learn (one track) is like the coach who has nothing to learn.

The 1986 movie *Hoosiers* offers some excellent two-track coaching insights. The story is about the Hickory Huskers, an underdog basketball team from a tiny Indiana high school that makes it all the way to the state championship tournament. When the championship game is tied and down to the last shot, Gene Hackman, the coach, calls a time out. In the huddle, Hackman prescribes a play that uses the best shooter as a decoy and gives the ball to someone else to take the last shot. You can tell from the players' expressions that they don't agree with Hackman's decision, but no one says anything—until the star player speaks up, "I'll make it." The coach, with nary a skipped beat, reconsiders and says OK.

Here the coach is the learner and is able to recognize the better idea, at least that it is for this team, at this time. Whenever I see this scene—the players huddled around the coach—in a standing room only crowd—I wonder about how a manager gets staff to speak up, to speak up when the pressure is on to say nothing, to go with the loudest voice or the most authoritative voice. What qualities did this coach bring to the team that enabled one of the players to speak up and, in the end, to help him be a better coach?

4. **Always/already.** Flaherty observes that "human beings are always already in the middle of something." I was aware that the library team leaders had their own way of doing things, their own ideas about what worked best in the running of their teams. I understood that to some extent, but also was prone to interpret "where they were" as resistance to team concepts. A more effective coach would have adjusted to this scenario rather than concluding recalcitrance. A winning lacrosse coach's understated style suggests his respect for what the players bring to the game: "He just kind of steps back," said a player in a story by Strickland (2007). "It really is our game. He doesn't tell us what we're going to run. He asks us, "OK, what do you think is working. He gives us a lot of leeway."

Bob McKinnon, coach of the Colorado 14ers, a NBA farm team, told me how he coaches his players (all just short of making a NBA team) to do their best. He's adjusted his coaching style to the "always/already" fact of "nobody wants to be here." At first, that may seem to be a rationalization for losing. Not for this coach. He uses the "nobody wants to be here" phrase in putting the focus on how his players can get to the next level. Farm teams that win statistically send more players to the NBA than do the farm teams that lose. When that sinks in, the 14ers play up to their full potential.

5. **Techniques** don't work (all the time) for Flaherty. I suppose my library team observations were a simplistic technique. Other coaching techniques, perhaps like those in the Inner Game series of books by W. Timothy Gallwey (1997), are too limiting and easily figured out by the coach's client. For example, the inner game coach will correct a flawed golf stroke by distracting the player so he doesn't think too much about the stroke. Often the player does better, but after a while he catches on to what the coach is doing and goes back to his errant ways. Gallwey offers the following example of his patented distraction technique.

   A sales team had the worst quarterly results of any in a national company. The manager talked daily to the sales staff and told them how to maximize performance results and increase revenues, but there was no improvement. The manager, figuring he had little to lose, suspended the mandatory quotas for the next quarter! The sales team would not be held accountable for missing target goals. It worked. Sales improved. Interestingly, although sales got better, the distraction technique really does not address the factors that might cause the low sales. What if the manager asked his sales team for their ideas? What if the manager listened and prescribed less? Flaherty is not completely negative about techniques—we all use them, he says—but we need to be selective and aware of when the situation and timing are right.

   To return to my observing case, I've concluded that going to one meeting and hoping for revelations to come tumbling forth was unrealistic. Likely, had I stayed with one team, gained trust, listened well, and worked hard at giving well-considered feedback, the outcomes would have been far more productive.

   Coaching well is more than just supervising less; it requires an extensive commitment from the coach and the person being coached. There is real potential for improvements when a willing manager coaches a willing staff member, as long as the manager and the employee being coached understand what they are getting into.

CHAPTER 17

Peer Coaching for the Postdepartmental Library

Not long ago, I envisioned scrapping a library's hierarchical structures, literally tossing out the old ways of working. Instead of the old hierarchy of boxes and solid black communication lines, we'd use circles and invent a form of wireless communication. This epiphany—my colleagues saw it more as a *momentary lapse of reason*—dawned on me while I was helping implement a self-managing team organization in a research library (2006a). Through this new, postdepartmental organization, we hoped to tap into the resourcefulness of each and every staff member. And along the way we'd somehow re-do the salary, communication, promotion and job classification, and discipline and reward structures!

Five years later we had achieved some admirable productivity goals and glimpsed the mother lode of what was possible, but had barely made a dent in the hierarchy. Entrenched resistance came from multiple fronts: the top-down parent organization, many of the library's managers; surprisingly some support staff, and the inherently inflexible reward and promotion systems.

Since that disappointment, I've seen some movement in more than a few libraries toward less hierarchy and more self-management; a subtle organizational shift is, I believe, underway. Much of the change is internal—sometimes unknown to the top leadership of the library, or more often tolerated in a détente with the executive group—and will eventually shift its way across the organization, where the real work gets done. Yes, the worst kind of heavy-handed, counterproductive library administrations still exist, but, even in the most rigid hierarchies, I've witnessed some positive changes from within, a burgeoning of the eternal human desire to control one's life.

Although the top boss may still think he or she is in charge, some units function more like teams than like the departments of old. These midlevel leaders appear to be comfortable with team constructs, entailing a loosely knit arrangement among the staff and an expected collaboration among all team members in working and decision making.

Externally, they deliver what Caesar demands, but internally they appear to be working in more liberated ways. This greater flexibility has evolved for various reasons—including heaps of positive evidence that greater productivity and innovation come through teamwork, especially when teams are *highly effective.* Another influential cause is that many new professionals (librarians included) increasingly demand or expect having a say in how to do their work. They prefer leaders to be more hands off than hovering.

Common sense suggests that people who are interested and engaged in their work will likely do a better job than those waiting for orders from above. To get results, a confident and secure department manager will give up some of his or her authority, share the power, and put that newly tapped energy to work.

These notions are not new. What is new is that several influential management writers believe that the old hierarchy is diminishing and that a much looser structure is, if not already here, on the horizon. All the more, our current global recession should promote more collaboration and less authoritarianism. Arguably, most bosses when battered as we all are these days, will have enough sense to call out for help, to throw out the organizational life lines. Only the most foolhardy will maintain the top-down delusion of absolute administrative control.

So my hoped for organizational changes, delayed a decade, may finally be underway. But the change is not the wholesale replacement model I'd envisioned. Rather, it appears to be evolving *parallel* to the existing hierarchy. My research on the conductor-less Orpheus Chamber Orchestra and Southwest Airlines indicates there is a *business* side and there is a *performance* side to this "new" organization.

This liberation movement at the team or departmental level has benefits for and requirements of tyro librarians. First, the looser knit arrangement gives them a work environment in which to thrive. However, new skills are required to make the most of a more innovative structure. With the loosening up of the hierarchical model, there may be less guidance and more need for resilience and linkage among participants. Although not exactly an entrepreneurial model, the new library does require a greater resourcefulness among its members. If a boss is truly less important in the day-to-day operation of a unit, then who makes decisions, and how are these decision made? New skills are essential, and in the case of new librarians, these skills may not have been acquired in their library science education.

Without the accompanying personal skills—an elevated *emotional IQ,* if you will—these new structures will not work at peak performance; teams will not be highly effective. We may espouse collaboration and teamwork, talk the talk, but if we lack team and collaboration skills, we may wind up with a superficially desirable structure in which members presumably feel better about each other, but get no more—or, more likely, less—done than in the hierarchy.

The Postdepartmenal Organization

Based on hundreds of interviews of young managers and leaders around the world, Marshall Goldsmith (2003) and his research team predict a major shift from traditional controlling structures to less firm, more fluid relationships in the workplace.

Goldsmith claims that the successful future leader will need to master some fourteen attributes. These qualities are not new, the emphasis is. Of the fourteen, I've listed below four that will require enhancing several interactive skills and understanding the new relationships between leaders and followers. The honing of these skills will most likely be on the job and they are probably best learned with someone's help. One way is through peer coaching.

Create shared vision.
Develop and empower people.
Build teamwork and partnerships.
Share leadership.

The Goldsmith research suggests we will work with peers in new ways. We will lead differently and, as followers, we will respond differently to being led. For example, to share leadership suggests *many leaders*. How does one share leadership? Are your subordinates capable of accepting their share? If not, how will they be enabled?

Another recent study shows the wisdom of loosening up versus ratcheting down. O'Toole and Lawler (2006) studied two types of organizations: Low Cost Operators (LCOs)—firms that shift the burden for health care, retirement, and education to others; pay low; and espouse *Theory X* leadership—and High Involvement Companies (HICs), and concluded that the tight controls exerted by LCOs actually wind up costing more than the freedom given to workers in HICs.

In a "bottom line" example, when an HIC like Costco is compared to a LCO like Sam's Club, Costco "does more with less." Costco, which pays a third more in salaries plus benefits than Sam's Club, has higher productivity among its staff. In one analysis, the 68,000 staff at Costco did the same number of sales as 103,000 staff did at Sam's. O'Toole and Lawler (2006) state that "when turnover costs and productivity were reckoned, it was cheaper for Costco to pay people more." Following are other noteworthy differences between HICs and LCOs:

HIC managers share decision making with staff.

HICs train staff for the big picture and expect understanding of the bottom line.

HICs give workers decision-making power in their responsibilities.

HICs, in hard times, look for alternatives to layoffs; they retain staff as a resource in good times and in bad.

And I would add another quality in which HICs outperform LCOs: *attention to customer needs*. This is a direct result of the decision-making power vested by top leaders in staff.

Another theorist, John P. Kotter, anticipated in 1996 much of what Goldsmith et al. concluded in 2003 about the new organization and the essential skills. Kotter's new organizational environment will have a sense of *urgency*—this will diminish the luxury of delaying needed change and help break down the traditional structures that often impede rapid response. A colleague tells me that change in his library is coming about far more quickly than in previous years. Only a decade ago, change in this library was resisted and dithered over. No longer. Now, he tells me, changes once regarded as too difficult to implement—the planning and discussion would have been interminable—can happen in a single meeting of participants. Unfortunately the new urgency in this library comes from reduced budgets (lost dollars) rather than collaborative and innovative use of existing resources for the greater good. The driver now is survival. Still, the new environment is far less confining, in particular for the new librarian, than it used to be.

According to Kotter, there will be genuine *teamwork* at the top. The one strong leader will be less important to the organization. Teamwork skills, if they are to be more than lip service, will need to be learned and practiced in the executive suite. Currently, libraries are still weak on this, assigning too much responsibility to the sole leader, more boss than team captain. Even libraries that are team based, and there are a few, often ignore the essential teamwork qualities to be truly successful at what they do.

There will be *broad-based empowerment* requiring effective communication with others. It is easy to say the library staff are empowered. Getting results from empowerment is the only real way to demonstrate empowerment. How much latitude do staff members have to do what needs doing without seeking permission from a higher up? How much praise or blame is heaped on someone who, when trying to provide the best customer service, makes a mistake? Phony empowerment does more to harm staff morale than probably any other unsubstantiated claim made by a library's leadership.

And for Kotter, the successful new organization will have an *adaptive corporate culture*. Adapting, adjusting, and anticipating all seem more doable in the loosely knit organization, with a wide spread of responsibility, than in a traditional organization with tight control over information and decision making.

One could argue that many librarians do not want to be overly engaged in the running of the library; a librarian may just want to do his or her job—the one in the job description—and to leave the major decisions to the bosses. Although some librarians prefer this model, I know many librarians who thrive in the participatory model and are happy to take part in the leadership of the library. And as I've already pointed out, the new librarian may expect to have a leadership role.

In my study of a women's college basketball team (1999), I asked the players (akin for me to the new generation of library staff members) about their expectations of team captains. What would they like to see captains doing *more of*? The players told me they wanted the captains to move the team toward *everyone* taking a greater share of team responsibility and authority. In keeping with this, the players asked the captains to give them more feedback and involve them in decision making.

I was impressed with the players' openness and their wanting to have a greater role (more responsibility) in the work of the team. I suspect this is the same result I might get if I were to ask a group of freshly minted and engaged librarians about what they want from their team leaders, their supervisors, and their department heads.

Another recent team researcher, Richard Hackman (2002a), espouses *five* necessary conditions for successful teamwork:

> The team must be a **real** team, rather than a team in name only.

> It has **compelling** direction for its work.

> It has an **enabling structure** that facilitates teamwork.

> It operates within a **supportive** organizational context.

> And, it has expert teamwork **coaching**.

Hackman is unique among researchers in that he highlights the value of coaching teams. His observations of the conductor-less Orpheus Chamber Orchestra in rehearsal for many years (2002b) may well have convinced him of the quintessential value of peer coaching.

HELPING NEW PROFESSIONALS

At first glance a musical orchestra may be an unlikely source for ideas on how to work in the new organization model. After all, is not the symphony orchestra the prototypical model for top-down management—a boss with a pointed stick telling workers what to do? Well, not really, and seemingly less so with a new generation of musicians who are less content with being told what to do. There is a trend underway among musicians, even in conductor-led orchestras, for more say. Both the newly constituted Colorado and Tulsa (Oklahoma) symphonies are thriving with extensive involvement by musicians in their management. Ronnie Bauch, an Orpheus violinist and former managing director, says, "You can see that the landscape (for orchestral organizations) is changing dramatically" (Schweitzer 2006, 40).

To this end, Schweitzer writes that Orpheus is working with student orchestras at the Juilliard and Manhattan schools of music in adapting their loose-knit, seemingly leaderless way of making great music. In the Orpheus/Juilliard/Manhattan collaboration, Orpheus musicians-as-coaches work with the students as they pursue a semester long project to produce a live, public, conductor-less performance. With Orpheus's assistance, the student players identify and develop specific self-management and peer-coaching skills that help the orchestra achieve its performance goals. At the end, it is the student orchestra alone on the stage delivering the performance. A student musician confirms, "[The Orpheus approach] changed the way I play in other ensembles and taught me how to use my voice to influence others."[1]

What Orpheus does in coaching new musicians for self-management and peer coaching is applicable to the new librarians in the "new library." Although new librarians may have done small group work from grade school onward, they may not have acquired the necessary team skills required for highly effective teams. At the graduate school level—in my experience—there is a prevalent aversion and disdain among students for working on team projects. They tell me they've had nothing but negative experiences in small group work. Good students feel taken advantage of by less able students and those who do not hold up their end of the bargain. They feel at risk with the team's receiving a grade rather than one for each individual. Frankly, they'd much prefer doing any assignment solo. As the professor, I persist and encourage, and usually the teams in my management classes work together and produce a good product. My overt objective is that the students get through the *how* of working together, at least this once, so they see (if not on their own team, then on other student teams) that highly effective teams can far surpass groups that never figure out the *how*.

These are the team skills I've derived from observing numerous student symphony rehearsals guided by Orpheus musician coaches. The students apply these coaching and self-management skills when working on their own:

Collective listening

Time management

Delegation of responsibility

Being prepared, taking responsibility, being proactive

Communication—talking—giving feedback

Collective Listening

Although listening actively is not a foreign concept to any professional, it is especially relevant to a musical group that strives to produce a particular sound. "You always have to be listening to what everyone else is doing," says one student. "This can be tiring and it can be fun" (Schweitzer 2006, 41). In Orpheus rehearsals musicians listen as audience members. At a Carnegie Hall rehearsal, I saw several musicians taking turns sitting some thirty rows back to hear what the music was sounding like and then giving feedback to the entire orchestra on how to fine tune the sound. While playing, they listen in their own instrumental groups to the sound the other instrumental groups make; they seek to balance the overall sound, not just fine tune *their* sound.

A *New York Times* review (Tommasini 2008) of an Orpheus performance mentions the importance of listening, a role usually commanded by the conductor, the boss: "The risky part comes in listening carefully enough in the moment so that pliant phrasing and impetuous flourishes can happen in a natural way."

How does collective listening relate to libraries? Do we librarians have to concern ourselves with "pliant phrasing"? Perhaps not in the literal sense; what about "pliant phrasing" when used in a figurative way?

Well, it's all in the quality of our performance. Do we strive for an A level or a "good enough," C level product, result, or output? We are different from musicians in not being on stage in front of an audience, but we still produce something for others to respond to, learn from, use, and consume. We still try to be the best we can be. Why are some libraries more productive than others? An accident! some would say in dismissing the varying results. *Au contraire*, in my experience, the best products, the best library performances come not from happenstance but from an ability to hear the "pliant phrasing" and to design and achieve a superior product, service, or way of working. When I talk with best practices librarians, I find positive energy attitudes, an openness toward different approaches, bosses who encourage experimentation, and truly empowered staff who are recognized for their achievement.

Another result of collective listening is that many students gain more confidence in their playing. They may in fact be hearing for the first time the overall orchestra. Imagine that, seeing for the first time the overall purpose of the library, not just hearing our section's music!

Time Management

Without a boss in the room (or even with a boss in the room), many groups are often prone to wasting time. Absent the boss, it becomes incumbent for the group to manage time. Unfortunately the traditional library model suggests that there is always more time. I have been part of groups who have gone far beyond the point of least diminishing returns yet still are short of a decision.

The self-discipline that occurs among musicians on a time budget, with a performance deadline, can be of great value to new librarians. This discipline adds focus, but there is a trade-off: the individual may have to settle for less than what he or she wants or is comfortable with, but at least you will have a product and probably a very good one.

Delegation of Responsibility

Student musicians learn to assign people to keep track of time; consider tempo, dynamics, and balance; and consider achievement and progress on a topic. None of these can be left to chance for a musical presentation, if it is to be the best it can be, anymore so than when a library team develops a new service plan.

Being Prepared, Taking Responsibility, Being Proactive

Self-management doesn't work if group members are not prepared. The first rehearsals at both schools of music are telling. If the musicians have not done careful preparation, then the process goes slowly and painfully—and everyone knows. A first step in the Orpheus process is the appointment of a core: key players from each section of the orchestra who meet ahead of time to develop the character of the piece and arrive at some initial agreement on the interpretation. This speeds up the process of rehearsal. When a group does not have a core, it is apparent in the hesitation and the lack of opinion among the players.

Richard Rood, a violinist and Orpheus coach, didn't mince words—"Do the core!"—and told each of the student players to listen to recordings, read reviews, and read the entire score—in other words, be prepared. It is no longer enough just to show up and scan your piece of the music for the first time.

How often does this lack of preparation happen in the library workplace? Was being unprepared a lack of interest, an unwillingness to take responsibility because it was *my* agenda? Perhaps it would have worked better if they prepared the agenda. An Orpheus coach alludes to what may drive wanting to be prepared, "The most important message to get across is how to establish musical goals" (Schweitzer 2006, 41).

Lack of preparation inhibits *being proactive*. When the music does not sound right, you need to get out front of the orchestra and listen. Then give the orchestra feedback. If the music is not going anywhere, say STOP! and explain why. This holds true for any small group: going along silently facilitates an ineffective decision. One critic (Holland 2008) observed that while Orpheus claims to play without a conductor, "Given the athletic body language emanating from the different parts of the orchestra, it really has four or five (conductors)." That's being proactive!

During a break in a rough and loud—all horns!—rehearsal of a Monteverdi selection, one student complained to me. "No one's in charge." That's the same criticism I heard about so-called leaderless teams in my library. There is someone in charge—the students, the team members. Once this concept is realized, ad hoc leaders will evolve.

Communication—Talking, Giving Feedback

Obviously this is central to most of these skills. Negotiation might be another way to describe what goes on in an Orpheus rehearsal.

Here's an example of an articulate student's feedback, in describing a Haydn piece: "It's boisterous, earthy—play it crass, (there's) some dirt in the sound . . . . It's *not* Mozart!"

Expressing what is on one's mind, without offending, is an acquired skill. Most of us have to work at using language that will have the intended effect and not the opposite, with people resenting our words and not really hearing our suggestion on how to improve the music or the library service plan. Becoming fluent in disagreeing agreeably comes only with practice, like learning a new language.

Richard Rood, the Orpheus coach, was pointedly clear about talking, telling the students, "Talk about the character more than you do the techniques of sound. What is the character of this piece?" He adds, "Talk and try out suggestions." "Come up with some ideas, some opinions (!), some convictions." As a highly effective coach, he elaborates on why it is important to have an opinion, an idea, a response. "The more everyone knows about it, that's the beauty, the influence, the group effort." Or, as a student participant summed it up, the "Process of bouncing ideas around is incredibly difficult and stressful, but ultimately worthwhile" (Schweitzer 2006, 40).

THE LIBRARY PEER COACHING INSTITUTE

There is a complication, of course, in my recommending the Orpheus coaching model. Unlike Orpheus, we do not have a corps of librarians who have refined their communication and peer coaching skills to the point they can coach consistently with a similar message to others.

Nor do we have an Orpheus way of working, one that would fit neatly in with my vision of the new library. Although some good efforts exist, there is no one I could actually point to and say, "Follow them!"

How do we get this cadre of library coaches, a nucleus like that of Orpheus?

First, keep in mind that the environment has to be supportive of coaching. Southwest's Herb Kelleher sums it up in the video *The Art of Coaching in Business*: "In order to make coaching successful, you first have to have the kind of culture that is receptive to it, where people don't feel that they're being criticized . . . . Feedback can be, in the wrong atmosphere, a code for a performance problem. In other words, you're calling it coaching, but what it really is is criticism. And good coaches don't coach that way."

So although we do not have a team of master library coaches, nor are we certain about the organizational climate to support peer coaching, I think an opportunity exists in schools of library and information sciences to inculcate good coaching skills.

I propose we establish a peer coaching institute at a library school, where for a semester groups of students are coached about the how of working together so they can be peer coaches—all the while working on a real and significant group project. This would be like the Orpheus model of a coach and symphony students learning to play without a conductor, akin to "leaderless" teams in a library.[2] Self-tests, along with other tools, case studies, and role plays, might be used before the group project to develop awareness of each person's strengths and needs for improvement as a team player and a peer coach.

Of course the most effective way to learn about peer coaching is the immersion model practiced by Orpheus. For librarians this comes down to designing an assignment as meaningful for library science students as an end-of-semester live and conductor-less musical performance is for the symphony.

CHAPTER 18

"You Have the Resources"

It's axiomatic. Managers are supposed to make the most of resources—budgets, materials, and people. But a straightforward call for the best use of resources does not guarantee it'll be heard and get a favorable response—it's more complicated than that. Staff may believe they are underpaid and overworked—and unappreciated. Asking them to do more with less—that's what they hear when you call for resourcefulness—will get you an earful about how they're at full capacity and the engine is smoking. Well, if their perception is not reality, how then do we get staff to consider possible new configurations of existing resources? How do we encourage staff to feel free and daring in responding to daily challenges?

IBM recently offered a series of "How Inventors Invent" days to its research lab staff. Those attending practiced tai chi or yoga and ran in a 5K race or played music. A master chef, a NASA astrophysicist, a cartoonist from India, and a fragrance chemist were among the speakers promoting innovation. When it was over, the participants were asked how they could heighten their creative productivity. There were no reported requests for magic mushrooms or trips to exotic places, just the mundane: meeting-free days, periodic bans on e-mail, and open office hours for drop-by visitors. To help mixing among researchers, they recommended breaking lunchtime routines and eating with someone different.

Perhaps in response to IBM's uninspired outcome, Hewlett-Packard issued an imperative: "Innovate." Similarly shortcutting the expense of a retreat, another company mandated: "Elevate." One engineering company reminds each cubicle's inhabitant: "Never Stop Thinking"—in headline-sized letters. Libraries are not exempt from exhortation. We've all been bemused by the consultant's counsel to work smarter, not harder; one library posted a sign above the door to its circulation department: "Think!" When I see these pithy, prosaic exhortations, no matter how benignly floated, I add a parenthetical expression: "Innovate (damn you!)." Isn't that what's really being said? When you have to remind a professional or any fellow human being to keep thinking, what assumptions are you making about that person? Is a futile berating the best managers can do to bring out our innate desire to do a good job?

Library staff development workshops ask participants to think out of the box, to move their cheese, and to catch a tossed fish or two—all this in hopes of inducing innovation, lowering resistance to change, and maybe turning a surly staff member into a prince of customer service. A tall order for any workshop, especially when you consider the underlying premise: Participants must not know how to think in effective ways, they must have some fundamental flaw like a repressed creativity gene. We keep forgetting the simple behavioral truth—just like motivation, innovation does not happen externally. I cannot make you more innovative. I can try to inspire or trigger your innovation, but innovative outcomes only happen when the person responds from within in a creative way.

The more confident a staff member can be about his or her resourcefulness, and the higher the management's expectations are about staff abilities, the more likely staff will be resourceful and more able to respond to the creative opportunity. The manager's role is to enable staff members to go with their creative impulses.

That brings me to the title of this chapter and my friend, Gordon Caudle, a former Outward Bound instructor who was president of Nekton, a research engineering company. Currently he is an independent start-up investor.

When out in the woods and confronted by unhappy campers about their inability to solve an assigned problem, he'd calmly reassure them, "You've got the resources." Once, as part of an executive leadership course, Gordon was guiding an overnight campout for MBA students. They were frustrated with their failure at a simple problem-solving task and were expecting him to solve it. The group was trying to make sense (and shelter) out of an ambiguous bundle of canvas and an odd assortment of tent poles and guy lines. Adding urgency were the fading daylight and the cold wind swooping off the nearby river. The campers were convinced parts were missing—there was no way they could put it up.

Interestingly, when Gordon encouraged them to keep trying, the campers paused and reflected. Gordon's "You've got the resources" triggered their taking another look, unfolding all the pieces and laying them out, and reconfiguring their assumptions. He was in effect saying: "You have the power, you have the ability." What was there in this situation that made the campers hear Gordon's words, take his advice, and reapply themselves? Respect, trust in Gordon? Yes, and more. Gordon could have shown off his technical skills and solved the tent problem, but he withheld the answer deliberately so as not to impede the group's learning. After all, the point of their being in the woods was for them to gain insights about leadership and teamwork. Debriefings would seek to make relevant extrapolations—the take-aways—from the camping experience to the workplace.

It's the same for leaders in the workplace. If we want to encourage resourcefulness, we need to display confidence in the staff's ability to deal with challenges. There are times when we should hold back and let people make mistakes, struggle some, and find their own way without intervention or blame. And we should take time to reflect on the learning in the struggle. A very successful management consultant told me a story about offering advice to his twenty-four-year-old daughter when she started a small business. He advised her on all the things that had to be done and what to especially look out for. He drew expansively on his many years of telling businesses, big and small, how to succeed. Finally, his daughter held up her hand to stop him: "Thanks, Dad. I know you mean well, but I want to make my *own* mistakes."

The camper's positive response is interesting, because often when I used Gordon's phrase in the workplace, I'd get an equally interesting, but negative, response: immediate disbelief along with some baleful looks at the miscreant (me), who obviously did not understand or appreciate the complexity of the work. Yet under the right circumstances, responses from some work groups were as positive as those from the campers—more of the "Maybe we can do it, after all" variety.

What are some of these right circumstances? What are the drivers of resourcefulness?

Trust has much to do with how staff members feel about you as a leader. The more trust they have, the greater will be their willingness to consider new ways (even better ways than you may have thought about); the less trust they have, the less willing they will be to confront change or deal with the unanticipated and unexpected. I recall how a lack of trust compounded an organization's prolonged e-mail crash. The systems staff were scrambling, haplessly rebooting, afraid to admit they were in over their heads. The administration was lashing out at the systems staff's seeming ineptitude. Instead of mutual support, there was mutual suspicion and disdain. Looking back, had the situation been less fear-driven, there would have been a quicker solution, probably in a matter of days instead of weeks.

There is our *innate desire* to succeed—call it pride. The campers certainly would prefer to pitch the tent on their own if they thought they could. We all would. Why not capitalize on staff's innate desire to do a good job? Present the problem in a way that appeals to pride, like when the musical conductor Simone Young got the all-male Vienna orchestra to buy into her musical interpretation. She told them, "Sure you can—you guys can do anything."

Surmountable adversities, like the cold wind and the settling darkness, can promote resourcefulness. However, you need to be reasonable and unambiguous about what you want. A 15 percent productivity improvement in titles cataloged is within reach. Doubling dollars donated annually is probably not. Erecting the tent was doable, and once they did, the campers benefited from its shelter and shared in the pride from doing it themselves.

Reward resourcefulness. An example from my experience is letting library staff put dollars saved into buying needed equipment. One year we saved enough money to buy more than 100 computer terminals for staff and student users, a move that reinforced innovation and laid the foundation for a technological surge several years ahead of other libraries. Another example was our encouragement and public recognition of a copy cataloger with a gift for simplifying complex but repetitive computer-cataloging procedures and boiling them down into utilitarian macro commands. Her work benefited other copy catalogers and resulted in an upswing in productivity.

Make use of team resources. If the staff knows *you* are not going to fix the problem, they may make better use of all *their* own resources—the team. If the challenge is sizable, those who normally take charge may have no choice but to be open to other ideas. I observed that Gordon's several take-charge MBA campers became less worried about asking for help from within their group. It is at times like these that the quietly perceptive member (every group has one or more) can come forth and offer his or her observations. I've been known to use a mildly facetious strategy when a group is at a decision-making contretemps. I tell them if they cannot make a decision, I will. *That* works every time.

Limit options. Well, what happens when we have too many options, including that of doing nothing? What happens when mañana is our only deadline?

One library director limited options and inspired staff resourcefulness. She did so by taking away shelving space for gift books. There was a valid reason to take the space—it was needed for people. But she had an ulterior motive: to get the collection development staff to make long-delayed decisions about years of unreviewed gift books. Her deadline was explicit: demolition starts in four weeks, and the shelves will be the first things to be scrapped. Gift processing would get some shelves in another location, but it would be 10 percent of the current number.

Collection development staff, overcoming their initial shock and denial, did find time to make the decisions to add or discard. The space was vacated. Since that legendary push, all new donations get a timely review. It was neither easy nor foolproof for the director—no doubt, a few good duplicate books were discarded—but the lesson learned about timely review far outweighs that cost. What good is a gift book out of sight, inaccessible, and unavailable? There is no value in unrealized potential.

Management has two obligations in pursuing resourcefulness, especially in traditional organizations like libraries. The first is to make certain staff understand—through our words and actions—that we believe they can be resourceful and are up to working through any reasonable challenge. The second obligation is to make sure that they can trust us to support their resourcefulness through thick and thin.

CHAPTER 19

A Gift from the Woods

A recent walk in the woods set me to thinking about the many insights—"lesser epiphanies" I call them—that occur to me while I'm outside. There's something about the wilderness that opens me to learning. Maybe it's giving up control: the remote, the thermostat, the car—all those comforts that, though nice, can confine our horizons.

Anyone meandering down a pine forest logging road, hiking in a desert's solitude, or on a brisk morning seeking out the first rays of sunshine gains a heightened awareness of self, an appreciation above the mundane. What, you may be wondering, does this have to do with the indoor work of running a library? If you are a manager who appreciates metaphors and alternate ways of learning, keep reading.

Experiential learning—going to the woods—can be a powerful tool in staff development.

Historically, the Outward Bound organization has done the most to make the outdoors a classroom for individual and team growth. It was OB's success in helping merchant seamen survive torpedo sinkings in World War II that eventually led to the development of adventure education as we know it today. The principles of leadership, teamwork, and service that were developed and practiced in the field by Outward Bound now extend far beyond the original clientele of prep school students. The founder, Kurt Hahn, hoped that OB education would promote the survival of these individual qualities: "an enterprising curiosity, an undefeatable spirit, tenacity in pursuit, readiness for sensible self-denial, and above all, compassion."

In the 1980s corporations, led by many executives who had experienced the twenty-one-day Outward Bound sailing program (a sort of coming-of-age ritual in New England prep schools) turned to OB-type wilderness programs in hopes of building better teams and identifying potential leaders in their companies. Although the corporate adventure education glory days of the 1980s and 1990s may have fizzled, there are still plenty of actors in the adventure education industry who will happily tailor programs for the corporate sector.

As you might imagine, in the corporate setting these offerings tend to be far removed from the rustic OB camps and from the desirable ethics Kurt Hahn hoped to instill. Corporate campers are cosseted in four-star accommodations and chow down on haute cuisine. The habitation is comfortable, but the curricula can offer plenty of personal challenge, from high ropes and "pamper poles" to rock climbs and whitewater rafting. Still, there is nothing quite like waking up in a damp sleeping bag, in a downpour, trying to figure out just where in your crammed and soggy backpack is that missing pair of dry socks!

To my knowledge, very few libraries engage in adventure-based programs. This is perhaps due to misgivings about spending scarce staff development dollars on what might be seen as exotic, and therefore potentially embarrassing, training. Or there may be genuine concerns about the physical fitness of graying participants. More likely the villain is the profession's unhealthy disdain for any training not patently pragmatic. Yet practical training rarely encourages the participant to stretch beyond existing boundaries, question professional norms, and reach out for the profession's brass rings. I once asked a recently returned trainee from a multiday library leadership program if she had been challenged. She was perplexed by the question. What did challenge have to do with it?

When wilderness learning is successful—and *it usually is more successful for the individual* than the group—the experience can alter what we think of ourselves and our work mates. The controlled risk and adversity, never found in the usual T&D venue, offers each of us a great opportunity to extract relevant lessons for how we lead and how we follow. In my weeklong OB experience on Maine's Hurricane Island, I was literally yanked out of my comfort zone and plunked down in an open "pulling boat" with a dozen strangers (along with supplies and two instructors) and expected to get from point A to point B in Penobscot Bay, regardless of fog, rocky shoals, or lack of sailing skills.

We cooked for ourselves and slept on an improvised deck. When we messed up, like sailing into a lighthouse's "red zone"—in other words almost certain disaster—we were responsible. Extreme? Yes, but those experiences did much to alter our self-imposed limitations. Things that were seemingly large and intractable in the workplace, diminished and appeared much more manageable. Surviving inhospitable weather, miserable sleeping conditions, and erroneous navigation changed us, emboldened us. Our newfound boldness transferred to our lives away from the pulling boat, heartening us to act rather than to react. Our camaraderie, developed in response to the lead instructor's martinet tendencies and the heated competition with another pulling boat, gave us insights into the workings of groups—both good and bad.

In this chapter I offer you three gifts from the woods.

"A Different Mountain"

San Pedro, an expired volcano, rises from the shores of Lake Atitlan to about 9,000 feet. Often ringed by a halo of cloud in a brilliant Guatemalan-blue sky, San Pedro looks placid, with its seemingly gentle, green slopes. When the sun hits the slopes on an angle, you see the deep ravines, like million-year-old wrinkles. It's been a decade since a friend and I set out on an ill-planned hike up San Pedro. Assuming it was two hours to the top, we started out in the afternoon from our "base camp," a hut in an avocado grove on the lakeshore. We figured we could make it back before dark. In keeping with the spontaneity of our decision, we tossed a few water bottles into our backpacks, added a snack or two, and headed out in our sneakers, shorts, and T-shirts.

Once past the *milpas*—a cubist quilt of family farms growing corn, avocados, and pepper plants, running midway up the volcano—the trail grew thin, eventually disappearing into a tangle of underbrush and towering trees. San Pedro's top proved elusive—each ridge conquered, each ravine traversed, led to another ridge, to another ravine. Bushwhacking, we'd reach a clearing only to slip and slide on the loose shale.

Taking a break on a massive tree branch laden with bromeliads and jutting out from the slope, we rested in the gentle breeze and admired the calm blue and sun-filled lake, far below us. We were heartened momentarily when we lucked into a muddy little trail—one cleared by the Guatemalan Boy Scouts, according to the peeling sign. Adding a dash of anxiety was a fresh paw print the size of my hand in the black mud. It was going our way, up.

At dusk we reached the top. The frigid wind cooled us off, but as it rushed through the tree tops jutting out of the caldera, we knew we could not bivouac. The temperature was probably already in the 40s and only going to get colder. As a propitiation—we had enough sense to know we were in trouble—we left a little tobacco in a crevice on the rim.

Our downward scramble took us only a few hundred yards when dusk turned into night.

Shivering, we decided to keep moving to stay warm and get away from the cold air. We had two tiny flashlights—the squeeze kind—but the small circles of light did not prevent us from tripping into bushes or slipping on the volcanic dirt. It was like walking downhill on loose ball bearings! Increasingly uncertain of foot, after numerous falls I was worried about the ravines. A misstep could send us over the edge, dropping into a tangle of vines, boulders, and broken trees.

Our tobacco offering must have mollified the Mayan gods. At 4:00 a.m., many hours later than we had figured, we made it down, begrimed and bone weary, embarrassed but uninjured. Some years later, I was reminded of that climb when I heard a story about a Buddhist teacher who takes his students on a hike.

"Come," he said early one morning, "We will go up the mountain today."

Without any special equipment or extra supplies, they set forth to master the mountain that loomed over their school. Their happiness about having a day off was short lived. To their chagrin they found themselves breathing hard in the high altitude, dripping with sweat, struggling and sliding on the loose rock. Losing the footpath, they had to bushwhack.

The students began to doubt the teacher—did he really know the way? The cliffs offered spectacular views but were perilous to cross. Yet the teacher persisted and slowly they made their way. At the top they discovered several other hikers, enjoying a leisurely picnic. They had strolled up a wide path on the other side of the mountain. The students complained to their teacher, "Why did we not take that trail?" The teacher's reply: "These others have climbed a different mountain."

Likewise, my friend and I had climbed a different volcano. After our nearly catastrophic venture, the farmers near our hut—no doubt amused by these *dos gringos locos*—pointed out that in the village of San Pedro, a mile or so around the bend from our hut, was a trailhead to a wide path leading to the summit. Whenever I contrast these two stories in my classes, I ask the students to reflect on the lessons in each. What does adversity—even when we bring it on ourselves—teach us? Are the consequences of poor planning, arrogance, and underestimating the volcano all bad? What are the costs and benefits of leaving a trail, any trail, and setting forth on your own?

THE ROPE

I was near the top of the cliff, secure as one can be on a narrow supporting ledge of rock eighty feet up. Below, blocks of granite littered the quarry floor, their sharp edges upraised like so many molars. I rested against my unreasonably thin safety line and wondered, How was I going to get to the top? Less rational was the incessant trembling in my legs.

The coach's voice invisibly hailed me from above.

"See the rope? Grab it and I'll pull you up!"

To the right, several feet away and up, he'd dropped a sturdy looking rope with a knot tied in the end. The kind of rope I never could get up in gym.

"You'll have to jump to catch it," advised the voice.

Jump?

"To the side. You can do it."

What? And leave the safety of my ledge?

"Sure. You're ready to stretch yourself. Try it."

What if I miss?

My first shaky try failed, and I scraped against the granite, cursing, scrambling back to the few inches of the ledge. I assessed my bruises and composed myself. I heard the encouraging shouts of my teammates below.

The voice came again from above. "Nice try. Think about where you want to go and how to get there. Use your resources. Now, tell me a joke."

I don't want to tell anyone a joke.

"OK, then sing me a song."

Go to $%^#@ hell. I definitely don't want to sing.

"OK, take your time." The rope slithered away out of my view.

It got quiet. The beauty of the late afternoon sank into me. There *was* a sky above me, and not far away I could see and hear the wind soothing the tremulous trees. Closer in, the quartz crystals locked in the cool stone face glimmered, coming into focus.

Gee, there's got to be a joke I can tell. Oh, yeah. The one about the armadillos.

My teammates hooted and hollered in appreciation. Feigned or not, it was a tonic, lifting my spirits.

My coach lowered the rope.

I thought about what it would take to make this leap, a leap of faith for my coach and me.

I told myself: "From the toes and up, over to the side, and close to the cliff."

With a prayer, I launched myself . . . and soared across the miles.

Participants in my workshops ponder these questions:

How does the coach help? Why does he do what he does? Why not drop the rope into the hands of the climber, hoist him up, and get it over with? What role does the team play? What moves the person to leap? Is the leap successful? How would you measure success?

Full Circle

In November 2004 the LAMA National Institute in Palm Springs gave me the opportunity to visit, at long last, the high desert Joshua Tree National Park. By car the park is 50 miles east and uphill, rising from Palm Springs's 150-foot elevation to around 3,000 feet. A library colleague preceded my visit by a decade. He was one of two library staff who took part in a rare library staff development event, a week at one of the Outward Bound schools. Travel and tuition were funded by a library board member. One chose the California OB school and joined a crew backpacking in the Joshua Tree National Park.

The other, a support staff member, opted for the school in the Pacific Northwest, and she trekked—in rain gear all week—along the magnificent Washington coast. On their return, it was his story and photos that planted the desire for me one day to get to the desert, to feel the sun on my back and the sand under my feet in that extraterrestrial landscape.

At the park's visitor center I asked the ranger what trail she'd suggest for a day hike. Her recommendation was a walk from the Cottonwood Spring Oasis to the Lost Palms Oasis, an eight-mile roundtrip—perfect! This time I had in my backpack three bottles of water, a lunch and snacks, a compass, sunscreen, a hat, and a jacket—you see, I did learn something from San Pedro!

The farther I got from the visitor center, the more enchanting the landscape became. The trail led me through sand-filled gullies, arroyos, and canyons, set in a landscape of borax colored sand and large tumbles of rocks, dotted irregularly with clusters of creosote bush and stands of spidery ocotillo and cholla cactus. A mile in I was out of sight of anything man-made, but for footprints of previous trekkers and the occasional contrail in the sky.

In a couple of hours I was dropping down into the canyon of the Lost Palms Oasis. I settled near a water puddle barely visible at the base of a sixty-foot-tall fan palm. Out of curiosity, I dug out a few handfuls of sand near the puddle, and sweet-tasting water seeped into the depression. That became a metaphor for how a harsh and barren landscape can nourish and flower when conditions are right, and by extension, for how my library's adventure learning program helped us achieve new growth and clarity of purpose.

We offered backpacking trips, rock climbs, ropes courses, orienteering, and several "days in the woods" full of team building and problem solving. Our program was built around metaphors and designed to show new juxtapositions and possibilities. Our point was that none of us was immutably fixed in place—we were all capable of new things and new ways of working.

Over the course of our adventuring, about a fifth of the total library staff volunteered to take part, mostly support staff. In my area of administrative responsibility—technical services—a much larger contingent took and met the challenge. That our facilitators were two former Outward Bound instructors raised the probability for success. Their background gave them an outstanding ability to challenge us and help us extract relevant, sometimes profound, meaning from each experience.

I've come to believe that our days in the woods had much to do with the success of my work group's change efforts, our rethinking traditional ways, and our questioning why we did what we did. Unprecedented productivity increases followed. I doubt it was coincidence alone that several of the people driving change in the library were active participants in outdoor learning. Of the many staff development programs we offered during those years, it was the outdoor variety that best moved staff beyond personal and organizational limitations. With the library's top leader encouraging risk taking and experimentation—while expertly fending off those seeking to keep the old ways—we were able to achieve major successes on behalf of the library's users.

I recently heard from the Pacific Northwest trekker. Although no longer with the library—with a leadership change, the library re-embraced the comforts of the hierarchy—she has gotten an advanced degree and was interning in a consulting organization, making good progress in her new career. She has not forgotten that soggy trek on the Pacific coast, nor what it taught her about herself and what she was fully capable of doing.

The hike at Joshua Tree National Park took me full circle—literally, from the Cottonwood Spring Oasis to the Lost Palms Oasis and back, and metaphorically, from my colleague's trip to the park (and what it meant for that library back then) to my visit in November and how it prompted my reflections on where we had been and how far we had come.

Happy trails.

CHAPTER 20

Leaving the Comfort Zone

Being on the tightrope is living; everything else is waiting.
—Karl Wallenda, aerialist

Those existential words—*everything else is waiting*—remind me that managers, try as we might, tend to avoid the metaphoric tightropes in our work and instead linger in our comfort zone—a waiting room crowded with routine decisions and predictable meetings. Too often, when intruded upon and surprised by the unexpected, we articulate reasons not to change, not to quit doing business as usual.

I recall when two college students appealed to me one morning to overrule a reserve room policy. In my assistant director role, I politely listened to their gripe. What I gathered from their assertions was that the policy was set up for the benefit of staff, was punitive to users, and probably needed to be rethought. Yet I found myself mouthing platitudes in rationalizing the policy. Why did I not do what was right—intervene, talk with the staff to get their take, make a decision, and then get back to the students? Why did I not move out of my comfort zone? For one thing, I knew the reserve room staff were difficult—to them, users were the enemy, spoiled children eager to exploit any advantage. I suppose it came down to avoiding conflict—my not wanting to leave more enjoyable work to fight it out with an entrenched staff. In conclusion, the two students went away unhappy, and I felt a most complete bureaucrat. My failure rankles still.

Managers of libraries, just like managers in any long-running business, can be seduced into remaining in the comfort zone, resisting the tug of doing what is right. We may never step out of it until we are embarrassed or forced into change—when the cost of not doing something becomes greater than the cost of doing what is right. Wallenda's *being on the tightrop*e is what I call the learning zone. An organization's well-being and growth develops in the learning zone—the organization stagnates in the comfort zone.

There's risk in the learning zone, of both success and failure. It is that risk that opens us up to learning by focusing our attention and elevating our learning faculties. Please understand that the risk in the learning zone is within our control—we are almost always up to the challenge, and we have the ability to solve the problem, provided that we care enough to make the extra effort. The risk level in my learning zone is akin to a balance beam I use on an outdoor exercise trail. That beam is only a foot or less above the ground, but it's enough to force me to pay attention to what I am doing, in order to stay upright. This is risk, but not the risk in the panic-inducing image of Wallenda wobbling on a tightrope a thousand feet above the roar and rush of Georgia's Tallulah Falls Gorge. That's the panic zone for all but the Flying Wallendas.

In libraries, as in most of life, learning zones are never far away. They lie only a step or two outside the comfort zone. By regularly taking on small challenges and gaining confidence in our ability to meet them, we heighten our risk tolerance. The more time spent in the learning zone, the greater your capacity for challenge. As I gain confidence and certainty in not falling off a foot-high balance beam, I become ready to walk the beam backward. I use what I've learned from walking forward, like keeping my eye on a distant tree for balance—a metaphor for the importance of having a goal, of knowing where I am headed, of having something that anchors me as I move backward.

Or, losing my balance, I stop and take time literally to center myself by putting weight on my back foot and feeling the play of my leg muscles and the solid beam through my shoe, savoring the sunshine streaming through the green leaves. Then, with renewed confidence, I take my next step back. Once I've mastered walking the beam backward, I'll try it with my eyes closed, shutting out all distraction, focusing on my inner goal. Eventually you may find yourself in a risk situation comparable to walking across Tallulah Falls Gorge, achieving the previously unattainable. The learning zone is elastic. Karl Wallenda raised the risk level on his 1,200-foot-high walk across the abyss—at the midpoint, he did two headstands—literal exclamation points to his achievement.[1]

I've had more than a few tightrope experiences in the workplace. And I have written about others who thrive in the learning zone, like the conductor-less Orpheus Chamber Orchestra. At their thirtieth anniversary concert this May at Carnegie Hall, they were not content to rest on their laurels in a musical comfort zone. Instead of opening with a familiar Mozart piece or something lyrically flowing and audience pleasing by Richard Strauss, they premiered a new composition by a living composer, Gunther Schuller. The learning zone can be an intense place—the faces of the orchestra showed their concentration, their listening to each other, their supporting each other as they worked their way through new juxtapositions and sounds. It was like a race well run—the players were visibly relieved once it was over and joyful in the collective result.

Equally relevant is my story about a young colleague in the electronic publishing field who is on her own tightrope. She's heading up a new project, taking on something never before done. Her boss told me her doing so is a stretch, but believes the young editor is up to it. The boss is betting on her to succeed where more experienced editors have failed. Her reasoning is paradoxical. Because academic book publishing is so paper bound, few professionals in the field are able to imagine a different way of doing things. For her boss, my young colleague's *weakness* (lack of experience in paper publishing) is a strength—because she is not bogged down in the conservative publishing tradition, she just might come up with radically different ways of doing the work.

As important as it is to be given the opportunity and to be supported, more important is the young editor's willingness to step out of her comfort zone, to undertake a major challenge. Her boss's support is invaluable—without it she cannot succeed—but it will be her inner confidence, sense of balance, and personal purpose and vision (a vision shared with the boss) that will make the project happen, that will keep her moving forward on her tightrope. Does this editor know what she is risking? Very likely she does. Does doubt about the outcome get in the way? Of course, but she is bound to prevail. A fear of failure alone will not stop her; it'll take more than a naysayer's litany of "it can't be done, it can't be done, it can't be done" to bring her down.

When we challenge ourselves to reach for the uncertain and ambiguous, to lift ourselves and our organizations to new heights, we are leaders of self. Being in the learning zone is about leading oneself. I encourage you to move out of your personal comfort zones. Here are a few suggestions to launch you:

1. Give a fractious subordinate your well-considered, supportive, and honest feedback on how he or she is doing.

2. Open a discussion with the person with whom you have the most difficulty working, your "least preferred coworker." Explore the issues together and seek mutual ways to improve your relationship.

3. When reviewing a process, ask "Why do we do this?" Don't let up until you really understand why. Find the root cause.

4. Take a "ropes" course for managers.

5. Learn about your level of risk tolerance, personal strength, and ability to help others and to ask for help.

See you in the learning zone.

CHAPTER 21

On the Road, Again: Lessons along the Way

On the road to Kata Tjuta (The Olgas), an Anangu sacred site, near Uluru in Australia's Northern Territory. Photo by Peter Lubans, 2002, used with permission.

Recreational travel, a uniquely human activity, can expose us to unusual ways of looking at common problems. Those observations can trigger rethinking why we do what we do. Travel can also lift us out of the cozy realm of the familiar and confront us with the discomfort of different views and life philosophies.

Library staff, when on their expedition with me in the woods, were amused (*bemused* may be the better word) by my preference for rainy and blustery days. Invariably, in my experience, a bad weather day raised the challenge level, and at day's end there was a larger sense of accomplishment.

The road to Kata Tjuta, in the picture, sings to me. It beckons me to adventure, the unknown, and the uncertain. Also known as the Olgas, Kata Tjuta is sacred ground with more than thirty rounded red domes among which to wander and ponder.

John Naisbitt, who writes about anticipating the future, encourages us to "Make uncertainty your friend"(Vogl 2006). For Naisbitt, uncertainty is where creativity and productivity happen. Travel can provide that uncertainty, that setting off-kilter our worldview to enlighten us with fresh perspectives.

My story is about a few triggering moments that stood out for me during a trip into Australia's Red Center, the outback and beyond. In my Australian cousin Peter's twin engine Beechcraft Baron, four of us (Peter and I, Peter's wife, Chris, and my wife, Sheryl) flew inland about 2,000 miles—during a two-week journey—from Australia's east coast and then circled back following a northerly route, including a bit of Australia's uninhabited northernmost coast line.

"We Don't Climb"

That's the headline on one of the Uluru–Kata Tjuta National Park "Notes" (2002), a two-sided colored sheet dedicated to why you, the visitor, should think twice about climbing the iconic Uluru, the former Ayer's Rock.

Barbara Tjikatu, a traditional owner, is quoted: "If you worry about Aboriginal Law, then leave it, don't climb it. The chain is there if you want to climb it. You should think about [our heritage] life and society, and stay on the ground. Please don't climb." The sheet goes on to explain that the chain and track are on an ancestral sacred trail taken by the Mala tribe's males on their arrival at Uluru for native rituals.

This is an empathetic appeal to our better nature to decide whether we will or won't climb. Uluru is no longer the white man's Ayer's Rock. It's ownership has been returned to the native people. They could easily close the trail to the top. Why don't they?

The Anangu's approach to enforcing policy intrigued me. I thought about our library policy efforts, from the laughable Nancy doll's *sieg heil* "shush!," to getting books returned on time, to discouraging food and drink in the library stacks, to limiting users' access to offensive—to passersby—Internet sites. I do know many of our policies are hardly successful—books come in late, people get loud, and people consume food and drink just about anywhere in the library building.

A story in *The Times* of London (Ahuja 2006) added a dimension to my thinking about how we enforce policies and how the native owners of Uluru do. The newspaper reports on a recent scientific study, which concluded that our human "moral code is so ingrained that substituting it with formal regulation can lead to worse behavior." The study tracks how two day-care centers treated parents who were late picking up their kids. One center fined tardy parents $3 for each occurrence. Over time, this day-care center experienced an *increase* in latecomers.

The other day-care provider reminded tardy parents that their being late inconvenienced the teachers, who had to stay late. There were no threats, no fines. This center saw no increase in late parents. The study concludes that penalties and regulation "may crowd out the good behaviour that most people, most of the time, follow," a theory expounded by Adam Smith in 1759: " [I]t is in our own self interest to behave morally to each other."[1]

What do we achieve with our fines for overdue books? Along with the burden of administrative costs, we often gain ill will. More to the point, books still come in late. Users have told me that, like the day-care parents, they equate the overdue fine to a rental fee, so they can keep the book as long as *they* need it, even when it has been requested by someone else. Given the option to pay a fine to justify antisocial behavior, the notion that all library users should share resources responsibly—"to behave morally"—somehow becomes irrelevant.

Twice in my experience, a fine-free policy resulted in no upsurge in antisocial behavior—or overdue books. Although I have little empirical proof, my guess is that we gained goodwill and probably less theft and other forms of vandalism that could easily be induced by resentment about fines. As a side note, we did earn the unexpected enmity of the budget officer, who saw the result of the "no fines" policy as a drop off in library revenues and lobbied his boss to penalize the library by subtracting the "lost" fine dollars from the new bottom line!

As the picture shows, the native owners have not convinced everyone to stop climbing. Yet observers say fewer people are climbing. At well over 1,000 feet tall and 6 miles around, Uluru is not the sanitized theme park challenge some may think. The fierce Southern Hemisphere sun, even in autumnal May when I was there, glares down, heating the textured skin of the rock, dehydrating and wearing down even the most physically fit.

I wanted to, but I didn't climb. Others scampered along the tailbone of this mammoth sleeping creature, up along Uluru's arched back. Then, later in the day, they descended, clinging to the chain. Legs atremble, cramping from exhaustion, many sat down and scooted, like a dog with an itchy behind, too tired to care about appearances. The ignominious descent suggests Uluru is exacting a cost. Indeed, a few climbers die each year. Probably next time, those who have survived won't climb again.

Like ants, people make their way up Uluru. Photo by author, 2002.

Mirage at 8,000 Feet

While in the copilot's seat on our flight from Broken Hill to Uluru, I spotted a rock outcropping in the distance that looked like my mind's image of Uluru. I signaled to Peter, our pilot, that it looked like we were there, sooner than we thought. Maybe a tail wind had pushed us along.

Still, the GPS device, clipped to the dash board, showed our programmed track to Uluru veering off to the west, while my rock formation, looming on the horizon, was in the east. I was not alone in being convinced this was Uluru—Chris, Sheryl, and Peter agreed it just might be. As we looked for the landing strip, the GPS started to beep in alarm. For a few moments we ignored the GPS, convinced we were right. Peter, only momentarily persuaded, had second thoughts. He pulled out the aeronautical chart he'd prepared for this leg of the trip and confirmed that we had a ways to go yet—Uluru was sixty miles to the northwest.

What I'd confused with Uluru was Mt. Conner, a crumbling mesa, unlike the rounded dome of Uluru. Others have made my mistake, have been taken in by this false Uluru. The erroneous sighting stands out for reminding me how easy it is to be convinced of something if we really want to be convinced.[2] I've made library decisions with the same conviction that I thought Mt. Conner was Uluru, especially when there were others around me reinforcing my wrong assumptions and conclusions.

I recall a building renovation that resulted in a loss of useable square feet. We wanted a renovation so much that we opted to proceed with a severely reduced budget for the renovation. Somehow we were convinced that the reno-vated space, though smaller and with no new furniture, would be better and we could make it work. So instead of waiting for better budgetary times, we charged decisively forward. We'd managed to beguile ourselves into believing that the result would be like the iconic Uluru, but what we got was the ignoble Mt. Conner ruins. We should have asked ourselves: "Do we want to move stacks and books around, demolish walls and floors, and experience several months of noise, dust and inaccessibility, while losing overall useable space?" As happens in group think, no one challenged our thinking.

Mt. Conner also took me back two decades to Penobscot Bay on the Maine coast. There I was with ten other worn out sailors in an open pulling boat on a befogged, soggy night trying to get to a safe harbor. I was the captain for the day, and someone else, equally unqualified, was the navigator. It didn't matter that we had nautical charts and compasses; we wound up in the lighthouse's red zone—the reddish sweep of light where you do not want to be, inviting certain destruction on rocky reefs and in the frigid sea. At this point the instructor in-tervened. A few of us learned from that experience—it took me down a notch or two, which was probably the instructor's intent. The lesson has stayed with me—if you don't know, say so. Don't fake it. But I still believed Mt. Conner was Uluru. As a colleague once told me, the popular view among some library directors that "Leaders have vision; followers implement," may be true, but so might "Leaders have hallucinations; followers have doubts!"

"The Esteemed Order of the Brolga"

And sometimes the influence of travel—or is it the jet lag or the lingering ef-fect of Australian wine?—can lead to fanciful ideas. Like awarding myself the "Esteemed Order of the Brolga."

Throughout my Australian odyssey, I'd been looking for a souvenir pin, the sort you stick on your hat or shirt pocket: there were koala pins, pins for kanga-roos, wombats, emus, echidnae, platypuses, and even a lyrebird, but no brolga pins. Brolga bumper stickers, yes; brolga postcards, yes; brolga tea towels, yes; but no pins.

True, my motives for wanting the pin, though not disingenuous, were a bit capricious. I planned to wear it in my lapel at the next ALA meeting. And when someone inquired, I'd smile mysteriously and relate how I had been admitted into the Esteemed Order of the Brolga by the Northern Territory Library As-sociation. I meant it to be a bit of a muted reverse psychology protest (What? *Another* award!) to the surfeit of existing ALA awards. I've come to believe that fewer awards have greater meaning for recipients. If we won't reduce the actual number of awards, then at least we can choose to make deserving awards every other year or preferably less frequently. If you are under an obligation to make an award without fail each and every year, there are times when you will honor the undeserving. Doing so, you dishonor the deserving.

A brolga out for a stroll in Australia's Northern Territory.
Photograph by Paul Thomsen (wildfoto.com.au), 2006.[3]

Why the brolga? The brolga is a large grey crane, with a loud trumpeting "garooo"—certainly an attention getter at ALA Council meetings or for greeting someone in the crowded exhibit hall. Also, the brolga is named after a great aboriginal dancer who was abducted by an evil sprit, who returned in the form of a beautiful bird. This brolga myth is featured at corroborees in dance and song, with brolga dancers taking long hopping steps and seeming to float on the air, a lovely image.

The clincher for me was the fact that brolgas are known to fly to high altitudes *to escape hot air.* I can see members of the Esteemed Order as a hardy lot of librarians who prefer action over talk and are able to soar metaphorically above the intoxicating clouds of inaction.

I'm still looking for that pin.

CHAPTER 22

Rock Castle Gorge

I have three stories to tell you, three threads to weave together. In May 2007 I was dismayed to learn that I had been without health insurance for a year. Adding to my concern was the bureaucratic fact that I would not qualify for Medicare Part B until the middle of 2008. So, unnervingly, no insurance for another year. A year of living dangerously, or so it seemed. My *free* eye exam was now over $300. What if I got really sick?

Life does go on. I made several phone calls to Social Security and my former employer, who had insured me for over twenty-five years. Their response: "Sorry, we can't do anything. You are at fault. Expect to pay big penalties, etc." Both agencies said I could appeal their decision, so I faxed in the appeals asking for a reconsideration of what was, demonstrably, a series of mutual misunderstandings.

Once the dust settled, I began to mull over my situation and my vulnerability. Although health insurance and other benefits have become an integral reason for us to work, they are a relatively recent phenomenon. The not-for-profit Blue Cross and Blue Shield dates back to the early 1930s. After the Second World War, health insurance became a must-have as health-care costs skyrocketed. Now over 25 percent of our salary package is benefits, with a big chunk going to health care. Is this why we work—to ensure and to protect our lifestyle? What is the price for our security?

There is a personal cost. Our need for security may draw us only to jobs with benefits. And we may stay in a job long past the time to try something new. When a hospital stay could bankrupt most of us, we are not eager to be in between jobs, even if we hate the job we're in. Instead we hunker down, keep a low profile, and hope for a change in the leadership rather than take on more risk. If we think for ourselves and have thoughts contrary to the organization's conventional thinking, we'll hold back. It's almost as if some bad managers count on this self-restraint and in some intuitive way gauge just how far they can push around a security seeking staff.

A cringeworthy ad recently came my way. It was from a mega-insurer and somewhat confirmed my views about how crucial benefits had become:

"Life is good. Let's keep it that way."

We can help:

Medicare supplement,

Final expense,

Fixed annuities,

Individual and temporary health insurance,

Dental coverage,

Medicare advantage health plans,

Medicare part D prescription drug plans.

"Be sure you have the coverage you need to protect your lifestyle and your family's future."

The ad assumes much: Our life style, our future, depends on "coverage." Does it?

I readily identified with the ad. At the same time, I was aware of its manipulation, of its playing on my exaggerated insecurities. And I wondered just how much I had allowed myself to equate "coverage" with happiness. Right about then—perhaps my unconscious mind was casting about for a calming thought— Rock Castle Gorge popped into my head.

I've hiked the Gorge twice, each time in winter. The Rock Castle Gorge trail is an isolated 10.8-mile loop off the Blue Ridge Parkway in Virginia. The Gorge trail peaks at 3,577 feet and drops, panoramically, to a low of 1,700 feet—the floor of the Gorge. When it's snowing and blowing up on the Blue Ridge Parkway, likely there is icy rain in the Gorge. When it's too hot to budge from your rocking chair overlooking the Parkway, it's a blessed 70 degrees down below.

The Gorge itself, carved out over the eons by Rock Castle Creek, is about five miles long, and follows the creek, its rapids, and its waterfalls. The Gorge is wide enough in places for cultivation, a water-driven mill, and orchards. Farm families lived along the trail—then a rough and narrow farm-to-market road— that criss-crosses the creek for the five-mile stretch.

Trekking on that rough road, I marvel at those people. I can hear their voices in the rushing creek. I can imagine the children playing among the trees, staying up late on summer nights, leafing through the Sears Roebuck catalog in the days before Christmas.

The Park Service says people lived in the Gorge from the late 1700s to the 1930s. Around 1910 some seventy families farmed in the Gorge. In the 1930s all but one of the families sold their land—with no threat of condemnation—to the developers of the Blue Ridge Parkway. Evidence of home sites, of what once was, exists along the trail.

Standing Tall: A Lone Chimney. Used with permission, Gordon Caudle, 2006.

Those seventy families lived out their lives—as best they could—without Social Security, Medicare Parts A, B, and D, Medicaid, or the Good Hands insurance people. Nor did they have home insurance, car insurance, boat insurance, or coverage for personal liability, personal property, and "loss of use." Since they obviously lived in a flood plain, they would not have qualified for flood insurance! Was their life then, a perpetual state of anxiety? A life lived in constant fear and jeopardy? Not exactly.

With none of our contemporary buffers against uncertainty and potential di-sasters, the families of the Gorge community lived happily at times. One Web site entry describes in nostalgic terms what it was like for children: "Gatherings at the Bear (or Bare) Rocks, a large tumble of huge boulders that thrust out of the mountains, included picnics for the entire community, singing, exploring of caves and a little courting while children scrambled over stones and into crevic-es with *an abandon unknown in today's world*" (Shelor 2006; emphasis added).

No, I am not suggesting we all hike into the wilderness and get a simple life. Nor am I suggesting a return to agrarian times. I am suggesting that we reflect on the price we pay for comfort, for certainty. Worse, we may harm ourselves when we stay in a dead-end job. We may even wind up in something akin to the creepy corporate world found in George Saunders novella, *Pastoralia* (2000). Saunders take us into a dysfunctional theme park with sly intimations of modern corporate life. The story is narrated by one of the two inhabitants of a cave di-orama. The two catch bugs, paint pictographs, and grunt cave talk. When man-agement is happy, the cave couple gets to eat the meat they've been grilling over their fire. If the boss is not happy, and this happens capriciously, plastic radishes and a predrilled (for the spit) plastic goat are all that slide through the food slot.

At the end of each day, there's a Daily Partner Performance Evaluation, the DPPE Form, for the cave couple to rate each other and fax in the answers to these questions:

Did I have any attitudinal difficulties?

How do I rate my partner overall?

Are there any situations that require mediation?

Our protagonist tries to do a good job; he consciously abides by the corporate mantra: "Thinking positive/Saying positive." He does not speak English in front of the few customers peering into the cave. He does not talk trash at them. He does his best to imitate what cave people would do. Jane, his counterpart, speaks English, occasionally curses the few customers, smokes, and calls in sick. She's a screwup.

The boss urges—in new age consultant talk—the protagonist to give Jane a bad evaluation so they can fire her. Apparently without his cooperation they cannot move against her. He resists, inexplicably loyal, calling her a friend. He himself has a dysfunctional family, a wife who faxes him about out of control credit card bills and of their dreadfully ill child. Cave mate Jane's son is a drug user and a parasite on his mother. If she loses this job, she lets the narrator know, she will have to go care for a dysfunctional parent—that's all that's left for her. The narrator, until the very end, gives Jane undeserved good ratings on each of the DPPE forms he faxes in every night.

There's another appraisal tool, the Client Vignette Evaluation, to be com-pleted by customers. Both the DPPE and the CVE correspond to real evaluation systems, including those to be found in libraries. In this bizarre theme park,

the DPPE and CVE take on an ominous quality, revealed as the tools management uses to discipline and terminate workers, to circumscribe personal freedom. Though we like to think our performance appraisals are not fear inducing
and controlling, we should understand they are indeed systems to hold people
accountable. Most managers trust all but a few staff to do the right thing, yet
we have designed an appraisal structure that applies to 100 percent of the workforce. Strangely enough, in my experience I've observed exponential growth in
performance appraisal structures for libraries. If a three-page evaluation does
not quite work as well as it might, we do not reconsider why we evaluate; instead we make the evaluation form into a six-pager. What dreadful things do we
fear might happen if performance appraisal was a blank sheet of paper or a long
conversation between leader and follower?

Pastoralia puts a price on dependency. The narrator does not think of leaving. He accommodates. He keeps his mouth shut. He does not stand up to his
goofy boss. He suffers; he endures. His is trapped with no exit. Why? We do
not know.

RESOLUTION

Several weeks after my insurance appeal, my former employer agreed, without explanation, to provide me with an insurance "bridge" to mid-2008. That's
a relief, because in round 1 of what may evolve into an epic struggle, Social Security lost my paperwork. In round 2 they denied the appeal, without comment.
In round 3, I wrote a personal letter to the Assistant Regional Commissioner of
Processing Center Operations (Now, there's a title!) to, please, please, not penalize me with the 10 percent Medicare premium increase—in perpetuity—for
enrolling a year late because of the misunderstanding with my former employer/
insurer. Her response to my August letter came in early December. She said,
"Uh, uh, no can do." Well, not really. Her letter reads like something composed
by the boss in *Pastoralia* or copied out of Aleksandr Solzhenitsyn's *We Never
Make Mistakes* (2004).

She told me, "Relief cannot be granted merely because of 'good cause'.... There
must be some erroneous action or inaction by the Government that is prejudicial
to the rights of the individual." The five single-spaced pages of boilerplate reminded me of the convoluted logic we would use in responding to library users
when they complained about an irrational policy—alas, we too have been guilty
of ignoring common sense, of "never making mistakes" or not doing the right
thing. Maybe this was that bad karma coming around? Although the ARCPCO
did offer to hear my appeal again, I decided against it.

So, while paying more for the privilege, I am back in the cozy fold of the
insured. Yet I'd already realized that although coverage is nice to have, its absence

is most akin to a pothole in the road of life. I really don't have much of a choice but to accept the calculated risks that come with living and carry on. Benefits have little to do with the "good life" regardless of what insurance companies and the government want us to believe. If you had to choose between the extremes of *Pastoralia* and Rock Castle Gorge, which would it be? "Safe and sorry" or "Insecure and living life"?

Pastoralia is the stuff of nightmares, yet most of us know real workplaces, and maybe a library or two, that are just as dysfunctional. These are places to leave in a hurry. Staying on for benefits only enables the disablers and delays your having a life of your own choosing.

CHAPTER 23

Sacred Teams

Teams intrigue me. I have worked with many teams and have discovered that truly effective teams (those that change things for the better) are rare. When that rare event occurs, there is a combined energy among the participants that exceeds that of individual team members. And there is a collective joy in the doing.

I've been part of accidentally effective teams that got the job done—we clicked. That success proved elusive when we formed other teams—even when we kept on most of the members from a successful project. I've come to realize that a team's success is more than personalities, more than the right blend of talents, more than the resources or support available to the team—it is a complex recipe. And sometimes, when everything is how and where it should be, the cake still falls flat.

This story takes place about the time my own library was nearing the conclusion of an experiment with self-managing teams. Since I was leading the initiative, I was puzzling a lot about the dynamics required for effective teams. Our experiment was a full-faith, top-down effort, but frankly, we had little return to show for the investment: a few qualified successes, but many of our so-called teams acted like the departments and committees of old. Not exactly failures, they were hardly the creative and energetic groups we desperately needed in the run up to the Internet era. So, during one Easter week in Guatemala in the mid-1990s, when I saw teams that supported each other, beamed with the glory of what they were doing, and made steady progress toward an ethereal goal, I was profoundly impressed.

I was in the city of Quetzaltenango (the buses tag it *Xela*—pronounced "shay-la") on the Pan-American highway; at 7,700 feet, its proximity to the Mexican border and to ancient, still active, trade routes keeps it an important provincial city, the second most populous in Guatemala. There's a lingering architectural grandeur from its 1900s coffee-boom era, buildings still grand, if cracked from earthquakes and a wartime economy. And adding an exotic appeal for many gringos like me is that Xela has always been a place of opportunity for the Maya, both sustaining the individual culture and blending the Mayan and Spanish heritages.

Xela sits in a vast valley. From the steps of the elevated Civic Theater, the bronze busts of noted Quetzaltecos gaze across an urban mélange of squat fortified offices and stores. Beyond looms the Santa Maria volcano, puffing steam clouds into an icy blue sky.

Tour books recommend Xela as a day trip base to indigenous villages for shopping for weavings and exploring things Mayan. A jarring bus ride away is Momostenango (just about 100 percent indigenous), with its prayer hills and a much-rumored school for shamans. In another direction lies the mist-laden Laguna Chicabal, a Mayan sacred lake in an extinct volcano's cone, rimmed with offerings of living wooden crosses entwined with fresh calla lilies.

Easter week (Semana Santa) had complicated my travel to Xela—most of the country shuts down during this time. I knew about the weeklong celebrations in Antigua and Guatemala City that date back to the 1600s and are televised throughout Latin America, but since I am serendipitous in travel, I did not know what to expect in a provincial capital. It turned out there were to be multiple sumptuous processions from the seven principal churches, interspersed with a number of unheralded and humbler processions, including some from brotherhoods (Mayan *cofradias*). The latter are less imposing, with music blaring from a boom box and a modest float (*anda*) shouldered by a half dozen people. At night a car battery pushed alongside on a U-Haul cart pragmatically powers the lightbulbs strung above. It seemed every group in the community was to be there—an expatriate American staying at my hotel averred that the town's prostitutes have a procession dedicated to the Virgin Mary.

But I am getting ahead of myself. It was late in the afternoon when I saw the first of the processions around the central square (the Parque Centro America). Amid the quietly observing crowds, I heard and saw the swaying approach of the massive wooden platforms. Each side of the *anda* rests on the shoulders of the people underneath. Often dressed in purple cap and gown, each follower bears his share of the burden in step to the doleful music from the trailing band. Slowly, ever so slowly, the *andas* make their way around the park and down the side streets, back to their sponsoring church.

The procession's ceremony, its solemnity and grandeur, and most important for me, the strong teamwork among the hundreds of participants, captivated me, drew me in to think about what I was seeing. Like a Guatemala tourism Web site prosaically puts it: "Lifting [the *anda*] takes a great deal of effort and cooperation." How and why do that effort and cooperation come about?

TEAM PROGRESS

A procession moves slowly; there is something elephantine in its movement, but there is steady forward progress with the burden they are carrying—the polished dark wood platform supporting a full-sized statue of one or more of the participants in the crucifixion, the Passion. The most memorable one I saw was of Jesus weighed down with a tree-sized cross.

Contributing to the slow movement are the dozens of participants, as many as thirty men or women (never mixed) on each side of the platform. Imagine turning a corner with 120 legs, some wearing high heels! But probably the major reason their progress is not as quick as it could be is that for every three rolling steps forward they take two back, and then move one step left and one to the right, describing the sign of the cross. This is done in time to the lugubrious music of the thirty-odd-piece band following each of the processions.

It struck me that this is not much different from how organizations advance—for every few steps forward, one or more are taken backward. Whereas the religious processions pursue the sacred, we librarians tend to believe our goals are of a purposeful high order, secular, but certainly in encouragement of humankind's betterment. If all of us carrying the load are to achieve the goal, it is going to be a long and arduous journey, with at times little progress. But, *poco a poco,* amid the smoke of the incense, the funereal music of the band, and the tinkling of the ice cream vendor cart's bell, there is progress, even if it literally takes all day to get around the park.

LEADING AND FOLLOWING

How do the people shouldering the platform stay centered on what they are doing? How is the vision communicated to them so they stay on course? On a side street, I noticed a man shooing people away from a tree along the route—at a midpoint where the load might feel the heaviest on sore shoulders and strained backs. Someone had nailed to the tree a framed picture of a saint—a reminder for those bearing the load that this was the reason for their labor; the purpose of their journey. Because they could not see beyond the base of the platform, could not see the statue on the *anda*, the picture offered a visual reminder of the point of the procession. And so it is for us in our day-to-day work to reflect on what we are about, to remind ourselves about the higher purposes of our work. Do we have a tree to look at and draw strength from? I noticed that many of the carriers and musicians seemed to derive comfort from that picture.

COMMUNITY

Each procession had sixty or so carrying a platform at any time, and probably another ninety men or women moved alongside—followers on a journey—ready to take up the burden. And they did, regularly, after so many blocks.

If a participant faints or has to step aside, the procession stops and one follower alongside the *anda* is asked to step in. Once in place, the procession starts up again. Much of this is more than happenstance—it is turn taking. Spots under the *anda* are negotiated for months—some churches charge a fee for anyone to walk with the float. Many are willing to pay a higher price to feel the weight of the *anda* on their shoulders, to lend their bodily support. Along the most visible parts of the route—when the *anda* emerges from the church and reenters at journey's end—the price of followership quintuples.

The community's support for those in the procession is made manifest in the side streets. *Alfombras* are street carpets, stretching from sidewalk to sidewalk for twenty or more yards. Created from colored sawdust and flowers, they can feature pre-Hispanic abstract motifs. Twenty hours in the making, it takes less than two for the *alfombra* to be obliterated by the processions shuffling across. Like the picture in the tree, the processionalists see at their feet the evidence of their purpose and the community's support.

There is also the strong support from the spectators. On Good Friday the central park overflowed with families, couples, and a few obvious *turistas*. On that night it was, as someone described it, hallucinogenic. The clouds of incense, the floodlights on each of the swaying platforms, under the full moon, with the thousands of spectators and the faces pressed alongside the dark wood of the platforms, seemed like something akin to a frieze by Goya. There was a determination in those faces that said to me each was there because of a personal belief. They were there because of a commitment to a purpose outside themselves, not because someone had *told* them to be there, to follow a priest's or *cofradia* chief's command.

Does my experience in Xela have anything to do with teams at work? We are on this journey together, and we are mutually dependent. The travelers in Xela supported each other. The many alongside and in the crowd encouraged them in their journey. How do we support each other; does one side move in the same direction as the other side?

A few weeks later, the events of Semana Santa contrasted sharply with a library experience. My library had an annual controlled catastrophe, the flood of books at semester's end. The returned books went into a sort of book purgatory, pretty much lost to the reader. Embarrassed more than usual by frustrated users, the circulation team, with the approval of the administration, put out a librarywide SOS: "Come and help us shelve," offering food and drink and other encouragements for volunteers. Of a staff of 200, about 10 percent took part. Ninety percent of the staff was too busy to help out with supporting a basic function of the library—ensuring that needed books would be found. Only the myopic could fail to see that thousands of unshelved books touched everyone's work, not just the shelving unit's. Had this been an *anda* in Xela, it would never have made it out the door. Where was our sense of purpose, our sense of community? Had we grown too proud to see much beyond our immediate circle?

I suppose once Semana Santa concludes in Quetzaltenango, the bonhomie recedes. But during that holy week, for that moment, when participants put aside their differences, share the burden, and focus on the task at hand, they achieve an enviable state of togetherness. The individual merges with the group to get to the goal, be there, and feel the joy of a collective humanness. Our work offers us the same opportunity.

CHAPTER 24

Seeking First to Understand . . .

> From the time I was a little boy, I remember one of the first lessons I learnt from [my father]. He used to speak very well of a guitarist from Granada, and finally this artist came over to our home and played for us. Afterwards I said to my father, "Papa, he is the worst guitarist I ever heard!" But he answered, "You didn't look, you didn't listen to the gentleness of his thumb."
> —Pepe Romero, guitarist, from the liner notes accompanying his CD *Songs My Father Taught Me,* which was dedicated to his father, guitarist Celedonio Romero

Something ineffable in Romero's tribute to his father has stayed with me. I made a point of saving these lines, knowing I would want to refer to them—in some undefined context. Initially, I assumed the quote was about diversity, about seeing differences and appreciating those differences. But that interpretation evaporated quickly—it was too superficial. Equally superficial was the notion that these words were about *superficiality.* Well, this time when I was drawn to the quote, I went back to the CD's liner notes for clues to my affinity. In words and phrases nearby, Romero talks of his father's transformational love and his enduring humility against considerable odds in fascist Spain, all the while seeking higher levels of accomplishment in the guitar.

Maybe that's what it is about—humility. And wisdom. The wisdom to be gained from looking and listening. A humility that opens you to others, not closing them out because their views are contrary to yours or they cannot make sense of yours. Metaphorically, from a manager's perspective, Romero's story is relevant to my not hearing someone else's music. Or their not hearing my music. The gentleness of *their* thumbs eludes me, just as mine eludes them. Is this humility a learnable quality? Probably. At the least we can all get better at it. According to the maestro, you only need to *look* and *listen.*

Probably it is as simple, as deceptively simple, as Augustine's admonition to us to seek first *to understand* and then seek *to be understood.* Open conflict often creates excessive noise (see the "spirited" discussion among any group of paid bloviators), making it barely possible to hear individual words, not to mention any melody or refrain in what is being shouted out. But even when conflict is low and manageable, we may find ourselves so at odds with our peers that we fail to pick up the wisdom of what is being said. Diverting our mental resources to defending our position, we diminish our capacity to comprehend external views. It is at times like these that we need that extra humility to remain open to hearing the unusual, the unexpected, the unimagined, and the fresh. It is a wisdom that derives value from something going against the grain. Out of discord, we may approach truth.

This makes me think about times when I was not heard or when I failed to hear another's wisdom. Let me illustrate my meaning. A friend with leadership responsibilities for a musical organization recently told me of a highly frustrating conversation with her codirector. She was trying to convince him of the necessity of their artists setting higher goals, experimenting, and taking on more difficult pieces. If the organization was to flourish rather than stagnate, she argued, it was time to raise the bar. Besides, she knew they had the resources and the ability. Her codirector's unenthused response was that he liked things pretty much the way they were.

She persevered and restated her observations and convictions—that the organization was at a plateau, well funded and comfortable but beginning to slip down the slope of a repetitive repertory. Most important, they were not attracting new, younger audiences—their future. Visibly irked, her codirector interrupted her: "You did not hear me, I guess. I said, I like things the way they are!"—end of discussion. She was dismayed. She knew there would be a similar response if she took her concerns to the socialite governing board members—they are of the "make no waves, please" species, comfortable in their positions. Yet my friend believes she is speaking the truth. I concur. How then can her truth be heard and understood by her codirector and her board?

Apart from a sympathetic ear, I had little to offer on how best to advance her agenda. In retrospect, her dilemma reminds me of several in which I have found myself. I recall a failure to gain support for what I thought was a loud wake-up call for action. This was at a time when few would admit that reference service in academic libraries had already undergone profound changes and was losing its clientele.

In the early 1990s I had begun to observe a sharp decline in traffic at the reference desk. Where once there had been lines of students waiting to ask questions, now there were a few people—not infrequently, the reference librarian was a silent sentinel whom numerous students streamed past on their way to catalog terminals and CD-ROM indexes (remember Infotrac?). But there we were, staffing our public points (in academic libraries) as if nothing were happening. It was like there were two realities——the users' and ours.

A few colleagues in the profession at large were in tacit agreement with me that change was upon us and we needed to adjust. However, one of these colleagues, who like me had been keeping track statistically, was afraid to publish his data—no help there. Another had begun motivating his staff to get out from behind the reference desk, to approach users at their point of need and forget waiting for them to approach the desk. This was a helpful starting point, one that I could have used to my advantage, but I failed to see this as a bold enough step.

Not unexpectedly, in spite of reinventing reference conferences, there was denial by reference departments that anything had changed. If numbers had dropped, well, the time to answer each question had increased. If fewer questions were being asked, they were more complex. Yes, users were happily using the technology, but there was a cost—staff time to help them learn how to use the technology. Adding to the cost was the request for more terminals at the reference desk to guide users confounded by the intricacies of CD-ROM interfaces.

But back to my being understood. I recall presenting my annual reference question summaries to the library's executive group. There was no missing the downward trend of questions asked—it was precipitous, each year dropping by multiple thousands. And since we had not changed our budgetary level of staffing the desk, each question was costing us more to answer. The same budget divided by fewer questions increases the cost of each question. I presented these results over a period of five years. Each year the response was the same—a polite acknowledgment of the information, a mild bemusement, but no action. I even tried humor, suggesting that at this rate, in five years we would answer one question, and it would cost us $2.1 million.

For some reason I was not being heard. Was it dimness on my part or theirs? I could suggest all sorts of nefarious reasons for what looked like stonewalling. But was there something I was missing? For one thing, what *action* was I seeking? In retrospect I see that was never clear in my mind. Like my musical friend, I found myself on the other side of moving a resisting organization forward—what for me was a trumpeted call for action was a muted and barely imperceptible sound for my peers. I suspect I could have done more. Lacking a Celedonio Romero in my audience, I needed to find out what was happening with that audience. They did not appear to be hearing me. To start with, I suppose I could have spoken up and said, "This matters to me, but I am not sure it matters to you. Are you not concerned? Am I overreacting? Set me straight."

My wanting to reinvent reference is a good example of presenting a mess (something is not right—it needs fixing), but not much more. I offered no specific ideas about what could be done or what the next steps might be. My ideas did not have to be the answer. More important is an idea's helping explain what effect a cause may be having. For example, I could have built on my colleague's idea to free up librarians to circulate through the reference area, approaching users and offering help. I'd seen a triggering idea in, of all places, a swank hotel lobby in Montgomery, Alabama. They'd done away with the long registration desk. Instead the lobby had three or four staffed, stand-alone, check-in stations. It sparked me to envision chain sawing our massive, elevated, wall-of-a-desk into a series of information islands.

Although a radical image, at least it was a "What if we did this?" My presenting the mess without possible actions is pretty much like putting on a play without plot or players. We set the stage and allow the audience to imagine whatever. Most theatergoers would walk out. Humility, like that of Romero's father, suggests I could go about things differently, seeking to be understood. Instead of leaving them guessing about my motives, I'd ask questions like these:

- Here is what I am seeing; do you have thoughts on what this might mean?

- Is there something to be done?

- If so, what should we be doing about it?

These questions would have made clear what I was after and that I did expect their help. Of course there are staff who do not want to hear and know full well what they don't want to hear. They prefer to keep their heads buried in the sand, like the codirector in my friend's story. But there are more staff members who want to be brought along, who only need to be shown what to look at, what to listen to, to better understand a need for action.

Well, I have explored what that "gentleness of his thumb" was saying to me. I find there are many things I would want to do differently—things I should have known, but did not. I keep learning, drawing wisdom from the successes and failures of the past. My writing about it, sharing it with others, is in the hope that someone like me, at any point of his or her career, will learn from this, that in these musings you will hear the gentleness of my thumb.

CHAPTER 25

The Stove-Side Chat

What's a *stove-side chat*?

The term seeks to evoke an old timey mood, one amenable to frank discussion of mutual problems. I use it to trigger an image still in the popular mind: a gathering of friends around a radiant stove, gloves, hats, and boots off, musing about the way things are or ought to be. Eons ago, hunters gathered in firelight to fend off the gloom and whatever was *hunting* them. While we've fast-forwarded to virtual fireplaces, we are still interdependent in our humanness.

Chapter 18 inspires this setting forth of a technique that can lead to resourcefulness: the stove-side chat. I use it in workshops for peers to make sense of a shared difficulty. Along that line, I will also take a look at the intriguing concept of self-organizing groups, those that succeed without overt supervision. Here's how the stove-side chat works:

At the start of a workshop I ask participants to think of a response to a statement about the day's topic. For example,

> *My biggest bug about* teamwork *is* _____.
>
> Or,
>
> *The worst part of* performance appraisal *is* _____.

To prime the pump, I declare one of mine, writing it on the flip chart as I want them to write it: succinctly and large enough to be seen across the room. Then, while I review the day's agenda, participants have time to ponder what they'll put up as their personal bête noire. I ask each person in turn. With little hesitation, the ideas tumble forth. Once the concern is out in the open, I try to help clarify, sometimes paraphrasing, to keep it specific and true to *their* actual concerns. I do this because the greater the clarity, the better the stove-side chats will be. It's best when the statement reflects the individual's heartfelt meaning.

I also work at moving it along. With two flip charts there's no waiting, even with thirty people. The lists are posted for the day and available for a participant to edit. Some do, wanting their statement to be a vote getter, to make certain they have captured what they believe. And a few simply have to add a second burning concern.

We hold the stove-side chat at the end of the day. The timing is deliberate. Everyone has worked together in mixed groups in several activities, including problem-solving games and case studies. There's an elevated comfort level; by now, each participant has a greater appreciation of the others. To counter the inevitable fatigue, I've learned to precede the chat with an energizing physical activity. If possible, we go outside and do something seemingly unrelated.

Before dividing into small groups, we edit the posted lists, aligning similar concerns, collapsing redundancies, and further clarifying. This helps the groups attend to what are now *their* lists. The filtering step is time consuming and challenging for me to keep track of changes, but the process reduces confusion and squandering of votes. There is a way to speed up this step: prior to the edit, cut up the flip charts so that each statement can be moved around easily.

Participants vote with dots. Each gets five dots and can stick all five on one or one dot on each of five statements. The statements with the highest votes are the ones to be discussed, one topic per group. The "multi-vote" is familiar for some; others see the value of this quick (and silent) way to prioritize. I tally up the dots—usually the top five vote getters are clear. If necessary, we can do a quick tie-breaking vote. Each small group spends about twenty minutes in the stove-side chat and then reports to the group at large on the first steps to take in resolving the problem.

Recent stove-side chats:

My biggest bug about teamwork *is* _____.

A few doing most of the work.

Teams in name only.

Norms (for how we will work together) are set but ignored.

Team members who are not team players.

Teams that do not value each member.

What really gets in the way of my leadership *is* _____.

Assuming that people will know what to do and (that they) will do it.

My reluctance to call errant behavior in subordinates.

Not knowing how to get others to follow.

Resistance to change by others.

Liking things done the right way, so I do it myself. But I don't confront you for doing it wrong.

> Tendency to micro-manage—I need to stay focused on the large picture, yet subordinates keep coming to me for advice on things they could handle themselves.

Not surprisingly, who's in the workshop makes a difference in how the session goes, how valuable the stove-side chats will be.

The ideal participant arrives open and flexible, eager to engage, not timid about asking questions, and ready to apply learnings to the real world. The engaged participant adds further value—they help pull along reluctant participants. Some of the reluctant are understandably skeptical—they may be workshop weary veterans with not much to show for their tours of duty. But if another participant's energy and enthusiasm can spark some residual interest and help them give the process a chance, some learning may occur.

Another brand of passive participant wants me, the so-called expert, to tell him or her what to do—resisting the real work of learning for oneself. I see participants not as empty vessels—they never are—but as co-explorers with their own work to do and challenges to meet. By declaring the workshop a safe zone, that whatever we do will be kept confidential, I encourage them to engage, risk their own idea formulation, and take a small step beyond the familiar.

Does my asking for their biggest and baddest concern promote an unproductive gripe session, an unending chorus of "A Sad Song Don't Care Whose Heart It Breaks"? Fortunately that has not been my experience. Why? Because, the stove-side chat has a built-in governor—reporting out. The negative slant serves to get out the problems—the work to be done—and instead of commiseration, participants understand they are to provide realistic first steps.

Why do this?

Many find it reassuring to know we all have the same problems. Their realizing that makes action less daunting. And the engaged participant is probably going to discover that his or her ideas are not off the mark—in fact, they may well be on target. That realization can be a big boost for the young leader. In workshops for a single library or a library cooperative, this sharing of collective wisdom reveals the best thinkers for networking and mentoring purposes at a later time when other problems come up and you need to talk with someone you respect.

Although most stove-side chat groups address issues head on and offer many good ideas, a few groups avoid. Their group dynamic leads to settling for the status quo and presenting lame first steps. For example, if their primary recommendation about a staff member's problem behavior is to send him to a workshop, never confronting him, the group probably could have done better. Again, engaged, thoughtful participants add unique value. By the end of the day, they are comfortable with challenging the inadequate solution and offering one or two that may make more sense.

Does the learning transfer beyond the workshop? Do participants practice the learning? That depends on the rigor and robustness of the workshop. My facilitating role is to add value to the process, to ask what people are not asking.

If participants are being indirect or avoiding, I press them for what they really are thinking, for what they are not saying. In this regard, I have come to regret whenever I ignore my intuition. Yes, the clock was ticking and others were waiting, but my paying attention to those red flags would have made the difference between a good session and one with profound learnings.

The stove-side chat builds on the notion of self-managing groups. The theory goes that if a group of people are left to their own devices, they can be productive without orders from outside experts or bosses. Much of what is done for groups by managers in the formal organization, self-directed groups can do better. Perhaps not in all circumstances; certainly when goals are unclear, the visionary leader shines and inspires others to see and work toward that vision. When the goal is clear and immediate, effective workers do not need outside guidance or a vision imposed—there is complete clarity about what needs doing.

Crisis brings clarity. Without waiting for orders from a command center or consulting a manual of procedure, staff can figure out and act on what's most in need of doing. People leave formal roles and do what needs doing, tossing aside the organizational chart.

I am reminded of a colleague's 1998 e-mail about how her research library responded to a disaster.

> The library flooded shortly after midnight; thousands of books were soaked. In less than an hour, staff were on-site, responding, calling students to come in and help. By 2:30 a.m., 100 students were helping move wet books. By 5:00 a.m. more than 200 students were helping. And when my senior administrative colleague got to the library around that time, she found her unit heads already at work: "The three of them were running the show when I got there, so I was happy to step back and take orders from them."

Although she was the formal leader, she trusted her staff and took on other roles to help them achieve the overriding goal: rescue thousands of books. Her leader did not fault her for stepping back. Would you?

Can the stove-side chat technique transfer to the workplace? Its deliberate streamlining is a plus. Instead of asking staff to contemplate what is wrong with some process and to list all that needs improving, the stove-side chat limits our tendency to produce endless lists. Each staffer gets to put up one or two concerns and then, after clarification, the top several are selected for action.

Ask your library department, "What is the biggest barrier to working more effectively with X unit?" Or ask more neutrally, "What one thing would you change in how we work with unit X?" What do you do with this list? Before you develop the list, make sure that X knows you are doing this, feels good about it, and will reciprocate with its own list about things to change in its relationship with you. The two units can figure out how to take actions steps on the key items. Probably a small task force of people from both units could rapidly implement changes.

Implicit in this process is trust and respect—both are essential. Obviously, if the organizational climate is fear based or avoidance preferring, then . . . well, you know the answer. Leaders who make a positive difference create conditions in which subordinates aspire to do their jobs better and better. For that to happen, a leader has to be explicit in his or her expectations about innovation and experimentation. Best of all is the leader who has corralled a few sacred cows and otherwise challenged the complacent. Staff seek an answer to a perennial anxiety: How safe am I if I question the way we do things around here? They want tangible assurance that those who covet the status quo won't easily undermine them. The more widely that is understood in the library, the better staff can do their work.

CHAPTER 26

"You Can't Build a Fire in the Rain": Sparking Change in Libraries

The word *change* often partners with *in opposition to*. At every workshop I give, someone asks, "What can I do about staff who resist change?" Similarly, when I ask, "What's your biggest bug about teamwork?" the most frequent response is, "Colleagues who *won't* change."

The cable news coverage from Paris of the youth employment law protest in April 2006 provided several images—some humorous and some irrational—of responses to the *threat* of reform. Like the one of the fractious young man, pants below his knees, mooning the gendarmes, the media, the world. Middle fingers extended, his waving hands were like quotation marks for his clichéd intransigence.

As unlikely as this may sound, the young man's antics evoked a memory of a Palmer House ALA Midwinter Meeting with directors of public services. My enthusing about some new program elicited a weary response from a peer: "*Plus ça change, plus c'est la même chose.*" Indeed, "The more things change, the more they stay the same," is near the top of the "Fifty Reasons Not to Change" chart.

We've all been there—the old way of doing something no longer works as well as it once did. Something different is needed and, being an intelligent workforce, we probably have a good notion about what needs doing. But as we start exploring the new ideas, like trying to light that fire in the rain, our well-intentioned efforts are swamped by a deluge of rationalizations for not changing. However Promethean our fire, the naysayers, the uncertain, and the fearful drench the sparks of change, until we're left with an ever-expanding puddle of doubt—and *no* fire.

WHY DOES REFORM REQUIRE A HERCULEAN EFFORT?

James O'Toole (1996) offers an explanation and a template for explaining opposition. A *dominant ideology* exists within each of us and affects our ability to change. Our cataloging code probably would qualify as a competing dominant ideology—consider how we cling to it while our users (and many librarians) almost exclusively use keyword searching to find books. Or consider the university presses' decade-long reluctance to move from print to electronic publication. Print has prevailed in spite of e-publications being feasible and offering possible cost savings along with other streamlining gains. After the 2009 recession, with library book budget cuts and receding levels of support, university presses may be forced to act. Although O'Toole is talking about fundamental change across wide populations, his theory still provides insights into why we resist change of whatever magnitude. He splits the population into the *Haves* and the *Have nots*.

Haves, those benefiting from the way things are, are unlikely to support change, especially reform that may reduce their perks. The Haves include *Have lesses*, who aspire for better but, like many of the Parisian protesters—students with welfare benefits, social networks, and family support—are unwilling to accept the risk and sacrifice that come with reform. In the case of the labor law uproar, these *Have lesses* reject the risk of being fired in the first two years of employment, a concession employers say they need to cover *their* risk and investment to remedy the chronic 20 percent unemployment among the under-twenty-five-years-of-age *Have lesses*.

Progressives, another category of *Haves*, support reform, but they too subscribe, if with reservations, to the dominant ideology. They are an interesting group because, to use a library example, some *Progressives* will vote for library expansion bonds or other public goods even if they rarely use the library, because they have other channels for their information needs, including personal budgets to *buy* almost any book they want.

Have nots include the many *uninvolved* who, sheeplike, accept the dominant ideology—the way it is. The *Have nots* also feature a working-class conservative group (called *Tories* by O'Toole), who have the most to gain from reform, yet defend the dominant ideology. Tories vote *against* library expansion bonds, even though their families would most benefit from greater information access and opportunity. Only the *Revolutionaries* in the *Have nots* reject the dominant ideology. But *Revolutionaries* rarely achieve a critical mass for change because the dominant ideology's centrifugal force spins them out to the fringe. Their rejection of the dominant ideology is made moot by the *Haves'* and *Have nots'* aversion to the revolutionary alternative.

WHY CHANGE? DO WE HAVE A CHOICE ABOUT CHANGE?

Each semester, on the first day of my academic libraries class, I read a geology quote used by Outward Bound: "Do not trust rocks. A rock resting on the rim of the Grand Canyon may give an impression of strength and permanence but as soon as a man turns his back the rock will resume disintegrating and sneaking off to California" (Kuller 1986).

The students readily grasp the metaphor behind the crumbling rocks—they understand their *campus* is changing, and the academic library is hardly isolated. While not exactly sneaking off to California, the campus library's role is disintegrating—call it *disintermediation*. My students cope well with what is a historically profound change for libraries (after all, this is a *class*), and our discussion of trends informs subsequent class assignments to envision the academic library ten years out. Invariably they design a merger of "bricks and clicks."

In my other class, management, I talk about the Sigmoid curve, the S-shaped curve. It applies to life, as Shakespeare illustrates entropically in his "Seven Ages of Man"—a span from "puking infant" to schoolboy to life's work, to "second childishness and mere oblivion." Organizations, and libraries, are on an S-shaped curve. I ask the students, "Where is your current employer on the curve?" A few draw organizations on the upswing, well out of infancy and approaching maturity. Some depict their organizations in a nosedive to "mere oblivion." Perhaps obviously, the best organizations anticipate the shifts in their business and make necessary adjustments to catch a new upward curve. Be it a new service, a new product, or a new challenge, all serve to reinvigorate the evanescent organization. Businesses that lose money close quickly—their S-shaped curve is greased. Not-for-profit agencies, like libraries, have less of a bottom line to worry about; they are less susceptible to cash flows. Funding agencies that renew our budgets regardless of our "productivity" tend to give us a longer ride on the downward slope, but it is still downward, however imperceptible. Instead of a few years, we may get a decade or two before we bottom out.

Any librarian working in the early to mid-1990s had to be aware of what was *not* going on all around: the numbers of reference questions were plummeting, fewer books were being checked out, and fewer photocopies were being made, while public printers connected to electronic resources were smoking. And then along came the World Wide Web. Disintermediation was upon us, as it was for almost every other service and business.

Back then, we were looking *down* the slope of the S-shaped curve, a dark precipice. How did we respond? Understandably, there was denial. We still hear cautionary tales about the shortcoming of search engines like Yahoo! and Google, and that most users are chronically duped by Internet charlatans. Some librarians regard our students as so many Pinocchios easily beguiled by any Fox and Cat Webmaster. Trouble is, the users are not listening any more now than they were a decade ago; instead, most are using the Internet in effective and efficient ways, probably better than they used the legacy collections in our libraries.

At the end of the first decade of the new millennium, have we caught a new curve, got our *mojo* back, like Apple with its iPod? Have e-mail reference, the information commons, ref-chat, information literacy programs, and our retailed-up, Barnes & Noble look put us on a new upward curve, a new beginning? Have we reinvented ourselves? Or are our new services *augmentations* that do not address the fundamental shift in the way people find and use information? Some claim we have turned the corner, caught a new curve: more students in the library along with increasing numbers of books borrowed. Certainly this seems to be the case in some public libraries, and I am told it is so in some academic libraries, especially those that have established learning partnerships on previously inaccessible faculty turf. Yet some academic librarians are less sanguine; they see empty rooms, deserted stacks, and unused, expensive e-resources. Even for those libraries that have budgets to pay for retail ambiance, it is unsettling to note what happens when a magnet service like an information commons moves out of the library: students follow.

How do we spark change in libraries? For much of my career, I believed change was simply what you did—it was intuitive. Like communication, change was too obvious to talk about. The important thing was to act. With some sad experience and mature reflection, I realize one can achieve far more with followers alongside. It was naive for me to think change would happen because it *must* happen for *me*. So, how do you bring others along?

Much has been said about strategies for implementing change. Some are superficial, like swapping out an old name, Circulation, for a new one, Access. Another of my least favorites is the call to reorganize—one embittered soul made up a quote, ascribing it anachronistically to a corporate sounding, first-century Petronius Arbiter: "We tend to meet any new situation by reorganizing; and a wonderful method it can be for creating the illusion of progress while producing confusion, inefficiency, and demoralization." I don't share the knee-jerk cynicism—nor do I consider all reorganizations wasteful—yet I understand what the unhappy author was talking about. Many reorganizations tend to be in name only, without tangible goals, glossing over fundamental *causes*.

Then there is strategic planning, the reigning model for introducing change in libraries. Strategic planning, honestly and courageously done, has great potential. From reading dozens of library plans, I have to conclude reluctantly that potential is rarely achieved. What I see is a clever strategy to retain the status quo. A friend at a university library told me they were at the conclusion of their strategic plan and that action steps were being written, *exclusively*, by the senior library staff—the Haves. One can only hope there are a few Progressives in the group. Perhaps no librarian knowingly does this, but, if you want to slow down change—change desperately in need of doing—there's probably nothing quite like well-orchestrated strategic planning to achieve "an illusion of progress."

For O'Toole, true reform comes through values-based leadership, led by someone who overcomes resistance to change by virtue of *moral leadership*. Such a leader is persuasive and principled and engages followers to arrive at mutually beneficial actions. O'Toole terms this leader, *Rushmorean*, as akin to the presidents captured in the mountain's granite (1996).

There is a change tool available to the values-based leader: the future search. I've been involved in planning and participating in a full-scale future search (FS) and in leading a FS at another large library. Both enjoyed a modest success; not seismic, but a shift in perspective that helped galvanize the staff around purpose and goals and engage them in the decision making to achieve those goals.

The underlying theory (Rehm et al. 2002) behind the FS is that if you get enough good people together, they can decide what needs doing for their organization and then go about doing it. Envisioning the future is the first step to getting there. The FS includes a large number of *stakeholders*: selected staff *Haves* and *Have nots* along with invited guests, like customers. For the academic library this group would include students, faculty, and board members. (My FSs numbered over sixty participants each.) This mix is the difference maker, because for an intense two days we sidelined the pecking order, with good and bad ideas coming from all over. Good ideas are supported on their merit, not by the status of the suggestion maker. Invariably, there are enough positive people in the mix to assuage the uncertainty and trepidation some participants—often proponents for the status quo—might be feeling. *Cannot* becomes *can do*.

Most of the first day in a FS is a reflection on the way we were and how far we have come. This includes addressing (and burying) the mistakes, our *sorries*, and celebrating the *prouds*, our many achievements. The required rigor shoots up on the second day when the group makes specific choices about resources and trade-offs—things you will do *without*—to get to the future. They do this after subsets of participants have described the future in scenarios of their design.

The long list of what is wanted can become like gridlocked strategic planning lists by which we accommodate compromise upon compromise in order to retain the old way of doing things. In both FSs, the lists became a sticking point, where we ran out of time before we reached conclusive steps. However, we did take away a much clearer idea of where we wanted the organization to be. We had not agreed on *how* to get there, or what we would do without, but we had agreed on the end result.

The positive conclusion in one FS was that *connectivity* was all important. And it was pretty well agreed upon, organization-wide, that connectivity was replacing the just-in-case model of book accumulation. Everyone now knew—however much it pained some—that there was a new model of information provision, one that was not going away. The unspeakable had been uttered. At the follow-up meeting of many of the original FS participants, we agreed to use existing budgetary resources to make a sizable down payment on technology. Without knowing it, we had shaken the dominant ideology, and change was underway.

Yes, you *can* build a fire in the rain. It is technically possible to do it without any help. Maybe not on the first try, but eventually a spark will cling to the tinder, smoke, and burst into a flame. Of course you may be the only one to enjoy it. The best kind of metaphoric fire for an organization is that made combustible with help from your engaged followers. They've gathered the tinder, worked with you in delivering a spark, and shelter you and the budding flame from the downpour.

CHAPTER 27

What? So What? Now What?

The title is shorthand for the "debriefing" process used in team-building activities. Whenever I debrief a group in my workshops or classes, I try to get answers to those questions. I've discovered there are people who take life literally; metaphor is largely lost on them. For some a candle is a candle, a lump of wax. When lit, the candle provides light. For others, the lit candle is that and more. The flickering light can represent life; when quenched, it represents an ending. These literal and figurative views are far apart. To narrow that gap among workshop participants, I've learned to be as explicit as I can be about why we are doing an activity and what might be gained. I take time to explain what the participants will be doing at the literal level and ask them to be alert to the levels of interpretation beyond the literal, the What?[1]

The What? is the activity itself. It is a summary of what happened; for example, for the Egg Drop, the What? could be this: Our four-person group wrapped, in ten minutes, a raw egg with twenty straws and a yard of tape and then dropped it from a height of five feet. Our egg broke. Although the What? is fact based, eyewitness accounts may differ vastly and can make for a rich, if limited, analysis, about differing perspectives.

The So What? is what you learned about yourself and others from the activity. What did you—yes, you—do? Wait for others to make decisions? How did decisions get made? Did your ideas for wrapping the egg gain acceptance, or were they rebuffed? If rejected, did you assert yourself? Did you or someone else take charge? Did anyone protest? If the egg broke or did not break, does it matter? Was the group ethical?

The Now What? is what you derive—the take-aways—from the group activity to apply to your life and at work. They are yours to take or leave. If you were uncomfortable with what happened, will you do things differently? If your ideas were ignored, will you assert yourself? If someone commandeers a future group, will you protest? If you believe a group is dishonest, will you say something?

189

My being explicit during the lead-in to an activity helps groups engage; it helps break the ice. Without this prior glimpse about the activity, you run the risk of the clueless remaining so. Some people, when unclear about what their role is, will not go with the flow. Instead, they will behave in a defensive way. Or they will go along like corks bobbing in a stream, going nowhere in particular. For example, a colleague and I did a team-building presentation to a couple dozen research library directors. Our introduction was minimalist—we were less explicit than what I would now regard as best practice. To illustrate team development, we had them do the "group juggle." It involves four tennis balls; everyone has to juggle the balls in a set order in the briefest time possible. More than a few of the directors were mystified about what they were to do; not only that, they had little idea how what they did could be linked to team building. Some jeered at the activity as so much foolishness. Maybe they only wanted/needed more information.

When presented with an unfamiliar task, we do not want to appear foolish, to lose face—all the more so if we are "afflicted with office" as Oscar Wilde once said. On hands and knees, in suits, trying to figure out how to best juggle tennis balls in the quickest time is vastly different from a comfortable position behind a desk surrounded with a multitude of other real and implied exaltations of office. If we are used to directing others, our having to do the task with no clear leader can lead to confusion or a stalemate.

In this case, the several groups got over their initial misgivings and began to offer ideas, experiment, and learn from mistakes; they made good progress. As I recall, some of the most reluctant participants had their "ah ha!" moment and made insightful transfers from the activity to the workplace. These directors may have realized that just as they had difficulty at first from a lack of information, so might their staffs back home. And although these directors struggled, they meant to do well. Would their staff behave any differently?

So how many clues should you give people ahead of an activity? The less you reveal, the more uncomfortable the participants, but that discomfort may precipitate valuable insights. The more you reveal, the more certainty in the group, but this cushioning might short change participant learning and runs counter to the real world's uncertainty. A group's failing can be a powerful moment for reflection, yet most groups want to succeed. They take failure as a personal affront—their group somehow did not get the job done—rather than as a normal group outcome on which to build and get better. This fear of failure—our national affliction?—affects facilitators as well. We are tempted to bend the rules so at least one group can succeed and claim victory. It's anticlimactic when no eggs survive a drop. There may appear to be little to debrief, but if we can get out from under the so-called failure, then we might have a healthy discussion about how we worked or did not work together in protecting the eggs. That may lead to a candid conversation about what promotes or gets in the way of workplace success.

DIAGNOSING THE DEBRIEF

As previously stated, I now lead off activities with thorough explanations. I try to make sure everyone understands the rules and knows what the game is and what the end result should look like. Yet after that effort and a practice round or two of the activity, I run into situations in which the learning is avoided and self-illumination is short-circuited. The question then becomes whether the group is unable to learn from the activity (the participants do not want to learn) or the activity has no learning to offer (the design is inept, inapplicable, or incomprehensible).

I recall one facilitator who ran an activity for library department heads. It was something that took group effort, touching, and a willingness to work with each other. Well, the group failed at the activity. During the debrief, the facilitator candidly said "your failure is diagnostic." It was exactly how these department heads worked with each other on the job, protecting their turf rather than improving the library at large.

I agreed, but one person took exception to the term *diagnostic*. No way, for her, could a failed activity suggest the group's dynamics in the workplace; the two arenas were separate. And yet the facilitator had sat in on department head meetings and simply was noting that the workplace dynamics did not change during the activity; just as mutual support was missing on the job, so it was in the activity.

The facilitator was blunt in his assessment, but the group was not open to his interpretation or to improving. So while these simple activities may confirm the issues in the organization, participants may resist making the connection from play to work. They deny the link and never get to the Now What? The big challenge for the facilitator is to reveal the truth so that the group learns about itself. The mistake this facilitator made was rubbing the group's collective nose in what was already known—they did not get along and they were OK with that as long as no one trespassed on *their* turf.

At times a workshop group is so dysfunctional, nothing less than disbanding the group makes sense. However, as we know, many organizations will mask their weaknesses and pretend they are trouble-free. The dysfunction is much more difficult to conceal when a group takes part in a workshop built on active participation rather than passive listening. Often a diagnosis based on small group behavior may be highly accurate about what needs doing if the organization *wants* to improve.

Frankly, I've come to regard my experience at one library as a nightmare—something I should have run screaming from in the opposite direction. But as is often the case with an outsider, there were few clues to suggest the troubles in this library—nothing to give me an early warning. Instead, as the day wore on, and I mean *wore on*, my apprehensions piled up.

The day's first outdoor activity—it was a crisp sunny morning—was the "rope push." Instead of pulling the rope, like a tug-of-war, each side was to figure out how to surrender the rope to the other side. Out of the blue, one of the participants ran off with the rope! He stood some fifty feet away, leering, like a delinquent child, all but sticking his tongue out. I was of two minds: give pursuit or sprint to my nearby parked car and head home! I did neither.

Abandoning the group would be akin to the captain of a sinking ship jumping into a lifeboat ahead of the women and children. Flabbergasted, I failed to call time and have everyone analyze the So What? That discussion, if honest, could have been eye opening. I suspect, given the group's subsequent behavior, no one would have been bold enough to say that hijacking the rope was a typical outlier behavior for this individual. From a cursory understanding of this library, I noted a few major service point redundancies that suggested a long-term failure to resolve uncooperative behavior—avoidance and accommodation drove this library's decisions. If you stop to consider the monetary costs of this behavior and the lost opportunities for new services, you glimpse the tip of this budgetary iceberg.

Next we did a group game involving tossing balls into boxes that required cooperation among four groups of internal and external customers. The goal was clear: achieve the highest level of customer satisfaction. One of the participants, Team Y's captain, suggested her team cooperate with an adjoining group. Quite sensibly (and following the suggestion in each captain's cheat sheet), she said to her team, "If we get Team X to agree to move their boxes closer to us we'd all have greater customer satisfaction (more balls in each box)." Remarkably, the team captain was ignored and the two groups would not cooperate—so the customer satisfaction was abysmal. Did they behave this way on the job? I asked this question in the debrief and got a few noncommittal answers.

Looking back, I fault myself in part for this nadir in my consulting experiences. The communication, the design, the planning, and the location all could have been better. And I could have done a better job facilitating. If I could do it over (my own Now What? moment), I would stop the group and give them feedback on what I was seeing. If my observations were ignored or judged irrelevant, then I'd walk away.

From a diagnostic aspect, their behavior pointed to real issues that were largely taboo. I was seeing a perverse organizational personality more than an incompetent workshop design. However, the latter always applies to some extent in workshops that *gang aft agley.*

Another example of the diagnostic value of small group activity came my way after a team-building workshop. It's been my custom to e-mail participants two weeks afterward, asking them to let me know what they learned. Usually a few respond. I got a Harry-Potter-Owl-Post "howler" from one participant, someone I did not expect to hear from because she had visibly disengaged herself from the group and looked, as P. G. Wodehouse might have put it, like an aggrieved vegetarian served up a plateful of bratwurst. Unbeknown to me, she was paying attention, or at least enough so to confirm in her eyes the hypocrisy of this library:

> What I picked up from the workshop was the reminder that there are people in the world who believe the end always justifies the means, and that breaking the rules is no big deal. We were given a set of rules by an authority figure (you) . . . . When it proved to be a more difficult task than people had anticipated, one or two began lying and cheating so they could "win." Others followed suit quickly, once they realized the authority figure (you) weren't going to penalize them for the behavior.
>
> . . . . What resulted was mob mentality, and a hollow victory.
>
> In the summing up, the people who had decided for all of us that breaking rules was okay spoke louder and more than those of us who were appalled by the behavior; I still don't understand what your purpose was that day.

I've forgotten what I wrote back to her, other than to say I was sorry for her experience. To be sure, I was dismayed that what needed to be said, never got said. I do recall elaborating that day about the ethics in this game—every group breaks the rules to improve customer satisfaction—but no one spoke up about how repulsive not abiding by the rules was for some or, for that matter, how some arbitrary library rules (*think AACR2 here*) beg to be broken. I doubt the discussion would have been as candid as the howler e-mail. The boss was in the room, and from what I could gather, my unhappy correspondent was describing her boss.

With more time we might have had the quintessential confrontation between the staff and the administration, a clearing of the air. But a one-day workshop is rarely enough time for an extrapolation of what is really bugging people. We'll get allusions to what's wrong, hints of an undercurrent, but rarely an open discussion. Trust takes time. And if the group does not regard trust as worthy of pursuit, or does not respect any other viewpoints besides the "official line," no matter how much time you have, candor will be missing.

To my correspondent's credit, she no longer works in this system, having landed a job elsewhere. I like to think that her Now What? moment may have been precipitated by what happened in my workshop. Then again, her passive aggression may be her normal way of dealing with conflict.

One of my most dreaded workshop participants is "He-Who-Has-Been-Sent." He (or, just as often, she) has been told, by a boss, to sign on with a workshop to repair—miraculously—some deep personality flaw.[2] The person arrives bearing a grievance, a chip on the shoulder—not against me necessarily, but against the boss, the organization—and of course the grudge plays out in a variety of ways.

Some sit silently nursing their resentment at having to be in the workshop; others try to sabotage the workshop—participating only to undermine it, looking for loopholes in the rules, denying, like Aesop's dog in the manger, the experience for themselves and for others.

On occasion, a dissatisfied participant will make an oblique reference to something not being quite what he or she thought it would be. If this comes at the end of the day—say, during a go-around in which each participant talks about what he or she will do differently after this day—there is usually too little time to probe the person's meaning. Still, to get full value from this Now What? moment, I probably should ignore the time pressure and ask a clarifying question, "What's behind your statement? Can you tell me more?" and then wait. One intervention like this probably will not take up too much time, but exceeding the stated end time may frustrate participants who have worked hard during the day and are eager for a break.

Debriefing at the end of each activity during the day has limits, as well. Some people, like my aggrieved participant, will let their hair down in writing but say nothing unflattering on-site. I've noted this difference between classroom debriefs and written reflections in my classes. While all was sunny in the classroom—Great teamwork! Terrific cooperation! Everyone participated fully!— the written reflections, done a week later, never failed to show a contrast. Many students felt much freer to express themselves privately than to take their beef public.

At the start of each semester, I make a point of assuring my classes that each team member has the power to stop a group and to say what is on his or her mind—there won't be a penalty from me for doing that. At least one team did stop and reflect, all for the better, but for the most part the confidences went no further than between the student and me. Regardless, the student's private realization of a problematic group dynamic was still important. I always coach each student—this is after all, his or her What Now? moment—to consider what he or she would do differently. What would he or she say? Some, I believe, did confront themselves and now resolve differences in a more open and satisfying manner.

PART 4

Techniques and Tools, Productivity, Climate

CHAPTER 28

Sherlock's Dog, or Managers and Mess Finding

Sherlock Holmes, the detective of short story fame, provides a splendid example of a mess finder at work. In "Silver Blaze" (Doyle 1953), Inspector Gregory initiates the following exchange with the sleuth:

> "Is there any point to which you would draw my attention?"
>
> "To the curious incident of the dog in the night-time."
>
> "The dog did nothing in the night-time."
>
> "That was the curious incident."

In this dialogue with the inspector, Holmes displays his knack for looking at complex problems by identifying what did not make sense and then coming up with an answer to explain it. Why was the dog's behavior curious to Holmes and no one else? It wasn't that Sherlock was a paranormal (not in this regard, at least); it was that he could see the incongruities others could not. Identifying what was out of place and applying his ratiocination process allowed him to get to solutions.

In my library career, I have often wondered about the many unquantifiable areas of our work.[1] What circumstances trigger in me the notion that something quite nebulous, like a passing remark or an unconscious observation that jars, in the rethinking may warn of a pending failure? Why do I react the way I do to what is clearly an ambiguous condition, sometimes acting on the impulse, other times not? Are there constants in this process of uncovering messes that might be shared with colleagues who are also concerned with improving work processes and services?

Here are some situations, drawn from real experiences, that might be useful in explaining what I am trying to describe:

> A staff member checks newly produced book orders for errors. He is unable to keep up, even though he claims to work fifty hours per week. The department head requests a new position to solve the problem.

> Since time immemorial, the end of each semester on this campus brings with it a flood of library books surging into the library that take several weeks to reshelve. "Why does it have to be this way?" is the frequent question heard from students and faculty. You're tired of reciting the same old reasons—lack of staffing, etc.

> A merger of the preorder searching unit with the precataloging unit (previously doing similar work at different points in the workflow) results in the same number of staff and longer turnaround times.

> Users complain frequently that they want longer library hours. Your studies show little use in the late evening. Although you share this information with anyone who asks, users still clamor to increase hours.

I hope these whet your appetite to continue reading and to adopt mess finding as a process that can uncover problems and bring about improvements using available resources.[2] This chapter is divided into three parts: definition, applications, and climate.

Definition

My purpose here is to show some of the ineffable qualities certain to be encountered in looking for messes. Categorically, it is safe to say that messes, though they may look like them, are not problems; rather, they may indicate a problem. Working through the mess, which takes time, may lead to an actual problem or it may not. Also, be aware that what looks like a mess in one setting may not be a mess in another. I first came across the phrase "mess finding" in a workshop on the creative problem-solving model developed by Isaksen and Treffinger (1985). The I&T mess finding step differentiates their problem-solving model from several others.[3] All purport to help managers think better and bring an orderly and disciplined approach to solving problems. Here are some of the first steps suggested by other problem-solving theorists:

> Ascertain the truth—Chester I. Barnard

> Define the problem—Peter F. Drucker

> Use intelligence (find conditions calling for a solution)—Herbert A. Simon

> Recognize a situation that calls for a decisive action—Joseph W. Newman

Select the problem—operations research approach

Observe—scientific method

Monitor the decision environment—Ernest B. Archer[4]

Obviously the first steps of most of these models presume that you know that there is a problem. The I&T model caught my interest because their unique first step, mess finding, captures the realization that sometimes the problem we thought we were working on was not really the problem we thought it was. Not infrequently, our solutions for some problems did not work. Instead the process of trying to find a solution that worked was a cyclical one like that described ironically by Eric Sevareid: "The chief cause of problems is solutions."

Likewise, Peter Senge reminds us that "tomorrow's problems come for yesterday's solutions" (1990, 57). We keep missing the target, and the problem keeps eluding our best efforts to fix it. For me, the phrase mess finding catches the fuzzy, ineffable first intimation that something is going or has gone awry and that missing or ignoring this first step might explain why our best efforts sometimes fail. Or why, more strangely, we never get around to working on a problem. I've gained a new appreciation for the person who said, "We need problem finders, not problem solvers." Taking the mess-finding step helps us get through the maze of dead ends to the real problem.

Mess as Process

The mess-finding step is worked through by answering several questions:

What's on my mind? What's nagging at me?

What's demanding my attention?

What have I been trying unsuccessfully to avoid?

What might happen if I don't deal with these concerns?

To these I've added a couple:

What's wrong with this picture?

I don't understand why we do what we do this way. Is it my ignorance, or is it obfuscation?

Why have we always done it this way? (And the many variations on this theme. "Because we have," is not the answer you are looking for.)

In researching this topic, I've discovered there is a lot written about problem solving; for example, total quality management is largely a strategy to solve problems. However, the mess-finding step continues to be more assumed, more implied than expressed by most writers. A few authors do lead us to a better understanding of mess finding. Marvin Weisbord (1987, 224) suggests that American managers are too impatient with reflection, thus indirectly explaining why mess finding is not much discussed. The implication is that mess finding usually takes time away from generating solutions and wastes it on considering incongruities.

Inspector Gregory openly mocked Holmes's ratiocination process, even knowing that somehow Holmes figured stuff out a lot faster than anyone else. Edward de Bono explains this as the difference between lateral and vertical thinking. In the latter, when confronted with a problem, one "moves along the widest pathway which is pointing in the right direction"; other paths are excluded. In lateral thinking, we avoid the most obvious solution, looking for the least obvious path in the hopes of finding a superior solution—an improvement over the vertical solution is at the end of the widest pathway.[5]

I can illustrate this impatience with an example from one library's experience with continuous improvement (CI). As part of that effort library administrators, working with middle managers, developed a list of list of librarywide problems in need of fixing. This list of hot topics included the following questions:

Why are books not on shelves when needed?

What should we be doing to provide document delivery service?

Each hot topic was assigned to a team to resolve. Once these teams finished their work, we asked them how the CI process could be improved. All of the teams strongly urged that future problem statements be clear and more specific than the ones they were handed. The teams were exasperated with spending too much time on uncovering the real problem hidden in the overly simplified problem statement.

The proverb, "He who hesitates is lost" means more than it intends. Because mess finding demands reflection beyond the superficial, it may not be well regarded in the hyperactive workplace. For those with a zest for fixing something, mess finding takes too much time. Yet in Weisbord's view, leaders ought to look at process as much as they look at task: "Both 'pictures' are there all the time." Process is akin to mess. "If you hear the same information recycled without being acted upon, that's a process issue. If you want to contribute something and hold yourself back, that's a process issue; if people run away or fight, abandoning the task either way, that's a process issue" (1987, 226).

Mess Taxonomy

Messes come in all shapes and sizes; some portend disaster, whereas others signify nothing. I have grouped and named below some of the messes I have encountered.

Mega-mess—or, Paradigm Mess

The whole system is a mess: nothing seems to work, everyone is suffering and complaining, and the only perceived solution on the horizon is "more," be it money, equipment, or staff. Usually staff are demoralized and uncertain about what is happening. There is a real sense of loss of control and the feeling that little can be done. Trust is absent. Some people set up a "them and us" gestalt, blaming others for their misery.

A directly relevant example, as true in 2010 as it was in 1994, is the stand-off between scientific, technical, and medical (STM) journal publishers and research libraries. Rapacious price increases are inevitably followed by library cost cutting. Why?

Inside many libraries the classic divisive gulf between public and technical services continues unbridged.

There is also the situation in which communication between a funding agency and a subordinate unit ceases or becomes highly formalized. In one instance, the library accepted status quo budgets because of its conviction that the university administration was opposed to any new initiatives. For its part, the administration saw the library staff as entrenched and unwilling to change. Neither could see any potential for improvement; hence the standoff.

Kick the Dog Mess

This is the urge to blame someone for something that's not quite the way it ought to be, for example, bad people (including "stupid" users). However, exploring this mess closely may reveal a bad boss or policy. At other times, there may have been a failure to train a staff member adequately or to clarify expectations for a job. The negative outcome can be a staff member who appears to be uncooperative and unproductive. This condition can be even more disabling when we have low expectations of staff and communicate our belief that they will fail (Weisbord 1987, 228). A believable tenet of TQM is that 85 to 95 percent of the time, difficulties in the workplace are caused by inadequate systems, not by deficient workers.[6] At times, I would include managers in the definition of inadequate system.

Kluge Mess

"Kluge" is computer talk for an unnecessarily complex piece of programming; it is the opposite of elegant. A kluge mess happens when over time a simple and straightforward process inexplicably becomes incomprehensible. It takes forever to get work through the bottlenecks of complexity and has defied years of attempts to improve it. A library example of this is the constant rehandling of a book moving through technical services. Usually this back and forth activity requires shelving to store books as they lurch through the process. The shelves add complexity because material is batched and may be unavailable for long periods of time. This results in systems to track and deal with what is out of sequence, further aggravating the complexity.

More than a little righteously we say we do this to reduce errors. In fact, because of the added complexity, frustration and the error rate go up more than if the extra steps were eliminated. When the rising error rate and customer anger is pointed out, the response is not to simplify but to build in additional inspection systems. In the kluge mess there is a fundamental failure to ask the questions: "Why are we doing this? What is this costing us? What is our purpose—perfect records or books for users?" The argument of flawed bibliographic records impeding access is largely fallacious. If there are any examples of this occurring, they are too few to matter. What does exist are countless cataloging absurdities that confound the user, fail to simplify our task, and in effect waste the time of the user.

Not My Mess

"If only they would do it right the first time," "they" being another department or division or the immediately previous person to handle something—usually an internal customer who supplies work and/or receives work done by others.[7] Shortcomings in timeliness, quality, accuracy, etc., are easy arrows to launch at another department. But they fall short because the real mess of a systemic difficulty is not addressed. It is obviously desirable that we have an improved understanding of our roles as customers of each other and what that means. The cop-out I've heard is, "If you did your job, we wouldn't be wasting our breath talking about this!" Far better to ask ourselves and the other unit how we contribute to the problem and what we can do differently.

The lengthy turnaround times for approval plan books from receipt to shelf illustrates the "Not my mess." Some selectors were convinced that these books went into a black hole, disappearing for several months. The catalogers felt they were being unfairly blamed because many selectors were dilatory in screening the approval plans and sometimes took these books away from the approval plan area for several weeks. The two groups eventually met and established , after some give and take, a smooth workflow and a one-week turnaround time for the benefit of readers.

Sometimes we victimize the user by arbitrary rules and regulations. Where we "understand" a policy or procedure, the user may not. Instead of our blaming (and fixing) the policy or procedure (i.e., the official dogma of our work), we blame the patron for not paying attention, not reading carefully our explanations, or being irresponsible. When we say the patron is wrong to have done something, we are usually right, but in a mess-finding sense we are wrong.

Must Mess

This is a subtle condition that emphasizes a single action that must be taken, when in truth the organization is faced with choices—including not doing something. This kind of mess is characterized by words and phrases like *mandatory, essential, absolutely, unconditionally,* and *utterly inadequate.* This overstatement and other exaggeration of reality can be benign, even humorous. Is hyperbole not overstatement in pursuit of the truth? However, once it becomes a way of doing business, it is usually a good indicator that problems exist in the concerned work unit. Consider the "utter inadequacy" of a school district that has no computers for student use with the "utter inadequacy" of a school district with nearly half of its computers unboxed and hidden away in closets, with more hardware on the way.

Stress Mess

Many people who work in libraries believe they are stressed, even burned out. Not to offend the many who are indeed stressed, I would venture to say that some of us are more stressed than others. Perception, we know, can contribute to one's reality. Some people really do believe they are working to their maximum. Since an acceptable minimum is never mentioned, it is hard to know just what the maximum is. No one ever says he or she is stress free. Most of us are probably in the 35 to 45 percent range of personal productivity, if one is to believe the research.[8]

Like most managers, I have heard pleas for more resources because of stress. More than once, high stress was the sole compelling reason that I should scour the budget for additional staffing dollars. When additional resources were provided, I got a strong signal that this was the last thing the unit needed. Invariably, stress was not reduced for very long, and subsequent appeals for more staff were already underway! When this happens, I am convinced there are difficulties lurking beneath the surface. Often the unit's members may be unwilling to give up doing something; instead they add more responsibilities to those already preoccupying them. Compounding this is the fact that an administrative edict to eliminate x so y can be done may not be sufficient. Not infrequently, much of the work done by the unit will qualify for the kluge category, and the group may in fact continue to do x camouflaged as w.

Attitude Mess

There's a list called "Fifty Excuses for a Closed Mind." These are "killer gotchas" when used in group problem solving. Each of the fifty put-downs can add something to our understanding of messes. Each represents a potential individual mess in the speaker's unwillingness to try something different:

"If we did that, we'd be out of compliance with the (voluntary) standards."

"So and so tried it and it failed, totally!"

"The customers won't like it."

"Let's all sleep on it."

"If it ain't broke, don't fix it."

"We're not a business!"

APPLICATIONS: ACTIVE WAYS TO FIND MESSES

Here are some traditional and some less conventional approaches to uncovering a mess—to realizing that something is not quite right, the organization's gears are clashing, and the engine is smoking.

Date records. It may be difficult to believe that something this simple and basic actually works. Putting a date on in-process materials (boxes, books, e-records, forms) not only gives you a data anchor, it permits an essential measurement of any work process: the time to completion. It harkens back to Ranganathan's (1957) mandate "to save the time of the user." Once we know the time it takes for a process to go full cycle, we can ask, "Is this OK or not?" Are we indirectly or directly wasting the time of the user?

Our failing to date materials may suggest a naïve belief that we are not a business, so we do not need to be conscious of how much time something is taking—how much it costs. And by not dating, we tacitly reduce the chance of being embarrassed by a dysfunctional system. Once dating becomes routine, look at the dates and use them to track turnaround times. Hundreds of gift books, all dated as received ten years ago and still not processed, require decisive action regardless of the many reasons—some legitimate—you will hear when you ask why.

Expect reasonable gains. When you introduce a process, especially one that makes effective use of technology, you should expect some gains in staffing and turnaround times. Perhaps not right away, but eventually. If gains do not occur, there's a mess in the neighborhood. Is the application a lemon, or do staff members not trust the new way and back up everything by running a dual system? Is there resistance to reducing staff just in case they are needed if the new way of work fails? Does the organization confer status on managers based on staff size rather than for keeping the FTEs at realistic levels?

Consult the user. Librarians, with some outstanding exceptions, rarely listen to their users. In spite of potentially valuable feedback, easily obtained with minimum effort, many librarians act as if users have little to offer them on how to do the job better. They are hardly alone in eschewing customer suggestions. This contempt confounds numerous service organizations in the government and business. I have been jolted by staff attitudes ranging from passive hostility to incredulous negativity to dismissive indifference when users have complaints and offer their ideas. In my library career, I've made use of a practical approach of getting user ideas: the "Suggestion Answer Book" (see chapter 36). Because we took user comments seriously, library services were improved incrementally in hundreds of ways.

Then there are user surveys. Many of my peers have never much cared for user surveys. They'd tell me the surveys were too subjective, not scientific, and not statistical enough. In my own use of surveys, I have always learned valuable, useable information. For me, the customer is always right, individually and in the aggregate. What does that mean? For example, irate patrons (that's our term for a category of user) who are fed up with our slow reshelving have repeatedly pointed out this mess to us. Our response? A rational explanation of slow reshelving. Instead, what the user wants—and we should want the same thing—is change for the better. Sometimes users can be very clear and helpful in stating what should be our own expectations, clear enough to help us find our service bearings. For example, one user stated her shelving expectations: everything back on the shelf by noon of the next day. Even with all the reasons I can offer why this is not achievable, the user is right. My rationalizing instead of taking action signals another mess, the "Yes, BUT . . . Mess."

Generate a bug list. This is a brainstorming procedure that elicits ideas for inventions yet to be invented. [9] It has immediate applications to the library. On surveys or in group settings, ask staff and users to list what is bugging them about the library. If they could change one thing, what would that be? The results ought to reveal several messes. Naturally, extra effort will need to go into finding what is of value in the list. Look for the low-hanging fruit to get the most return for your effort. Do enough of this, and categories for improvements ought to create recognizable patterns.

Value your statistics. Even though statistics are hard to come by in libraries, they can be useful signposts to what is or is not happening in an organization. [10] Examine statistics closely before using them, and only if you can trust them. When the staff say they are overwhelmed by service demands and your frequent observation is an empty room and idle staff, there may be a mess. Look for incongruities in different statistics. How many hours or staff does it take to shelve how many books? How many staff are shelving? A caveat: always look at statistics as potentially wrong headed. For example, comparing one month to the same month a year ago is risky because it begs misinterpretation out of a longitudinal context. If you are fortunate to have several years of statistics, then you may be able to perceive realistic trends.

Encourage the sharing of statistics among similar institutions as a form of benchmarking. For libraries, this would represent a major leap forward to appreciating, finally, high-quality performance. Even share statistics from purportedly incomparable specialties. Resist unflinchingly the argument that some areas of our work are outside human knowledge, too sublime for measurement, and therefore not quantifiable. When you hear that, you're getting a whiff of the sacred cow mess, so get out your lasso and shovel.

Be concerned, appropriately, when monthly statistics go up after you have questioned a statistical decline over previous years. An ongoing example is the considerable variation in reference statistics among peer institutions. Because of Internet self-services, most have experienced a drop off in reference questions of well over 50 percent. It is odd when a comparable library claims only a drop off of 15 percent. Why? Does this library offer new services that drive up reference use, or is it simply keeping track of reference in different ways? Any workflow numbers that show extensive variation over time are well worth looking at for causes and to determine whether less variation is possible. This is an important concept because variation in one part of the system causes variation throughout. Delays at the front cause equal, if not greater, delays at the end of the process.

Walk around. Open doors to people's ideas. An impromptu comment from a staff member can lead to amazing improvements if you can hear what the person is suggesting. Often, the comment is about a mess. Look for complexity: processes that add little value to the outcome. Birds leave a feeding field when the energy required to stay in place exceeds the amount of food they find. There's some food still in the ground, but the birds will starve trying to find it, so they leave.

We ought to be aware when we encounter one of the many points of least diminishing returns in our work. Sometimes we take pride in the complexity of a process, not realizing that complexity tends to become an end in itself when unconstrained and unquestioned (Fuller 1985). Ask questions of the staff working in an area about what they do. If they are unable to explain what they do, there may be a mess.

Look for cyclical and predictable messes. An unresolved favorite of mine is the wildly fluctuating book ordering pattern in academic libraries. This mess leads to an unpredictable workflow in technical services, not to mention the "inexplicable" delays for users who are seeking new books. Usually this mess is accompanied by numerous rush requests for delayed materials on order or in process. If you track rush requests and find there is a constant monthly number, for example, 20 percent of the total requests, what does this mean? What would happen if all requests became rush?

A perennial example in large libraries is the moldering exotic language backlog. Few of us can take any pride in how we control and manage it. There is usually a nagging realization, an afterthought, that something does need to be done about these books. If it only were possible to assign extra resources, we would catalog them immediately and get them into the hands of our exotic language clientele. Of course, the extra resources do not exist.

So break out of this mess and similar ones by giving yourself a deadline. In x months the temporary shelves that house these collections will be gone. Think of all the time you will save, all the simplification that you can achieve by giving up those shelves. In libraries, many messes reside on shelves. Figuratively and literally, take away the shelves to isolate and resolve the mess. If this strategy is too extreme for you, give yourself a decision-making deadline: at the end of two months, you will implement a process to integrate these materials, at a rate of so many per month, give them to a library that can process them, return them to the donor, or discard them.

Teach ways to find messes. Make it part of your staff development to teach about right- and left-brain thinking. Help staff see the incongruities in processes and provide an appreciation for both linear and vertical thought processes. Help them hone their ability to listen actively. How else do you think staff will learn to flip back and forth between what Weisbord (1987, 228) calls "task" and "process"?

Workshops on the tools of mess resolution can be useful. Teach leaders how to stay out of the way of others dealing with messes. Avoid the expert who claims an ability to size up a problem and fix it. Acquire the person who sees the learning opportunity for the group and does not squander it on ego-tripping. Open people to metaphors by providing opportunities to leave the workplace and engage in play and fun activities that are replete with metaphors, such as those that can be found in adventure-based learning. Teach them to write haiku, not memos.

Listen for the moo. No one will admit to keeping a herd of sacred cows, those decorative but wasteful creatures. To be truthful, most of us have a few grazing in our own pastures. We can all name several cows in other pastures, but have trouble seeing any in our own. Look in the valleys. Enable people to see a sacred cow when it is there, even when dressed as a useful creature.

What to Do about Them (Messes)

So what do you do when you think you have a mess? What steps do you take toward making a positive difference? My work in adventure-based learning has introduced me to wilderness medicine as used at Outward Bound. The training provided to instructors features a mess-organizing process called SOAP.[11] It is a disciplined approach for assaying messes, after immediate dangers have been cleared away. SOAP suggests practiced ways to look at any mess and to organize one's thinking. SOAP stands for:

Subjective—What is happening? What do you see is happening?

Objective—What information or data are available? What are the vital signs?

Assessment—anticipated problems—What possible scenarios/complications may occur? What is the problem for the moment?

Plan—What will you do about the problem(s)?

Like most other problem-solving models, the I&T one has data gathering as the next step to confirm the mess. Data, for I&T, include feelings, observations, information, suggestions, complaints, and impressions. Before tackling the mess, ask yourself: What can I observe (read, watch, see, study, learn) about this mess? Into what categories does what I am observing fall? What issues run through the data? Ask others about it. Test it, rigorously

Another valuable process is the straightforward cyclical evaluation model developed by Ishikawa (1985) and Deming: Plan, Do, Check, and Act (PDCA), the "Deming Cycle," or as Deming called it, the "Shewhart Cycle." It has been used successfully in programs of total quality management.

There are other tools, easily learned and used, for uncovering a mess and defining the underlying problem. These tools, like the Pareto chart, the fishbone chart, the "five whys," silent brainstorming, nominal group technique, and the flow chart, permit you to count, categorize, approximate size, and identify workflow disruptions. And these tools allow you to display what you find in graphic and ordered, factual ways.[12] Although they do require a time investment, they can rapidly move a group forward to substantial work with quick gains, certainly with some assurance of gathering the low-hanging fruit.

CLIMATE AND CONCLUSION

Anyone who has a few years' job experience knows that some organizational climates are more encouraging of individual initiative and question asking than others. An ideal climate would promote mess finding by more than a few key leaders. Because of their official authority and responsibility, managers and team leaders play a crucial role in setting up a climate that permits, even encourages, mess finding. Leaders have a real opportunity to be proponents and teachers of mess finding. The leader-as-expert (wizard) is less effective in the teacher role than the leader who identifies messes and works through them with input from others. The latter models the finding of messes so that others learn how to do it.

Hierarchies and infrastructures like performance appraisal and centralized budgets can inhibit mess finding and limit the possibility of improving the organization to a few people. Infrastructures are like sacred cows: they build figurative walls around some issues and restrict discussion and exploration. A less hierarchical and more team-based organization can result in many more empowered people who have responsibility for doing a job well.

This in turn increases the possibility for identifying and following up on messes. In high-performance teams, all team members know how they play their role makes a difference for the team. For this to happen, the leader has to make clear his or her expectation of each staff member playing an intelligent and active role. They can't all shoot the ball.

Specifically, leaders can demonstrate an awareness of the mess-finding process by taking the time and encouraging that time be taken to reflect on organizational issues, large and small. Better yet, the leader can help staff encounter and engage the unfamiliar and uncomfortable and otherwise push at the boundaries in the workplace. Doing so in a safe and considered way moves the leader and the staff into the discomfort zone. Once there, most people find it highly conducive to learning. The leader can also encourage staff by questioning assumptions, spotting sacred cows, and more important, welcoming questions about the leader's own assumptions.

Leaders can demonstrate and defend that is it permissible to make mistakes in the pursuit of improvements. Mistakes are not something to be dreaded; rather, failure is a gift for learning. This figures large in mess finding because that process may require taking many wrong paths before the best way is uncovered. Although teams are better able than bureaucratic hierarchies to find messes and to do something about them, mess finding can occur under any organizational structure. Taking the mess-finding step has the potential of making our services and resources more available and useful to our many users.

"Excellent," I cried.

"Elementary, my dear Watson, elementary."

CHAPTER 29

"Deterministic, Highly Reductive, and Transient"

Allen Veaner's cerebral take—in the title—on what he calls "business management derivatives" is a perfect lead-in for this discussion of business fads; why we embrace them or eschew them, and what, if anything, we can get out of them.[1]

FADS

First, what about the word *fad*—what does it cover?

Not all fads are created equal. The word *fad* is not the best term with which to span, in one breath, a wide range of workplace strategies, from the foolish to the savvy, from simplistic—"highly reductive"—adages to well-researched conceptualizations of how people are most productive. *Fad* suggests something short lived, soon to be replaced by something equally ephemeral, like the annual fashion shows that dictate the new fashion color for women and tie width for men. That's a fad. In the realm of the fad we can find fad phrases, adages, buzzwords, and exhortations. We've all used a few of these. Like most clichés, they are open to ridicule and may be used to serve the opposite purpose of the original intent. For example, "If it ain't broke, don't fix it" was never far from the lips of one director who used it to dismiss staff attempting to improve mediocre systems. Some others are:

If it ain't broke, break it!

Do more with less. (Or, as happens in some applications, "Do less with more.")

Work smarter, not harder.

There's no "I" in "team."

Open-door policy

Change management

Paradigms (greatly enhanced when prefaced with "shifting")

Customer-centric

The learning organization (versus, presumably, the unlearning organization?)

Who Moved My Cheese? (One organization's grapevine: "Who Cut the Cheese?")

The FISH Philosophy

One Minute Manager

Think outside the box (TOTB).

TOTB is now immortalized in airline-seat-pocket sales catalogs. One purveyor offers a $40 "sculpture" of three thinkers—stick-figure Rodin—hovering on thin brass poles above an open-sided brass box. The tag plate on the wood base profoundly claims: "Only those who see the invisible can do the impossible." That the TOTB thinkers are tethered to the rim of the box by three brass balls apparently does not impede seeing the invisible and doing the impossible.

And there's a vast subset of the business fad industry: books. Not about a system of work, but titles written by celebrity leaders like Donald Trump, Jack Welch, and others bent on explaining how they got to be as good as they decidedly are and how you too, if you follow their advice, can make it to the top. Mr. Trump's latest, *Think Big and Kick Ass* (2007), probably defines the genre.

Non-Fads

Often lumped together with fads, there are systems of management (SoM), like management by objective, total quality management (TQM), strategic planning, and teamwork. As well, I'd include the golden rule concept. These SoMs represent well-thought-out, proven, different ways of doing business, always moving away from top-down management. These are non-fads, and they are not of the quick-fix variety that beckon to us sirenlike, promising heightened library productivity with minimum investment.

The SoMs have some traits in common: they change the nature of fixed boss/ worker roles and offer different, more informed ways to make decisions. SoMs do threaten the status quo by decentralizing an organization's decision making. These "new" systems tend to disintermediate managers, including those in the executive suite—making them less essential to daily decision making—and leaving the micromanager with too little to do, other than to . . . lead! SoMs often share a liberated philosophy that respects workers as intelligent collaborators, partners them with managers, and expects all workers to understand what they are doing and be able to make informed decisions—within the goals of the organization—about what they do.

Almost always these systems are up against the inherited pecking-order model—the organizational chart—that consciously or unconsciously ties the hands of employees (presumably to ensure consistency and quality), requiring approval of any deviation from established procedures. Eventually the constant permission seeking exhausts staff and they go on autopilot, doing much less than they could. Very good staff members leave, but other good staff remain and waste their energy in developing work-arounds to circumvent the inflexibilities of the "system." Work processes harden and resist improvement. The system then becomes more about defending why something is done, more about why change is not possible, and less about getting better.

Obviously, if a top-down organization declares itself a team-based organization but sustains the hierarchy, nothing much beyond vocabulary will change. When nothing changes in the executive suite, nothing will change in the organization. In that circumstance, teamwork is relegated to fad status. The same can happen to TQM, strategic planning, and other SoMs. I have seen TQM become totally *quagmired* management, and I have flipped through piles of strategic plans that were in reality status quo plans.

Often critics will use the nonresults of such half-hearted applications to dismiss the overall concept behind a new way of work. In reality, the concepts are robust; it's the application and the leadership that are weak. In my experience, well-integrated applications of continuous improvement and teams have delivered on their potential. Innovation and productivity skyrocketed, and, yes, I am talking about a library.

IT'S PUPILLARY, MY DEAR WATSON, PUPILLARY

Why do librarians distrust so-called fads, including SoMs? What promotes this distrust? I have often wondered why some people simply don't get it. By "it," I mean an intuitive way of working: a supportive environment, teamwork, and people encouraging each other, with little need for the superficial authority. Yet some folks seem to be about appearances and titles, the corner office and the rug on the floor—as if, what else have they been working for? Like the well-known Theory X and Theory Y that split managers into two camps—hard-nose, hands-on supervisors or hands-off, empowering managers—perhaps it is our personal philosophy that matters most. We embrace or reject the new ways of work on the basis of who we are and what we believe is important, regardless of potential improvements in adopting new ways of working.

I have had the good fortune to return to my native Latvia and teach several leadership workshops. I was intrigued that the Latvian librarians were more resourceful and willing to collaborate than many other librarians I have met during my career. Until 1991 Latvians were repressed by a totalitarian—as in Stalinist—rule. Some observers confirm that a generation of leaders was lost during fifty years of communism. Then, in 1991, Latvia became exuberantly independent. Who, then, would lead? Droves of expats helped out. Now a new native generation of leaders appears to be emerging.

This generation's parents include mothers and fathers sent to Siberia and otherwise punished and harassed for questioning authority. So from what I saw in my workshops, this new generation of leaders had an unparalleled collaborative spirit, a can-do attitude, a willingness to help each other and take chances. Was this new spirit in reaction to the highly central, stifling, and fear-inducing communist way? Maybe post-1991 library leaders, with individual freedom regained, would desert the hierarchy, preferring instead a much more liberated and participatory process of work.

I got in touch with a Latvian economist in Riga who studies labor–management conflict, including recent dustups at the national symphony and the opera house. These two were of note because their leaders are heralded in the European art scene as highly innovative and liberated. When I pitched her my idea that there was a newly invigorated, freed-up leadership, she would have none of it. What she sees among the new leaders is, to use her term, *pupillary* leadership, a pupil-like, slavish attention to doing what Western leaders are thought to do. Rather than integrating and developing their own style, the Latvians are imitating Western ways.

Integration might come, but in the meantime, whatever they are doing, the economist says they have yet to put their own stamp on it. The all-too-familiar hierarchy is the fallback, as it is for most libraries. I hope by giving the Latvians a chance to experience how positive teamwork and collaboration can be for an organization, they will keep in mind alternatives to the old.

When Southwest Airline's president Colleen Barrett asked me recently if I had a PASSION FOR CUSTOMER SERVICE, I heard the conviction (and capitalization) in her voice. If some consultant guru had asked me that, I would have been thinking, "You gotta be kidding!" She *knows* customer service. After all, Southwest is the perennial industry leader in customer satisfaction.

For most organizations, customer service is a marketing ploy, a pretense that the customer is important. That lack of conviction comes through in the corporate voice, and it is most obvious when staff are not given freedom to resolve customer problems. When staff have to literally *stick to the script,* there is no passion for customer service. There's a quote in a customer service book by Ken Blanchard and Barbara Glanz that Ms. Barrett gave me: "When the heart is in the right place, the ego gets out of the way" (2005, 72). Simple and complex, it explains to me why some new ways of work catch on and why some do not.

CHAPTER 30

"From the Gutter to You Is Not Up": Worst and Best Practice

That wry country and western song lyric suggests the duality of my experience in finding best-practice libraries. Certainly, amid the many adequate ones, there are best-practice libraries with highly motivated and productive staff earning deserved recognition from their clients. But in my experience, finding those best-practice libraries is a bit like hunting for Euell Gibbons's elusive wild asparagus—you can expend a great deal of effort and not have much to show for it. And if we can't find these best practices, we don't benefit from the lessons in their good qualities and achievements.

WHAT ARE OTHER LIBRARIES DOING?

When we do look to other libraries, it's rarely initially for best practice. Confronted by a new service problem, we instinctively ask: "What are other libraries doing?" Unfortunately this leads to imitation rather than best practice. It also promotes the adoption of least-risk solutions. Worse, since we do not need to think very much about a solution, we lose the benefit of grappling with the issues and being held accountable for our own decisions. If everyone imitates, innovation has no chance.

Our preferred low-profile style reflects little in our best-practice looking glass—the landscape is flat with nary an outcropping of excellence. When we do something better than most we become exceedingly bashful. If we achieve major cost savings in how we process materials, answer reference questions, or shelve our books, we exhibit a disconcerting modesty. This may be due to the fear of being labeled a rate-buster, labor's derogatory term for people who exceed tacitly agreed-upon norms.

215

For example, let's say the productivity norm for an original cataloger is 100 titles per month. Any cataloging department exceeding that standard risks being singled out for criticism by those many who stay within the norm. Invariably critics will claim that quality has been sacrificed in the name of quantity. I remember an agitated history professor fuming at me that we had abandoned standard library cataloging practices in our misguided streamlining. Someone on the library staff had convinced him (wrongly) that we tossed out quality for quantity.

Public libraries, in the last few years, have had the benefit of finding best-practice organizations through a national stratified index. *Hennen's American Public Library Rating Index (HAPLR)* is based on data from nearly 9,000 public libraries (www.haplr-index.com/). Although it does not mention electronic services, this valuable index uses meaningful measures such as circulation per visit, reference per capita, cost per circulation, and expenditure per capita. Libraries that score in the top ten of these rankings are likely to be extraordinary.

If I wanted to find the best public library Web sites, I would go to the top few libraries in the *HAPLR* list. Because these libraries are getting most things right, they probably have done a good job with their individual Web pages, especially while designing for the quintessential person-to-library interaction. I would expect that they would translate the positive elements from successful person-to-person interactions into the virtual patron/librarian realm.

Academic libraries do not have a comparable quality index. For many, the one driving quality measure is volume. The drive for ever-larger accumulations of books results in buildings bursting at their seams, crowded and disorganized stacks, and floors cracking from loads exceeding architectural codes. Relief is on the horizon—electronic resources and user demand are squeezing book-budget dollars toward electronic access and away from physical volumes.

PEER PRODUCTIVITY WAKE-UP CALL

My experience with genuine best practice in academic libraries has been limited but insightful. I have twice participated in what could be called a listing of best-practice libraries. Both listings were productivity surveys (five years apart) among the technical services divisions in the twenty-five largest research libraries, the so-called Big Heads group. The survey was simple enough—each of the several technical services work units, such as serials check-in, divided its output by the number of staff to show how many pieces were processed annually by each staff member. Since it was a survey among homogenous institutions, skewing was limited. We all were pretty much doing the same kind of work, but the results showed some of us were far more efficient than others.

In the first survey, my institution finished at the bottom. But sometimes bad news is good news: we were in our first year of trying to figure out ways to eliminate backlogs and become responsive to getting materials out in time for readers to use. In spite of external criticism about inefficiencies, we knew we were the best. Indeed, in our own way, we had achieved a best-practice condition. Somehow we had come to believe that our purpose was to produce exquisitely error-free records. By doing so we added complexity to an already complicated process. The more loops and curlicues we could build in for checking and re-checking for accuracy, the better we thought we were. It was like we had never heard of the Law of Diminishing Returns. The peer-productivity survey jarred and shifted our priorities.

The survey results were coded (are you surprised?) to be confidential, but I was able to ferret out the top performers. On-site visits revealed how these libraries were better. While we borrowed a few workflow ideas, the most important take-away was our knowing it was possible to streamline our work and retain good quality standards. That emboldened us to ask questions about what we were doing and why we were doing it. We reduced costs, eliminated all but a few exotic language backlogs, and radically improved turnaround times. Five years later, the follow-up survey found us at the top. We had good cause to be proud. But with the euphoria of getting to the top of the hill came the question, "How do we keep getting better?"

Getting better, we realized, was something we had to want as a total organization—the notion of competing to exceed your peers' standards will only get you a little above that level. To exceed and excel requires a genuine shared commitment in the organization to getting better. Individual staff must understand what that will take.

In our streamlining, we discovered that many of our redundant practices were developed in response to our internal customers. Unless they worked with us, we could not get better. For example, imagine the traffic jam when a public services librarian dumps a massive book order on acquisitions at the end of the year. Or consider what happens to a promised one-week cataloging turnaround when book selectors remove approval plan books to their offices for weeks at a time.

These experiences taught me some fundamental lessons about creating and sustaining the getting better environment; organizations that engender trust and value individual staff (each-to-all) have the best shot at continuously improving. Self-only, the opposite organizational culture, may claim pockets of excellence, but that excellence will rarely flow across departmental lines because of that culture's mistrustful and competitive qualities. Only the each-to-all supportive culture encourages *systemic* best practice.

As a side note, a few years after I had left the Big Heads, I remained on their chat "listserv" on technical service hot topics. To keep my hand in, I'd eavesdrop on the discussion. Someone proposed to repeat the productivity survey.

Perhaps suggestive of our reluctance to be in the limelight, the prevailing senti-
ment was "No"—each technical services department was incomparably unique!

BEYOND LIBRARIES

Attending the ALA Annual Conference in a bitterly cold Philadelphia, I
found myself between committee meetings. I wanted something hot to drink,
a cup of coffee, but I could not find anything resembling a coffee shop. I was
at the sumptuous Four Seasons hotel, which boasted a sweepingly grand dining room. What the heck; I asked the maître d' if he would serve me a cup of
coffee. "Of course," was his response. I sat at the bar and griped to the female
staff member there about the miserable weather and my inhospitable experience
while checking into another hotel that claimed to have no reservation for me.
Meanwhile, a waiter-in-training began to tear away the foil around the neck of
a bottle of wine. The woman behind the bar stopped him, explaining to him that
was not how to do it.

"What difference does it make?" asked the waiter-in-training.

The bartender replied, "This is the Four Seasons!"

I was impressed. When it came time to go to my committee meeting and I
asked for the bill, she said, "There's no charge. Welcome to Philadelphia!"

Well, I still can't afford to stay at the Four Seasons, but that was a best-practice moment. Although there is no literal transfer from this story to the library,
it is still relevant. What does this incident suggest about the hotel's leadership?
How did this staff member know she had the authority and the expectation to do
what was right? I tell this story to underline what we can learn about our own
organizations from nonlibrary organizations (NLOs). When I am impressed by
an NLO, I look for clues—those intrinsic values or behaviors at the heart of the
organization that permit it to be the best.

FINDING THE BEST PRACTICES

How then to track down those libraries that achieve performance break-
throughs? I've developed a personal guide to discovering libraries worthy of a
second look. Though not a surefire, works-every-time method, these are some
organizational qualities that hint at best practice. I look for the organization that

1.   innovates,

2. experiments rather than plans,

3. emphasizes doing better,

4. has positive staff attitudes,

5. has an unmistakable clarity of purpose in its published information,

6. backs up accomplishments with quantifiable differences,

7. is regarded as a maverick by its peers, and

8. has strong external community relationships.

Organizations like this will offer fresh perspectives on how to do our work.

Happy hunting!

CHAPTER 31

"I'm So Low, I Can't Get High": The Low Morale Syndrome and What to Do about It

Employee morale surveys are fairly frequent in the business world. But although morale is much talked about, it is rarely assessed in a formal way in libraries. I once took part in a "real" morale survey. It was done librarywide with an anonymous questionnaire on how staff regarded their work and the workplace. Naturally we sought to harvest ideas for improvements. The results (the report's cover depicted a "thermometer of satisfaction," with the mercury at below freezing!) were more jeremiad than road map. This storm of dissatisfaction left the organization reeling.

Were things really as bad as they were made out to be? If they were, what were the causes? And most important, what actions could move the mercury to a satisfactory level? Thinking back on that experience, I believe that the perception of low morale among many respondents was influenced and overly magnified by what's been termed a "culture of complaint" in library organizations. If "attitude is a choice," a fair number of the responding staff chose to believe the worst. I can understand why a morale survey is not a top priority for many library managers.

Certainly there are genuine morale and work satisfaction issues to be worked on in every library, but library management consultants say they are hampered mightily when staff cannot move past dwelling on organizational wrongs. This paralysis, the consultants observe, incapacitates staff from even imagining what an improved status would be. Efforts to improve are met with predictions of failure. What has been your experience in this regard? At library conferences I've frequently encountered the "If you think you've got it bad, wait till you hear this!" phenomenon, where people seek to top each other in just how awful their job or their professional situation is.

Is this just the usual and, some claim, psychologically beneficial venting tradition? I wonder about how therapeutic it is when I hear woeful tales repeated with no desire to seek solutions or take "next steps." It's as if it is all in the telling, not in the resolving. A solution or explanation would be anticlimactic.

One library has a story that repeatedly appears in confidential debriefings of staff morale. As told, a deserving staff member was passed over for a promotion and, adding injury to perceived insult, was demoted. The promotion went instead to a buddy of the department head. This story illustrates the alleged unfairness and favoritism in that workplace. A little digging into the circumstances of that story would reveal that it never happened, but that is never done, and to my knowledge that one-sided story is still told and accepted as gospel. It appears impervious to truth.

Another component of extremely low morale (or low morale syndrome) is evident in this situation. A staff member tells everyone, including her supervisor, "I despise this job," but makes no visible effort to move on to something better. When a job move is suggested, the response is, "I would, but . . ." (fill in with an appropriate rationalization). And alas, this person is not leaving any time soon. Most managers would be worried, and rightly so, about the impact this person is having on the organization and its clients.

What can managers do to combat these extremes? How do problem people become part of the solution? More important, how can you get a realistic picture of the state of the organization's morale to try to do something about it in a pragmatic way?

First, What Is Morale?

It's elusive, this idea of morale. Do you know high morale when you see it? Is low morale symptomatic of an organization's culture? Is morale inherent? That is, do unhappy people bring low morale to the job? Or is it something acquired on the job? If new hires are inducted into low morale by old hands, can the new hires be inculcated with high morale? The business world has noted several influences on an employee's sense of well-being. These influences are evident in the questions used for taking an organization's morale temperature. Not surprisingly, many of the questions relate to the worker's

- perceived importance of his or her work,

- opportunity to develop new skills,

- availability of continued growth (a future),

- clarity of purpose in his or her work,

- elbow room for decision making,

- sense of trust, and

- being recognized for a job well done.

Most readers will recognize these as essential elements of effective workplaces. An organization with more than one or two of these missing is unlikely to get good morale scores. Also, several survey questions will ask about communication and relationships. These touch on how a worker is treated and regarded in the organization. For example, questions ask for feedback on the degree to which

- leadership is genuinely concerned about employees' thoughts and opinions,

- there is general support for differing points of view,

- there is support for new ideas,

- people are given an opportunity to present and try new ideas,

- there is cooperation among departments,

- staff is involved in decision making,

- managers listen, and

- management is clear about the organization's long-term goals.

Usually, a small number of survey questions will relate to workplace environment, including quality of workspace, equipment, safety, etc. Presumably the workers' rating of all these questions becomes a gauge of the actual morale in the organization. A low score equates, under normal conditions, to low morale, and a high score reflects high morale.

WHY MORALE MATTERS

"It is in the darkness of their eyes that people lose their way, and not, as they suppose, in any darkness that shrouds the path." This bit of Native American wisdom attributed to Black Elk has much truth in it. It speaks eloquently to me about why I should be concerned about morale and the crushing effect negative morale can have on productivity and purpose. It probably never really was this easy, but early in my career one simple management formula advised: "You can have unhappy staff and high productivity or you can have happy staff and low productivity." We've come a long way toward believing (and understanding) that high morale can be an equal partner to high productivity and creativity.

Morale matters because low morale affects process. In libraries the process usually involves clients and staff. Because of our strong service tradition, with many points of service, we are especially vulnerable to the impact of low morale. Consider some of the extreme behaviors all of us have observed at service points (hopefully not our own!). For example, leadership that is distrustful of staff's decision-making abilities may cause an excessively rigid interpretation of the rules that offends clients. Or that strict interpretation of the "rules" may be a means for unhappy staff to "take it out" on clients.

Good people, when caught up in the low morale syndrome, may give up and leave. The balance remaining either can't leave or are active contributors to the dissatisfaction and the predictable downward spiral into dysfunction and marginalization. The price of the unwillingness to let go of the complaint is the failure to take action. Naysayers can and do repress good ideas from surfacing in formal and informal settings.

WHAT TO DO ABOUT LOW MORALE

If I were to change one thing about the morale survey in which I participated, it would be to make the questions more specific to the individual. I'd ask far fewer general impression questions. Instead, I'd focus on the individual and how he or she is doing, on his or her experience, and on his or her ideas for improvements that matter most to each one as individuals. Why? Because after the morale survey came out, I heard from several people that their morale (individual and unit) was more than OK; it was the low morale of other people and units that caused them to give a low ranking to the general questions—a sort of unanticipated sympathy vote. Along with this, I'd construct questions that get closer to the locus of low morale. Examples from the business world include the use of provocative metaphors, for example, "Librarywide meetings have the atmosphere of 'a king holding court' or 'a mud wrestling match,'" etc. Or, "In my department I feel like 'a cog in a machine,' 'a member of a family,' or 'a valued member of a team'."

Clarity about people's roles and decisions can do much to raise morale by taking away uncertainty and suspicion. The "favoritism" story I referred to above was based in large part on misunderstanding and misinterpretation—the communication could have been better. The manager and the affected employee should have fully discussed what was happening and why. Although that discussion would not have assuaged the disappointment of the employee, it would have provided facts for her to consider why she was not selected for the promotion. She still would not like the decision, but perhaps she would have understood it and been able to deal with it in constructive ways.

Management has a responsibility to say that attitude matters. If someone's problematic attitude is obvious and borders on incivility, it needs to be discussed. After engaging in active listening in order to understand what is bothering the person, the manager can motivate (or try to change that person's behavior) in four ways: reason, inspire, support, or confront. All four ways should be available to every manager, and each manager should have a good understanding of how to apply them.

A hands-off approach (avoiding or accommodating) is a mistake when dealing with staff with extremely low morale. You may need to say the unspeakable (in private, of course), "Since you are so unhappy here, how can I help you find a position somewhere else?" In my years in organizations I have come to regard as bizarre the notion that the workplace has responsibility for my happiness! Attitude is not a genuine difference like race, or background, or sexual preference. Attitude is a choice, as has been said before. If leadership is to get results, then people who are in opposition to change because of profound attitudinal problems ought to be encouraged to lighten up or leave as graciously and quickly as possible.

If you observe a staff member repeatedly undermining committee meetings, knocking down suggestions from others, do you do nothing (avoiding or accommodating)? Or do you tell that person (with helpful elaboration) to get some balance in his or her viewpoint? Do you do that in front of the group or in private?

Finally, however you assess morale, you need to do something about the results. An explanation to the organization about what actions can or cannot be taken is essential. This assumes that, prior to the morale assessment, you have some idea of what can be done—the questions you ask will indicate that. If your results show that the upper administration does not believe in or respect the staff, what action will be taken? The point here is to give some consideration up front to what you can or cannot do. Making public the resolve to work on a few of the most important results (even just one!) can give an immediate boost to morale.

CHAPTER 32

Productivity in Libraries? Managers Step Aside

"Wanted: A Few Good Departments"

So ran the caption on my call in June 1990 for productive workplaces in libraries. Optimistically, I expected several responses from people interested in taking part, anonymously, in a study of factors contributing to productivity in the library. My research, as part of a study leave, was to look at why some departments perform better than their peers. Is it a matter of such factors as communication, recognition and reward systems, leadership, climate for creativity, organizational structure, and the incorporation of technology into the workflow?

To help clarify what I was pursuing, I provided a stalker's guide to finding the best departments in any library. The guide was based in large part on experiences in the pursuit of excellence at a research library, during which several departments made strides in being highly productive. These departments were characterized by

an indomitable, positive attitude toward customers, internal and external;

innovation and ready adaptation to change;

an ability to add responsibilities without automatically requiring more workers (resourcefulness);

good output and rapid turnaround (sometimes approaching the phenomenal when compared to other units) with quality as a throughput, not an afterthought;

A "can do" attitude, and relatively high staff morale with a sense of humor;

Open communication, where decisions are transparent and conflict is addressed constructively; and

porous, not vitreous, organizational boundaries.

That no college or university library answered my call didn't surprise me all that much. For one thing, the literature search on "libraries and productivity" described an empty landscape. Apart from a paper by Waldhart and Marcum written in 1976 and a few references to the importance of information and our supporting role in achieving higher productivity nationally, I found very little.[1]

Furthermore, my talking with colleagues, including several directors, resulted in few leads for follow up, with some questioning the validity of such a qualitative study. It's as if the topic were both unfamiliar and uncomfortable. One colleague, looking at recent reorganizations in several libraries, said he found none restructured overtly for productivity gains. All this is not to suggest the nonexistence of productive workplaces or even a lack of concern about it; far from it. It only suggests that no one was talking about it, at least to me.

This perplexing silence compounded my curiosity and provided, to a large extent, the conviction that the topic was indeed worthy of pursuit. So, instead of touring library departments in search of elements common to successful organizations, I delved into the abundant for-profit literature and thought considerably about its relevance to libraries.

The chapter covers the following:

A definition of productivity

The opportunities/barriers for productivity in the workplace

Implications for managers/leaders.

A basic definition offered in the literature is that productivity equals output divided by input. In other words, it is meant to be a neutral ratio of the costs involved in the production of an item among many items of the same kind. It is numerical. Following is a simplistic example in the library setting. (It is simple because it does not take into account the several potential differences among transactions or the costs of supplies, automation, training, electricity, heating, furniture, etc.)

In one year, five reference staff provide answers (output) for 40,000 questions, with each one dealing with 8,000 transactions. If the average salary (input) is $30,000 (including benefits), one could say that the average unit cost (and productivity ratio) for that year is $3.75. If I know what this activity costs in other libraries, I can then attempt to make comparisons of productivity levels. I can also compare individual productivity among the staff. The more years' worth of such data are available, the better.

It is here at the comparative level that the term quickly loses its neutrality and makes some managers and staff reluctant, even with extensive qualifications, to discuss openly how productive their departments are. Why this is so suggests there is more to the word and its interpretation than is at first apparent. Too often one sees "more" or "improved" irrevocably linked (stated or not) to the term *productivity*. Often staff see this as an irrational mandate from a martinet management, only to be fulfilled by speeding up a work process with a proportionate loss of *quality*.

It should be noted that within universities all of the library staff, including upper management, may have the same response to a presidential or legislative mandate to increase productivity—to do more with less, to work smarter not harder, etc.—that is normally, but unfairly, attributed to line level, nonsupervisory staff. Not infrequently, that response is to ask for more workers and more pay. Likewise, during these fiscally stressful times, it is not uncommon for upper university administrators to deny the problem and to persist in seeking additional funding from an empty treasury (hence the constantly increasing fees for tuition) just to maintain the status quo.

ECONOMIC, BIOLOGICAL, AND PHYSICAL ASPECTS

Katz and Kahn, writing in 1966 (14–29), look at organizations from a scientific perspective, in fact linking terms from the biological and physical sciences to describe what happens in organizations over time. For them, the organization is an "energetic input-output system in which the energetic returns from the output reactivates the system." They were among the first to dispute the idea of organizations as closed systems; rather, they argued convincingly the notion of the "flagrant" openness of organizations—some libraries might even qualify as promiscuously so—and reasoned that the organization's well-being is tied to "transactions between the organization and its environment." Simply put, they regard organizations as living entities subject to the same demands and requirements as are the ecosystems of a salt water pond or the human body.

Productivity or efficiency makes the difference between the survival or failure of the system over time and marks the quality of that survival. Katz and Kahn term this "negative entropy," whereby the organization is able to achieve surpluses (no, not backlogs of books to be processed!) to sustain its future. For example, a library is able to make a savvy computer application in processing books that then releases money (energy) for new services. Unlike many biological systems, the workplace, if willing, has the ability to influence in an intelligent way internal processes to make the best use of resources and feedback.

Productivity in this sense is not as numerical as it is how we approach our work, that our decisions in all aspects of the job are based on deriving a surplus for healthy organizational maintenance. It is a matter of "quality." In my interpretation of this model, backlogs of books or questions represent unrealized energy, a drag on the overall enterprise. The organization that ignores feedback, resists essential change, and embraces tradition as the only way of doing business, is hastening to the grave.

A METAPHORIC APPROACH

A game, the group juggle, can be played to show individuals how efficiently they and the group problem solve. The challenge is for them to "juggle" as a group with no balls dropped and everyone touching the ball at least once. First comes the establishment of an "order" or "process" by which to accomplish the task. Usually this means setting up the routes for the ball (or rubber chicken) to travel around the circle. For large groups, this first step is characterized by confusion and uncertainty; occasionally some question the activity itself—what's the point? Rarely does any group, small or large, immediately fire the ball back and forth and achieve an immediate solution. Obviously, in a game like this the traditional individual roles of department head or expert are obscured, even suspended. This activity serves as a forum for observing how ideas are brought up, treated, and respected; who says what; and how the group experiments to reach a solution.

As the second step, I add the concept of "quality" by asking the group to define the term and its cost. Often the participants settle on quality as not dropping the ball in its course around the circle. The cost is starting over whenever the ball is dropped. The third step is "capacity." How many balls can the group handle within its quality and process definitions? When the group has reached three or four balls, I time the process and announce the time to the group.

With the announcement comes the fourth segment, the challenge for them to juggle productively. Usually the group elects to reduce the time they take in sending the balls around the group. Soon the balls are flying rapidly across and around the circle and yes, the group does become more productive, often reducing by 25 to 50 percent the time they take. At this point, to the group's disbelief, I ask them to improve their time by another 50 percent. Some would prefer to stop the game, believing that whatever they have achieved is good enough; that management (me) is once again asking for the impossible. Others accept the challenge—after all, it's just a game, right?—and begin to innovate. After a few minutes to discuss ideas, the group looks about for available resources (including gravity), exerts its creativity, and/or adjusts its shape or configuration within the limits of the game. More often than not, the group dramatically reduces its time, sometimes exceeding the stated goal, and by working smarter does do more with existing resources than any in the group previously thought would be possible.

As the above should suggest, productivity in groups of people is a complicated notion that involves, among other things, the individual values of the participants, process, cost, quality, and creative problem solving. When we are productive in the true sense of the word as I use it, we are being the best we can be.

It is tantalizing to consider why a group can be productive in a game and then far less so in the work setting. A game is not work, yet at times I encountered such strong resistance to change that wrong ways prevailed even when we knew them to be wasteful and unproductive. What are the forces that inhibit us from behaving at work as we do in play? Better, what are we presently doing that with a little shift of effort or direction could result in increased productivity? What are some of the opportunities for and barriers to productivity?

Sweet are the uses of adversity.

—William Shakespeare

Adversity. The sense of being on the brink of dissolution is a useful one to inspire our creativity. While we are not subject to the extreme swings that for profits endure, we do, from time to time, find ourselves tottering on budgetary precipices. (As I edited this in 2009, many universities were cutting back—there was no choice. Public libraries were closing branches and taking double-digit percentage reductions off the base budget. Although not exactly a panic, we have not seen reductions of this magnitude in several decades. When I wrote this in 1991 an economic contraction was underway. It led to a sense of urgency about cutting positions and budgets that permitted staff and managers to consider real actions that made a difference, however short lived.)

Some observers view the changes as driven less by short-term economic disruptions than by a transformation in upper management's perspective of corporate size. Namely, there is now tacit agreement that small is better and that corporate survival hangs on trimming away the excess, an approach that is far more painful now than it might have been if corporations (and libraries) had considered the consequences of how they were doing business when budgets were always on the plus side. One cannot but wonder if there were ways to avoid the extreme measures of 1991 (and the far more extreme ones in 2009). A position thought to be superfluous now was probably excessive at the time of the hire. I noticed in 2009 a tendency that if supplemental funding could be found, it was used rather than reducing and living with a 20 percent cut. Some would say the use of the supplemental funding is more humane than the latter. However, it only avoids and delays the day of reckoning once the supplemental is used up. I'd recommend saving the supplement for a genuine emergency in the future.

I visited one of my neighboring institutions where a budget freeze had left several departments short staffed. As I talked to the staff in one department, they displayed several of the attributes which for me characterize productive workplaces: they were working together to overcome the difficulties confronting them, and they were looking at what they were doing and asking how to do it, if at all, better. As well, boundaries that had delayed needed changes for many years became surmountable in the budgetary downturn. Staff had begun to learn other jobs and were exploring and implementing streamlining measures. Fortuitously, a new department head had transferred in from another department and came with an agenda of questions in need of answers. These questions revolved around why some things were done the way they were. The fiscal urgency gave the staff an excellent atmosphere in which to explore questions of relevancy for any procedure and to look closely at alternative ways of work. At the same time I observed the quintessential role played by genuine positive leadership in adversity.

A mandated fiscal alert may also promote a greater willingness to accept mistakes as a natural part of finding the best answer and a lessening of the temptation to spend time on the useless function of fault finding and blaming. Just as some administrators use the cover of a budget crunch to transfer or modify unproductive positions, so can staff look rigorously at how they work and seek to improve workflow, through restructuring, consolidating, or otherwise streamlining the work within and *outside* their units. The crisis mutes the most anti-change person and may even bring him or her into the process of dealing with the problem. Adversity is the traditionalist's greatest enemy and the productive manager's best friend. If the library has a market force, it is a budget cut. We may resist many other subtle market forces, but a drop off in revenue can't be ignored any more than a corporation can ignore red ink on its balance sheet.

It's almost a maxim—hard times bring people together. Coming together, relationships can be strengthened, new ones formed, and cooperative ventures started and completed. "We're all in this together," becomes a common realization that permits implementing the previously unthinkable. One Japanese scholar (Taira 1988, 58) suggests that it was hard times and the common goal of getting ahead of the United States that brought Japan's labor and management together a few years after World War II.

Some readers may regard the above as heartless in tone, easily capsulated as "lean and mean," but my intent is not to trivialize a valid path to corporate health. The sharper a unit's focus, the clearer its goals and purposes, the more fit it is to sustain the travails of a fiscal crisis. My experience has been that within a climate of self-imposed and controlled adversity, no one has to be cut from the payroll. Through normal attrition, without any layoffs, major changes are still possible. What is required during hard times is time, purpose, and flexibility. When events preclude these "luxuries" and jobs must be cut, the anxiety level is much higher, and changes will be made under fear, never the best motivator for creative improvements. If one has a choice, the self-initiated reduction or streamlining program (call it continuous improvement) is far superior to the external mandate from on high. Although the former is rare, it is management's greatest responsibility and to date its greatest failure.

There is no more alluring social power on earth than the mystique of doing good.

—Larry Kennedy (1991, 111)

Goodness. Our profession believes we do good. Broadly, we are indeed well regarded by our clients. Often the library is rated as the best service facility in the city, county, or campus. Library surveys often reveal the genuine affection and respect of our users. Much of this high regard is a result of our service commitment. For the most part we actually deliver service better than most other agencies. However, we have been known to accept backlogs, resist technological change, engage in time-wasting discussion with resolution of the minutiae of our work, and be overly zealous in playing by the policy book, like AACR2. When backlogs or bottlenecks or other service failures are questioned by anyone, the reasons for their existence invariably involve the magnitude of our goodness and preclude any solutions within existing resources. In other words, we are doing so many good things it makes it impossible to take time from doing one good to do more of a second good. Under this type of thinking, the only way to unstop a bottleneck is by additional funding, and not by streamlining, combining, or eliminating.

These last three actions are difficult for us to accept, specifically because they beg the question of our doing something differently, and they do unleash the question of WHY we are doing it in the first place, a question that shakes the tradition. Although there is a genuine goodness in what we do, outsiders will tell us it is so in degrees and not all the parts have the same value. We should be less resistant to market forces. Demands for our services do vary, as does the supply. I often say the user is part of the organization. How many readers share my belief? Our profession is as prone as any to believe that for the most part we know better than the customer, internal or external. In reality, most library problems could be better solved with the assistance of users. By plugging the user into the decision-making process, it is possible to think the impossible, to do what few thought could be done because of politics or other hidden barriers to change. Naturally enough, it depends on mutual trust and respect, but I have found that user ideas, explored and taken in the right spirit, result in beneficial changes in how we work.

For example, what would be the situation at the Library of Congress with its gargantuan backlogs today had they chosen as an outcome of user surveys and work simplification studies to shorten the cataloging record in order to catalog more books? How many more cataloging records and the books they represent might be available to the nation's libraries (and to Congress) had someone chosen not to further enhance an already good thing? Instead, according to Dennis Carrigan (1989), the average length of the LC record "in number of characters, increased 24.5%; the number of entries grew 130.2% ; the number of fields essentially doubled; and the number of subject heading subdivisions increased by 156.2%."

Was this done knowingly, as a trade-off between backlogs and improved access? Or did it just happen since something *good* could only get better by making more of it, even if we were already in 1991 seeing users preferring single-term searching (KWIC) rather than the exclusive controlled access set and taught by libraries?

The issue of goodness also appears in the popular assumption among many staff that productivity improvement always carries with it the loss of quality. It is as if to do it differently and faster means to degrade the process in quantity at the expense of quality. Well thought out ideas with the varying options considered and all sides heard regarding improvements should carry no loss in real quality. That a leader seeks to measure some good activity does not mean he or she undertakes a heretical process, akin to conjuring up some antiintellectual quality reduction. That of course is not the intent in any ethical approach to work measurement. Surely our definitions of goodness should embrace any factual evaluation techniques, like work simplification, decision-making processes, or workflow analysis that just might produce higher quality and quantity. A very good example from work flow analysis in 1991 is that of downloading data (copy, cut, and paste) so as to avoid the errors that come with manual rekeying of records as they make their way through our various processes. That this was debated in 1991, when copying and pasting was feasible but on occasion spurned because of "tainted records" produced by lower tier libraries, is as absurd in 2010 as it was in 1991.

The creators of this world—after God—are Gutenberg, Watt, Arkwright, Whitney, Morse, Bell.
    —Hank Morgan, *The Connecticut Yankee in King Arthur's Court*

Technology. As Hamlin Hill (1963, xvii) tells us, most readers of Mark Twain's book are unprepared for the sad failure of the "marvels of modern science" to reform the cruelties and inequities of sixth-century England. The status quo prevails in spite of Hank's "splendid necromancy of the nineteenth century"—technology. Sometimes we expect too much of technology, sometimes we lose sight that it is people that do or do not get the job done.

That said, we are realizing, at long last, some of the promises of the electronic age. Stan Davis (Davis and Davidson 1991) says, "Information-based enhancements have become the main avenue of revitalizing mature businesses." Electronic access and delivery do indeed provide libraries (mature businesses) with numerous opportunities to make sizable gains, but only if we choose to work in an intelligent way at getting the economic most out of each computer application. One immediate, but unintended, effect technology can have in the library setting and elsewhere is to force managers to work closely with staff. It is of course possible to install a system and keep its use limited to the face value of the system. That is, take what it gives you and no more.

The savvy manager will listen to the staff using the equipment/systems and will seek to improve on the status quo. Doing so takes the manager out of the role of expert into the role of listener and someone who facilitates staff ideas for improvement based on their experience with the system. Technology permits staff to have a larger role in designing processes to get the most out of them. The supervisor, unless he or she is already someone who works alongside other staff, must rely on what the staff have to say about what is needed and what is or is not working well. Because of its inherent complexity, technology can be helpful in promoting a team approach to solving problems and overcoming challenges.

And technology can greatly enhance communication within large organizations. One such application is an e-mail network in the workplace as a nearly instantaneous way to communicate among everyone. An example that brought this home for me was a series of mailings of notes taken by me in meetings with library units about things they had on their minds and that they wanted the library administration to know about. I have such meetings about once a year and have shared the notes with department heads. That year I e-mailed the notes under the caption, "Things Needing to Be Said and Heard," to everyone on the staff, more than 200 people. The response to do something about the concerns expressed was dramatically more than when I sent my paper notes to the department heads. Technology clearly enhanced the process of letting people know what was being faced by many departments in the library on dozens of issues, from job reclassification, to leaking plumbing, to complimenting staff for jobs well done. Several staff members said thanks for sharing the notes—they were read.

> We hunger for community in the workplace and are a great deal more productive when we find it.
>
> —Marvin Weisbord (1987)

Teams. We are on the right track in many libraries, and have been for a long time, in recognizing the value of people being informed and seeking their say in how we go about our work. We have room to improve, but we are probably less culpable than many other professions. We may be more enlightened, but we still have numerous opportunities to promote an environment for productivity. Following are several approaches.

Organizing for teams. I recently proposed to a middle manager that we replace the vacant department head position with a self-managing team of unit and section heads. It would function like a department head, making decisions for itself. This self-managing group would report to me, and I would support its work. All members of the team would be equal in the management of that department, their only difference being in expertise. He rejected the idea, candidly telling me he would have nothing to do, because what he did as a manager was make decisions. If we took that function away and gave it to a group, we'd be taking away his job. Besides, this was an ultimately foolish idea because the other department heads would take advantage of this leaderless situation. His response sums up much of why self-managing teams are not easily put into place.

Committees are teams of sorts, yet they do not enjoy much of a reputation for sorting out what needs to be done and then going ahead and doing it. Usually committees send up recommendations, not unlike quality circles. When those suggestions are shelved, as they were with most quality circles in industry, the effectiveness of the group is seriously undercut. When those recommendations are made *within* the group itself and it has to decide whether to act or not, we have a very different set of dynamics in play.

A team of experienced managers with which I work closely has been given full decision-making capability for its area, the workflow in technical services. After some six months of shaking off (with facilitation help) the way they used to do business—competitively, *not* collaboratively—the group is moving forward. They are implementing new methods rapidly, enlarging the pool for feedback, including users and devising more effective routes for materials to travel in order quantifiably to enhance turnaround times and access to materials.

Why are self-managing teams a rare occurrence in libraries and elsewhere? Is it part of our culture to be organized in competitive departments? If that is so, what can we do to break that mold?

Delegation. As the middle manager told me, his job is to make decisions. In his case, I know that he actually delegates many decisions to his staff. But it is his perception that he gets to make the decisions, that the buck—the responsibility—stops on his desk. All of us have been in situations where bosses wind up making decisions that could be made much further down in the organization, at considerably less cost and time. While it's good for someone to know that the "buck," the responsibility, stops somewhere, it should not inhibit lower-level decision making. It does imply a trust on the part of the leader in the staff's ability to make decisions as needed. If the lower-level person makes a mistake, then the leader has to accept the responsibility for that mistake. And there's the rub. Some leaders firmly believe that if they personally don't make the decision, then the right decision won't be made.

There is a splendid little film by Kurt Lewin (ca. 1938) that suggests strongly the most effective method of making decisions and leading groups. Lewin studied boys' groups and how they responded to three styles of adult leadership: democratic, autocratic, and laissez-faire. The most productive style was that of the participatory or democratic approach, wherein the adult leader offered advice on projects when asked, listened, and otherwise encouraged the boys in their decision-making process. The democratic leader was more of a guide than a boss. At the end of each session, cleanup was shared by the boys and the leader.

The autocratic leader, a Kick in the Ass (KITA) manager, made all the decisions, closely supervising and telling the boys what to do.[2] A troublesome outcome of this was aggression among the boys. There was so much scapegoating that two of the participants dropped out. Productivity did hit high peaks in the autocratic model, but only as long as the KITA leader was in the room. In his absence, productivity plummeted as the boys became idle and counterproductive. In the democratic model the boys stayed on task, making steady, self-directed progress. The laissez-faire model, a fair caricature of the Theory Y concept carried to the extreme, proved to be least productive, with boys and leaders on an aimless course.

Do not forget that the popular perspective of "the Boss," like Dagwood's Mr. Dithers, is one shared by many staff, and they mark down as indecisive or soft a manager who does not live up to the KITA, my way or the highway stereotype. In most traditional workplaces we have routines with a clear line of command and several stops for "signatures" (for example, a committee must approve a recommendation first). A new library director told me: "My staff do not know how to talk across departments—only vertically through their bosses."

Then there is the manager inured in the belief that if the idea does not originate with him, it cannot be particularly good. I had an interesting learning experience in the woods one day as the cofacilitator with a team of MBA students. Of the ten students, two of the males dominated the group's problem solving. We muted both during a game called "Hot Stuff," a complex activity. The group was now on its own in spite of the wild gesticulating by the muted twosome. Not surprisingly, the person who had been quietest that afternoon took part in the group discussion and came up with a very good solution. At the end of the activity, the two muted students did not accept the solution as the best one— instead, they claimed had they not been muted, their solution would have been better! Perhaps. Little wonder that at one graduation ceremony all the recently crowned MBAs chanted while the science and engineering PhDs got their diplomas, "You will work for us."

One observer (Mooney 1982) says that attitude of managerial omniscience is what has killed most of the quality circles, once numbering in the thousands. What killed them was the unwillingness of managers to share their responsibility for coming up with ideas to improve the workplace. Instead, thousands of QC ideas were filed away, awaiting someone enlightened and daring enough to say, "Let's try them and see what happens."

Luther Gulick wrote in 1937 that one of the functions of the executive was directing "the continuous task of making decisions and embodying them in specific and general orders and instructions" (Gulick and Urwick 1937). Although that was written decades ago, many current managers and management theorists still regard decision making, especially budgetary control, as the exclusive territory of the manager, and believe that dire happenings are in store for any group that attempts to subvert this essential truism. The delusion of control persists. A colleague who facilitates change in an international company gave me an insight into how far some managers have yet to go in this regard. In mild exasperation, she told me, "If the manager did just one thing it would be a giant forward step." The one thing? "Regular staff meetings."

> For every human problem, there is a neat, plain solution—and it is always
> wrong.
>
> —H. L. Mencken

Implications for leaders: So the good news in all this, despite the war stories
each of us could tell to the contrary, is that leaders and staff, for many reasons,
are casting about for better ways to manage and be managed.[3] There is an unprecedented appreciation that the KITA approach works less well than others
do. But the question remains, What does work? This question applies to such
allegedly non-KITA approaches as TQM, management by objectives, participatory management, or even the elderly process of zero base budgeting, wherein
an organization has to justify its existence every year. Was it not just a few years
ago that we were advised to follow closely the now pot-holed roads mapped out
in books like *In Pursuit of Excellence* by the ubiquitous Tom Peters?

All these attempts, old and new, have some intrinsic value. But if the decision-making structures remain about the same, the new way fails to have a life
beyond the exhortation phase. The classic exposé of management "solutions"
is that by the ill-tempered Frederick Herzberg, "One More Time: How Do You
Motivate Employees?" Written in 1987, it remains relevant because of Herzberg's fundamental findings about what staff want and need to be productive
and involved in their work. Largely, it is a combination of authority and responsibility that fit the position. The most resented aspects of corporate life are those
that remove achievement, recognition, and responsibility from the individual,
that stifle the worker's creativity and his or her say about the job. People want
to make decisions that affect their work. No, not to "run the show"; rather, when
problems emerge and are open to discussion, the staff want to be trusted to have
a say and may likely have the best way to bring about positive results, and often
the solution will involve more freedom for decision making on their part. The
sense of achievement staff members say they want is only obtainable if they
have the freedom to make choices.

Certainly there are staff who have no interest in taking responsibility for their
work; they want to do the job, but if the heat comes, it's management's job. I
contend that a major responsibility for leaders is to hire and encourage staff who
want to become shareholders in the enterprise and want to participate in finding
solutions to problems.

A 1982 study by Marta Mooney is notable here. It is drawn from a survey of
people in very large corporations assigned the task of improving productivity—
no small task! The 200 or so productivity managers interviewed identified the
following elements as the several fundamentals to have in place if productivity
is to improve:

> Focus directly on raising productivity. (No more beating around the bush,
> please; don't fail to ask how any idea will affect productivity—use the word.)

Strengthen line responsibility for productivity. (People doing the work have the best ideas for improving the work.)

Obtain top leader commitment. (It can't be done in a vacuum or without management's help when the process becomes painful; if the vice president for computing is the roadblock, will the leader make the necessary change?)

Maintain a multidisciplinary approach in trying out prescriptions for improvement. (Take the best from several approaches and keep looking for more. Invent your own application.)

Maintain open communication. (Trust can't happen if people are kept in the dark; devise ways for staff to take ownership of information.)

The startling learning from Mooney's study is that for many of the respondents, resistance to change *among the managers* was their most serious obstacle. As one put it when asked about line management's view of decision making by staff, "We expect them [employees] to act like adults at home but treat them like children at work." My most important realization from all that I have heard and seen is that leaders and managers need to get out of the way, more rather than less. Most strategies for management success imply this, albeit they do not come right out and say it. The reality is that delegation is still strongly resisted by library managers. Here's some substance to my apprehension. Total quality management is much acclaimed, yet one application (*Total Quality Management* 1991) of this way of working in higher education states: "TQM does not change the authority structure for major decisions, nor does it remove from administrators the responsibility for organizational leadership. TQM imposes additional responsibilities for leadership and decisions that will improve quality." More recently I listened to several reports from the university library field about TQM implementation efforts. This was at an ALA professional seminar. There was some noteworthy positive feedback, such as, "TQM gets people talking" and "Everyone [in TQM] has permission to ask Why something happens." At the same time, the studies suggested that the TQM process—like so many other good ideas when implemented—was being transformed into a narrow problem-solving technique rather than a campuswide, genuine empowerment of staff with an overriding emphasis on pleasing customers.

The speakers provided some illustrative quotes: "The director may choose not to delegate, we're not real good at that" and "I'm not ready to empower my staff (to simplify the cataloging process." This is not what Herzberg has in mind in his plan for employee motivation. Our culture appears to demand decisive and controlling leaders. It also demands multitudes of managers, so many that it is no small wonder it is difficult for staff to have more of a say. LeBoeuf shows that a contrast can be found in Japan, where in their automotive industry the ratio of supervisor to staff is 1:200; in Detroit it is 1:20 (1982, 267). If we really value our American tradition of self-reliance and independence, why do we have so many overseers?

What I suggest is that leaders may find that adopting attitudes and new structures (circles with interchangeable parts, not hierarchies) that build trust and openness will go a long way toward improving our productivity. The conceptual goal of doing the best job possible within existing resources is pretty clear, but it needs to be stated and practiced consistently by top leaders. With this mandate from the top, middle managers can do much to promote improvements in all that is done at their level and by their workers. Doing so will require library managers to move away from expertise in the technical aspects toward that in people and team-building skills, like coaching, listening, creativity listening, question asking, and trust building. All these skills are essential for corporate boundary bashing, risk taking, and decision making by staff unaccustomed to doing so. Herzberg observes that when supervisors are forced to give up the routines of checking duties, they "may be left with little to do" (1987, 116). However, "the supervisors usually discover the supervisory and managerial functions they have neglected or which were never theirs because all their time was given over to checking the work of their subordinates." The better we know this and act upon it, the less important numerical goals become to the primary goal of doing the best we can with what we have to work with. Numbers matter in the process of getting to this latter, more important goal, but they are clearly secondary.

These are my way-finding directions for greater productivity; I do not provide a formula, nor do I seek to imply that the path is clear of hazards. It will be a wrenching journey. There are circumstances that only you can rise or fall upon; no one else can help you, but be assured that the notion of the team is in the long run as right as any direction can by. The mix of what we do as leaders needs your individual touch. I recommend the emphasis be shifted to one that openly says we seek to be productive in all that we do and that the help of the staff is essential. We can show our productivity in many ways, and when we achieve it we should celebrate it.

CHAPTER 33

"She's Just Too Good to Be True, But She Is": Recognition Ceremonies and Other Motivational Rituals

Of late, I've been noticing the employee-of-the-month (EoM) displays at businesses like hotels and grocery stores. Usually what I see is a bank of color photos of the winners, shiny brass name plates pinned to a polished walnut backboard, or a choice, reserved parking spot. But what really stands out are the frequent gaps in the displays: it's June, and the last EoM was for February. When you look close at the brass plates, you realize that the most recent EoM is from the previous year!

What happened? Are there really no more outstanding employees? Why do well-intentioned recognition efforts like this run out of steam? The theory behind a recognition program is that it is unarguably good for an organization to recognize its staff. Recognition by one's peers fertilizes genuine growth for the individual. And, the reasoning goes, even if our efforts don't always work quite as we hope, they do little harm.

Well, not really. They are surprisingly costly in time to administer, the dissatisfaction (between the few "winners" and the many "losers") can be widespread, and the happiness (job satisfaction) they endow may be elusive. I've worked in libraries with recognition ceremonies ranging from elaborately orchestrated to none. My productivity and creativity (or anyone else's, it seemed) did not depend on the recognition program. For me, supportive relationships mattered the most. Yet since many of us work in large organizations, we are encouraged by HR departments and frequently our own staff to develop formal recognition systems. It is often the prescribed medicine for a diagnosis of "low morale." This chapter reflects on why managers put their faith and backing into recognition systems. I also will try to derive some lessons from my experiences in recognition efforts that worked and those that did not.

239

RECOGNITION AS ORGANIZATIONAL ARTIFACT

There are at least three categories of recognition:

- **Individual, tangible:** Cash bonuses, parking spaces, paid days off, a prize for best performance, paid lunch on your own, and a raft of things like pen knives, clocks, necklaces, watches, etc.

- **Individual, intangible:** Picture on the wall, write-up in library newsletter, one-on-one lunch with the boss (yes, some think this is a reward!), and public announcements (with certificates signed by the corporate leader) for years of service.

- **Organizationwide:** Fully or partially paid lunches, dinners, or picnics, sometimes including staff-produced lampoons of the past year's highs and lows. Longevity often is recognized at large staff meetings and/or at banquets.

Frederick Herzberg's (1964) classic research on what makes workers happy and miserable provides some insights. He assigns a high value to "recognition for task achievement" as a "job satisfier" or motivator, along with some others like "intrinsic interest in the work," and "advancement." "Dissatisfiers" include "company policy and administrative practices" and "working conditions." The conundrum in Herzberg's findings is that while good company policy and working conditions do limit dissatisfaction, they do not result in job satisfaction.

No matter how hard you try to get the air conditioning just right or work toward making parking affordable and convenient, the best you can expect is a *lessening* of dissatisfaction. Fine tuning the environment in which one works is not the same as improving what one does. Illustrative of this is the frequent criticism I have heard about the venue of the library's recognition programs. Better-financed organizational units rent out the ballroom at the five-star hotel, whereas the library has its recognition potluck in the staff lounge! This is a classic dissatisfier. Changing the venue will decrease the complaints, but it will not affect true job satisfaction.

While looking at Herzberg's bipolar chart of satisfiers and dissatisfiers, I was struck that recognition (second only to achievement as a positive, upside motivator) has the largest negative, downside value assigned to any of the motivators. What causes this duality? My theory is that when we institutionalize recognition, it becomes an administrative practice, a potential dissatisfier.

Scene One

Two staff members in technical services were singled out for recognition by their colleagues. The two had worked visibly and assiduously for the past several months on ensuring a swap-out of computer hardware and software used by each of the more than eighty staff.

The spontaneous celebration occurred shortly after much of the work was done and systems were up and running. Most of the installation, though complicated and tied to production systems, was nearly flawless! Everyone benefited, and everyone understood. In some ways the celebration party was as much for the staff as it was for those being rewarded. It was a milestone event, marking a transition shared by all staff. Administrative involvement was noticeably absent.

Scene Two

It is the eleventh annual staff recognition banquet. The winner of the best performer of the year, a cash bonus, is about to be announced, sometime during dessert. The award, named after a highly esteemed librarian, is meant to be a genuine honor. The awards committee solicits nominations and prepares a recommendation for approval by the library director. The chair of the awards committee reads a glowing and lengthy rationale for this year's winner, which is met by muted, hardly jubilant, applause. The moment feels anticlimactic. There is much consternation among the staff for several days afterward. They are disgruntled about the winner, who is someone reputed to blame mistakes on staff efforts outside his specialized area of responsibility. Most of the staff, regardless of the award's eulogical write-up, remain ignorant of what this person actually does. Their perception is that someone who was "part of the problem and not the solution" has just been rewarded.

IF YOU MUST . . .

You say your organization just has to have a RP? Then here are some pointers. Communicate broadly, with clarity and persistence, all of the following:

- **The purpose of the award.** Make it significant and bolster its integrity. If it is for longevity or the fewest sick days used, consider abandoning the formal recognition. Resist the award's becoming a spoil of political battles.

- **The nomination process and who has access.** Requirements should not be weighed in favor of staff who work with users or technology. That is their job; there has to be something more deserving of recognition than doing a good job with the public or converting manual processes to computer-based ones.

- **The reason a team or person is getting the recognition.** No platitudes. If inflated rhetoric is necessary to justify an award, think again.

And, for the recognition program, ensure that there are the following:

- **Frequent turnover on the recognition committee.** This may help ensure new ideas and freshness in attitudes.

- **A moratorium on any award when it begins to flag and fade** (usually after the second time it is given). My working ratio is 500:1. By this I mean that for every 500 staff, only one genuine and heartfelt award can be supported by the organization under normal conditions. So if your organization numbers 100 people, an award once every five years is supportable. This ratio is derived from an unscientific analysis taking into account statistical variation in performance—the fact that most people (85 percent) are doing a good job, and when they fail or exceed extraordinarily, it is often the result of systems or situations beyond their control.

  Spontaneity is essential for increasing organizational energy and avoiding somnolence. Every award has yawn potential. I know of an organizationwide recognition dinner that costs at least $50,000. Many (90 percent of the several hundred participants) would be happy to see it come to end, but the built-up inertia, including that of the planning committee, repels reform. Change efforts bounce off the solid facade of this doddering annual tradition.

  Right up there with spontaneity is organizational support. The more careful the planning, selecting, and awarding, the better received the reward will be among all participants. Those awards done in haste or as an afterthought suggest a lack of sincerity.

- **An assessment of your RP from time to time.** Assess not with a questionnaire but with conversations among committee members and staff. Managers should ask who and what we are recognizing. What is the message we are sending? If recognition is usually of individuals and teams that do not rock the boat, persons and groups that "go along to get along," that is what you are going to get. Ask pointedly, "What has the recognition program done for management lately?" If you want to promote contrarian views, to maintain an environment that's safe for making unintended mistakes, celebrate the best questions asked (e.g., Why are we doing this?) and the biggest mistakes made. The "task achieved" that's being recognized must benefit a sizable part of the organization. If not, then have specialized awards or don't bother.

LAST WORDS

Although I do know of one extraordinary successful RP—it stands alone in its organizationwide commitment and passion—I still think it is probably best to avoid a formal, full-blown RP—which is sure to sag under its predictability and incremental fatigue. There are few better sources for nourishing staff cynicism than recognition ceremonies that have become routine and tiresome. When recognition committee members and staff have to be flogged with repeated appeals for monthly recommendations, that's a sign to move on.

The best recognition is when we pay attention to each other and give frequent pats on the back and constructive feedback. If there is spontaneous recognition for task achievement, two things happen: The boss has to be more aware of what is happening, and the employee's thinking (based on the self-improvement recognition promotes) can help get the job done better.

CHAPTER 34

"I've Closed My Eyes to the Cold Hard Truth I'm Seeing": Making Performance Appraisal Work

Let's face it: Managers hate conducting performance appraisal discussions.
—Dick Grote (2002)

In my management class, the segment on performance appraisal has students doing an imaginary assessment. They are to create a problematic individual—a least preferred coworker—for their written evaluation and imagine the dialogue they will have with this person in the face-to-face assessment. Many find this the most difficult assignment. Completing the ninety-day work goals form, for follow-up with their problem employee, is no easier.

Once they've survived this assignment, I ask them to consider an organization with no formal performance appraisal system. How will they, as supervisors, communicate goals and development needs? My method is to move the student into questioning the unquestioned effectiveness of the commonly accepted performance appraisal (PA) process. Does PA really make a difference? I ask them to think about some of the underlying operating assumptions of PA:

Without control, most people will withhold their best efforts.

Most people will not of their own volition take responsibility to develop and improve their performance.

Most people will not improve without tangible targets and goals.

I ask the class if these assumptions apply to them. Is this how they want their bosses to view them? Most say no—they do not need the outside controls to do a good job. I then ask, OK, why would these assumptions apply to others, to the people you may be evaluating when you are a supervisor? Systems of performance appraisal are emblematic of twentieth-century organizations, with probably more than 90 percent of all libraries of any size using PA. The version

244

they use can be customized or one required by the larger organizational entity, like a county government or university. PA is evidence of what many would term "well-run" and accountable organizations. Then again, some firms, even libraries, ignore PA, and their staffs do amazingly well. They are productive, flexible, and creative. How can this be?

Does the research evidence support the sizable investment and effort of PA? A review of the literature (Coens and Jenkins 2002) reveals much written about PA techniques and strategies, but little about results. Discussions of applying PA systems in libraries (Stueart and Moran 2002) are no more enlightening, because they do not mention productive outcomes.

A few years ago I came across an airline magazine ad hawking *the* answer for surviving obligatory personnel evaluations: software, at a modest cost, to make writing the PA routine and gain the manager much-needed time for "real work." Not only would the software supply paragraphs of evaluatory prose, the words were guaranteed litigation proof. Shortly after, I came across another indicator that PA had become an established industry: a low-tech approach available in teacher supply stores—evaluation phrase books for use on student report cards.

At best, PA is an imperfect approach. Its application probably does encourage communication "for the record" and can benefit staff unclear about job expectations. But the process can become superficial and a ready source for feeding corporate cynicism.

This chapter considers the reasons we often rely on PA, some of its conundrums, and suggestions for making PA a positive experience for managers and staff.

WHY PA?

It appears that organizations abhor a PA vacuum. PA has industrial-strength tenacity. If a PA system is abandoned or ignored, its advocates, inside and outside the organization, begin to press for a formal evaluation process. And why not?

We want staff to know what is expected. We want staff to have up-to-date job descriptions. We want supervisors to talk with staff and vice versa. We want staff to be recognized for doing well, and we want them to improve, develop, and change with the job. Or do we? Sometimes we choose, or have chosen for us, the least direct path to get to where we want to be. Let's consider a typical scenario:

At Library X, there is no formal PA system. The conventional wisdom has it that there is too little communication among staff and supervisors, with much conflict avoidance. This perceived insufficient communication is attributed to the lack of a performance appraisal system. Therefore, instituting PA will ensure communication between supervisors and staff. Without exploring other options, Library X adopts a labor-intensive PA apparatus so that people will talk to each other.

This example demonstrates the organization's willingness to believe in PA as a good thing, an essential building block in the organization's structure. David Whyte (1995), the poet, adds to our understanding of how common sense can be suspended when management begins to rely on prescribed and ready-made solutions. It is as if "[t]he complexity of the world could be accounted for, [corporations] fervently hoped, by a simple increase in the thickness of the company manual."

WHAT CAN GO AWRY AND WHY: UNINTENDED CONSEQUENCES

PA has the potential for improving the organization. Results can be good if, according to Herzberg (1987), the PA process emphasizes achievement, recognition, the work itself, responsibility, advancement, and personal growth for the individual. If PA is imposed on employees as company policy, then it can become one of the primary sources of dissatisfaction in the workplace. That can occur because management unwittingly seeks to retain most of the control over the PA process.

Sometimes we want PA to do too much. For example, coupling PA with salary decisions may seem efficient. But invariably the two processes work against each other. Money is largely a budgetary decision for the organization, whereas performance appraisal is about individual development. Studies show that this "stick and carrot" form of motivation is less than effective. When a large sample of American workers was asked to name the best way to motivate workers for quality and productivity, here is what they said:

> Let me do more to put my ideas into action: 33 percent
>
> Listen to my ideas for improvement: 17 percent
>
> Pay me more: 27 percent
>
> Give me more recognition: 19 percent

More people said they would be motivated if their ideas were heard and they had opportunities to apply them. Although important, money alone is not as important a motivator as are the freedom to act, recognition or achievement, and being listened to (Coens and Jenkins 2002, 184).

William Deming, the statistical genius who brought Japan into prominence as a producer of quality goods, despised PA. He entombed it in his list of seven deadly corporate diseases and, never a believer in understatement, declared:

> [The annual review] nourishes short term performance, annihilates long term planning, builds fear, demolishes teamwork, nourishes rivalry and politics . . . . It leaves people bitter, crushed, bruised, battered, desolate, despondent, dejected, feeling inferior, some even depressed, unfit for work for weeks after receipt of rating, unable to comprehend why they are inferior. It is unfair, as it ascribes to people in a group differences that may be caused totally by the system that they work in. (quoted in Coens and Jenkins 2002, 308)

His disdain for PA was not just curmudgeonliness. He proved statistically the limitations of focusing on the individual as somehow independent of the systems in which he or she worked. Deming pointed out the numerous errors to which PA was prone, including those known as the central tendency and range restriction errors: Central tendency is often induced by administrative intervention, which requires the clustering of most people toward the middle. So on a scale of 5, some will rank people as a 3, even when the worker's performance warrants better or worse. In industry, the notorious "rank and yank" systems restricted just how many of any staff could be in each rating level. For example, General Electric, under Mr. Jack Welch, restricted ranges to 20 percent at the top; 70 percent in the middle; 10 percent that need improvement. Those in the last category knew their jobs at GE were finished; they'd been yanked.

Less draconian is management's setting quotas (e.g., only 25 percent of staff can be scored at "exceeds expectations" for the salary increment, the carrot). This policy forces supervisors and staff into a tacit collusion of "turn taking" for "merit" pay.

Well, with what would Deming replace PA? He recommended an annual half-day conversation about goals and aspirations with each staff member. Your role is to listen. Deming does have his critics. James Hoopes, for one, did not go along with Deming in his debunking of PA:

> Evaluation, ranking, and merit pay do frighten employees. But there are other soul killers besides fear, such as the hurt felt by high achievers when their earned rewards go to the undeserving. Elimination of merit pay will show fear the door, but achievements may leave with it. Getting rid of evaluation is not a way to improving management, but rather of abolishing it. (2003, 228)

Mr. Hoopes would retain PA—an improved version, of course—but never does spell out how he would overcome its numerous errors in practice and rampant malfunctions.

DOING WITHOUT PA

At my urging, a library where I was part of the administrative team gave up doing performance appraisals for about five years. Productivity in selected units, quantified by numerous work measures, showed steady gains, soaring in some cases (even when controlling for computer applications). Was there a cause and effect relationship? Can the absence of PA result in better performance? Not exactly. What made the difference for this library was a strong leadership emphasis on team goals, clear expectations from team leaders, attention to team development, and an emphasis on coaching and challenging rather than directing.

However, in many other units in this same library, eliminating PA made no discernible difference. So while the workplace absent PA was no worse, it was also no better for those units. Why not better? Well, we simply eliminated it in those units and did not replace it uniformly with something better. Had we done more with conversation, honest feedback, and genuine coaching, I think we would have seen much more trust and mutual support, a healthier workplace.

Still, many staff did better without the annual performance appraisal. Why? Because we focused on teams and productivity, which after all was a new way of working. We were engaged in doing better, freeing people up, soliciting and implementing ideas, and taking pride in our accomplishments. Five years later, our appraisal system came back. As often happens, it came from above. No, it wasn't divine intervention. It came from the top executive office, where a particularly fastidious staffer had convinced the organization's leaders that it needed a uniform PA system.

This new version of PA was "improved" and industrial strength. The evaluation form was a complicated, nine-point scale for a dozen significant standardized performance behaviors, competencies, and job responsibilities, about six pages long. Most aggravating was that this new system required six annual meetings between supervisors and employees to plot progress. In my area, with 100 staff, this meant six meetings per staff person for 600 hours. Because they were not meeting alone, this meant 600 hours of supervisory time as well. So we would expend a total of 1,200 hours a year to satisfy the new process.

Fortunately, when word got out that this uniform PA system would not apply to the top administrative staff, the administration backpedaled and put off its implementation indefinitely. But in the meantime, the leaders mandated that some PA system must be in place. Our not having one was now viewed as radicalism by the chief officer and assorted others in the hierarchy. So in spite of five years of evidence that suggested not having a PA system made no difference or was instrumental in raising productivity, we returned to the familiar, the way we had been doing PA five years previously.

How to Make PA Work

Make PA work by budgeting enough time for the manager and staff to reflect on individual performance. In too many libraries, assessment is an add-on, squeezed into crowded schedules. Grote (2002) suggests a "Four Step Strategy-based Performance Management system," which emphasizes mutual responsibility for the evaluation process between supervisor and employee and encourages extensive and relevant communication.

- Let PA do what it is meant to do, no more. Keep in mind that more complicated forms, more frequent reviews, and more signatures do not solve communication or feedback problems—rather, they aggravate them.

- Solve communication problems separately from PA with coaching, counseling, and training. What is needed is less administrative control and more training for managers to become more adept at talking with people, about checking in, seeking to understand, and support.

- Use group assessment tools that facilitate feedback among team and departmental members.

- Emphasize staff development, not evaluation, like Lois Jennings (1992) implemented at the University of Canberra ("regrowing staff" is their term). At UC, PA has been supplanted by an annual session for every staff member with the library director, to gauge where each one is in his or her career and what training and development is needed.

- Experiment with the plus/delta approach for giving staff feedback. At a workshop I attended, each participant was asked to list his or her strengths and areas for development (deltas) on a flip chart. Then each person went over the list in front of the full group. The group amended the list, adding both plusses and deltas.

  Those amended lists became an affirmation of strengths and a confirmation of areas for development. Individuals showed keen insights into their own weaknesses, often listing them, thereby permitting other participants to agree or disagree. On occasion, an individual's perceived "weakness" was rated as a strength by the group.

Most important, what any manager should do and can do is to give feedback in timely and caring ways. I've learned that the best feedback

- is intended to be helpful;

- includes positive elements (not just negative);

- deals with issues that are within the control of the receiver;

- is specific and clear;

- is cross-checked with the receiver for understanding;

- leaves the receiver free to determine his or her own solution and corresponding behavior (now, there's a challenge for the workplace);

- is solicited, not imposed (another challenge!);

- is given when it is needed; and

- if nothing else, is clear, concise, caring, and constructive.

CHAPTER 35

"To Save the Time of the User": Customer Service at the Millennium

Not long ago, the business media declared the dawning of the age of the customer. Corporations embraced this, at least in their advertising, assuring us customized service, immediate resolution of problems, and even direct contact with the boss. A few organizations rehoisted and saluted "The Customer Is Always Right" banner and boldly promised 100 percent satisfaction or "Your Money Back." New York City went so far as to give courtesy training to subway employees and taxi drivers (with some positive effect—I no longer get cursed at when I ask for directions in the subway kiosk! However, the directions still need improvement. Unless I already knew how to get there, the directions would not get me to where I wanted to be.)

Well, in spite of these efforts, the customer service experience remains a mixed one, varying greatly from extraordinarily fine to abysmal, with a bias toward the negative. Consumer research shows that every victim of a negative experience retells the story seven or more times, hence the extreme skewing. You and I, no doubt, could rant for several pages about personal encounters with poor service. The same media that declared this the customer era regale us daily with horror stories of abused customers. Among the most frequently told stories are about robotic telephone recordings, directing us à la *Waiting for Godot,* to choose from a menu of buttons, never listing the one we need.

The Internet is said to be customer driven. Give e-customers a bad experience, they're gone. And because of their rising impatience, e-customers (including e-library users) are gone faster than they would be in pre-Internet days. Worse, they may mount a competing Internet site ("sucks.com") in retaliation for poor service. Still, a prevalent rant in the Internet press is e-commerce's failure to deliver on promises made to the consumer. Clicking on the help button on most e-commerce sites is a bit like yelling SOS in the middle of the Pacific. Since

I work in the information services world, what's happening in other customer realms sensitizes me to what we are doing in libraries, online and off. All too often, when librarians discuss information services quality, it is with the smug certainty that our service is far superior to the lame efforts of, say, information technology. At one time we could afford to sneer at their so-called help desks.

Well, we do have a fine tradition, one totally foreign to most e-commerce sites, but we have our less-than-splendid moments as well. True, few of our public service points operate from behind bulletproof glass, like Medicaid and IRS offices, but then there are those heavily attended library workshops about "problem patrons"—our name for enraged and maddened users. All is not right. Is it within the realm of possibility that we somehow contribute to our patrons becoming problematic? Let's take a look at a recent interaction I had at the circulation desk.

My father (eighty-nine years old) had an overdue library book. He had been in the hospital for more than three weeks after emergency surgery and was about to have follow-up surgery. When I explained this to the library staffer, she said that she understood the situation, but that there were no exceptions, per the branch head, for overdue fines. My father must pay the fine of $2.80.

For some stressed-out psychological reason, I found this response hysterically funny. Over my chortling disbelief, I asked the clerk what they'd do if he'd died? I've thought about that silly episode and wondered how could this happen. The obvious, intuitive thing was for the staff member to thank me for returning the book, say forget the fine, and wish my father well—he's a regular at this library. Instead, the response was right out of the pages of pathological bureaucracy. Why?

Later in the year, I met a remarkable public library director who has made it simple for her staff to know how to respond when faced with something like the above situation. She's very clear about what she values: the staff have her support for things that please the public. And the staff know they will not have her support for things that make the public unhappy. Of course, these are not just her personal values, but ones reflective of the community and the library's philosophy and purpose. I cannot imagine a repeat of my overdue book fiasco in her library. For those prone to dismiss this director's way of leadership as impossible to apply: it works.

The staff members love the clear simplicity. They know exactly what it means and when to use it. That clarity is reinforced by the director's daily leading by example. She demonstrates and interprets what this simple policy means, and middle managers and staff gain an understanding of expectations and how to respond in a multitude of circumstances.

A cautionary word—although the circulation desk in public and academic libraries is often the user's and librarian's favorite whipping boy, it's well worth remembering that there are other parts of the library that contribute to user unhappiness. In fact, certain unpublicized policies and practices do far more damage than any passing incident at the loan desk.

Getting to uncommonly good customer service, I'll start with a rhetorical question: "What can an organization do to ensure good customer service?" Following are some difference-making answers.

UNTIE THE HANDS OF THE STAFF

Make it a positive thing for library staff to take ownership of customer problems, intra- and extra-departmentally. Anyone who crosses unit boundaries to satisfy and resolve a user's question should be applauded (and protected). Middle managers are central to this form of staff empowerment. It is essential that middle managers understand and support staff crossing departmental lines to help a library user. Make people aware that this level of effort is the expectation organizationwide. Send anyone who says, "It's not my department" or "My hands are tied" to the stacks for a mandatory three-hour shift of shelf reading.

Certainly educate staff about customer service, but do so with practical training that explores the best ways of responding to real-world situations. As a supervisor, make clear what resolutions you favor and why. Avoid customer service workshops that assume that staff or the patron is the problem. When good people do stupid things, workplace research shows that the system is at fault 95 percent of the time. The "system" includes administrative policy, equipment, facilities, staffing decisions, etc.

So you see, a workshop designed around teaching staff lessons about respecting differences and applying common sense and courtesy assumes that their shortcomings create the problem. Instead of addressing ways to improve the system (a 95 percent payoff!), these workshops invest in trying to convince the hardcore problem staff (a 5 percent or less payoff) how to treat other people. This latter training wrongly treats symptoms, not the disease.

In fact, once you ask staff and users about customer service issues, you probably won't need a workshop. But you will need a process by which to bring about change in the system. Staff who are verbally abused by customers ought to have a lot to say about the causes of dissatisfaction. And they likely know just what is needed to improve the situation. Why not ask them what is it that gets in the way of pleasing patrons?

My assumption is that staff know exactly what they are doing within the boundaries mandated by policies, culture, and personal on-the-job experience. If they have too little or too much discretion in solving problems, the results may be unsatisfactory. The less confusion about values, goals, and roles, the better the communication with customers and problem resolution. Clarity promotes the quintessential factor for freeing up the staff to do the right thing: a climate of trust in the organization about the capacity of the staff to do what is best.

Most important, there has to be in place a strong value about how we support each other. Systems that practice and understand the "each-to-all" mode of support, rather than "self-only" will have much more success in ensuring a beneficial response to customers.

GET RID OF THE BAD APPLES

The misanthropic do not have a place in a service industry like libraries. If problem staff still can't get it right after counseling and training, they won't ever. If a staff member is tone deaf to the nuances of human communication, he or she will invariably respond from personal preference. That "go-to" preference is the one that gets people in trouble.

For example, a reference librarian who behaves condescendingly to users should not be at the desk. I recall a case in my early career when users frequently criticized one librarian for his overbearing manner. Counseling and constructive feedback, over a period of years, did not improve this librarian's interaction with the public.

Actually, the individual never did agree that he had a problem, so each counseling session never got past the denial phase. Yes, he did give accurate answers to reference questions. However, imagine the kinds of messages our tolerating his negative behavior sent to other staff and library users. This person needed to move on and to leave interactions with faculty and students to the many librarians who enjoy helping people and providing good information. All that said, let's get real. Most of us inherit the sins (and bad hires) of our administrative forebears. The librarian in the above example had been in the organization for several years. At least two other supervisors had failed to address this person's poor public interaction. I believe his vigorous denial of any need to change exhausted those supervisors.

But that's reality. Many of us in a leadership position find ourselves looking to the employee's retirement as the only way of getting rid of someone. One of the most frequently consulted personnel documents is locked in the director's desk—the list of hire and retirement dates of all staff. All too often, avoidance seems to be the preferred model of conflict resolution. Over time, avoidance can distort performance appraisals to such an extent that no written record exists about an employee's problematic behavior. Rather, the written appraisal winds up describing a contributing and positive staff member (a total stranger to his peers!). At best, a limp double entendre or two may be buried in the written review. That said, documents like this are of enormous value to the aggrieved when they resist removal and the process advances to a personnel action hearing. It is ironic, but the blanket of workplace protection shelters the undeserving and the deserving.

What does work, in my experience, is several months of steady and regular pressure on a person to modify problematic behavior. The problem behavior and the sought-after change should be in writing. And there should be a written plan for improvement, with realistic goals and milestones. When the supervisor does this, resolutely and constructively, the individual knows what is expected, has a realistic chance to improve, and may indeed move on to more compatible work.

LISTEN TO WHAT YOUR USERS ARE SAYING

Several years ago I attended a Disneyland customer workshop. One workshop concept has stayed with me: "There are no stupid questions." At Disney, staff are trained to hear the unasked question. For example, a hot and frazzled parent, with kids in tow, asks a Disney staff member, "What time is the parade?" Because parade times are well publicized, we might dismiss this as a "stupid question" or refer the parent to an information booth somewhere in the distance. But when you think about the real question, you may have the opportunity to help the parent enjoy the day. What the parent may be really asking is where is the best place to view the parade when all the kids and parents are overheated and cranky.

A system to get suggestions from users can be a useful way to find out what they are thinking and what they would like to see changed. The "Suggestion Answer Book" that I edited at two university libraries gained us hundreds of helpful insights and suggestions from our users. I was careful never to respond in a way that could be interpreted that I thought the suggestion was "stupid." This was my deliberate strategy, because I'd learned from experience that when I thought the suggestion or comment was lightweight, it turned out to be more than normally useful. And my cavalier dismissal of one comment would be read by other users, who would of course hesitate to write in their ideas. The Suggestion Answer Book allowed us to share in the user's experiences, in his or her words and terms. We got to walk in others' shoes. The book gave a much needed voice to the user, one that we heard loud and clear.

BE CLEAR ABOUT YOUR POLICIES AND THEIR INTERPRETATION

Policies need clarity. If the policy's purpose or rationale is unclear, interpretations and enforcement will be equally muddied. For example, restricting food and drink makes little sense to most users and even some librarians. Predictably, it will have various interpretations among staff and users. Some staff will be more conscientious (some rabidly so) in enforcing it than others, adding further confusion to the policy.

Like that communications game we played as children, where a message is whispered from ear to ear with hilarious transformations around the circle, so goes an unclear policy. Unless you work at policy clarification, you can expect confusion. For example, at the staff's request, you create a policy that staff do not need to help readers empty bags of books they've brought to the desk. Does your policy really deny help to parents who are carrying small children and people with disabilities?

Talk through policy interpretations with your staff. My rule of thumb is that unless a policy is crystal clear to staff, you, and users, it is best left unimplemented until clarity is achieved. Certainly, trying out a policy is one way to discover hidden problems—just make it clear to all that the policy is an exploratory one. In short, because circumstances change and the unanticipated happens, policies should be flexible and responsive to situations.

This chapter's title refers to my favorite of Ranganathan's Laws of Library Science: "To save the time of the reader." That "law" fits all libraries and applies to the information side of the Internet. This law has been a fundamental value to me in making decisions about how we do what we do in libraries. It has influenced what I do in designing services and seeking to improve existing ones.

Yet I've been dismayed and frustrated by the numerous policies and practices that "waste the time of the user." At the same time, I've come to realize that what Ranganathan's axiom means to me (and others of my persuasion) does not mean the same thing to all librarians—especially those more concerned with conservation and accumulation. It is unfortunate that the tension between these two views has never been relaxed. In many ways, that root-core difference in philosophy suggests just how far we have to go before we can gain the requisite clarity for the best customer service.

CHAPTER 36

"Where Are the Snows of Yesteryear?" Reflections on a Suggestion "Box" That Worked[1]

Most of us in the workplace know that customers can be an excellent source for improving what we do. Even if we don't believe that the "customer is always right," we know they are right more often than not. So to listen to them is to take a positive step toward improved library services.

The ubiquitous forum for gaining customer feedback is the locked "Suggestion Box." Why is it a box—a locked box? One cartoon of a suggestion box has it centered over a waste paper basket. The box has no bottom, so suggestions drop into the trash. Not to be too cynical, but this method is indeed more efficient than taking the suggestions to someone's office for that person to "recycle" via his or her own circular file. The box design has its limitations. In fact, most suggestion systems of the "box" genre don't work because they are closed. Public posting of selected responses to suggestions from the box is a step toward accountability, but the inevitable screening of what gets posted still results in many suggestions never seeing the light of day.

Because of those known limitations, I conceived and introduced the "Suggestion Answer Book" at the University of Colorado in the early 1970s. The SA Book was deliberately an open system. My working assumption was, and continues to be, that users are our allies. They are not the enemy. User education also influenced my decision. I was one of many librarians consciously seeking to liberate users, to help them become independent users of information. And this was Boulder, Colorado, in the early 1970s, with its 5,000-plus hippie "street people." Our users were into major liberation of all kinds. When I started at a new job at another research library in 1982 as the head of public services, the Suggestion Answer Book was one of the first things I introduced to help make the library more proactive. I answered thousands of questions, gripes, kudos, and suggestions.

Was it smooth sailing? Hardly. Remember, there are reasons most organizations prefer a locked box. More on that later. This chapter reflects on why the book succeeded, and suggests that the SA Book format is one of the best ways to get user input. But recognize that an open book is, well, an open book. The SA Book is a public forum; there will be graffiti and "flaming" amid the polite and helpful commentary.

WHAT DOES A SUGGESTION ANSWER BOOK LOOK LIKE?

Mine was rather homely: a three-ring notebook, with about 100 numbered pages, located in a heavily trafficked public area.[2] Each page was formatted for three suggestions (A, B, C) and three answers. A small sign above the opened book stated what it was, inviting users to contribute their questions, concerns, gripes, and suggestions for improvements. We'd usually try to keep a pencil on a string attached to the book.

Users wrote their comments on the numbered pages. We periodically took out the current pages (usually three or four at a time) to answer or refer, via photocopy, to staff members that might have information for the answer. Once an answer was obtained it was typed directly below the written suggestion and the pages were returned to the book. Any recently entered suggestions were gathered to start another cycle. Updates were inserted in the SA Book as they appeared. We began to insert an "update index" page to let regular readers know what suggestions, some fifty or more pages back, had been updated.

The SA Book is ancient technology (paper), involving several labor-intensive steps: handwritten comments, referring comments for answers, typing and dating answers, and replacing pages. My responses were anonymous. Why? To give the process objectivity and a dash of mystery. In some ways, the SA person was an ombudsman. If certain library policies displayed pettiness or foolishness, the SA person would try to do something about it on behalf of the student. Of course because I was an administrative officer I really could encourage and sometimes implement change for the better.

Also, my anonymity appeared to free up students to express what was on their minds. After all, they wrote anonymously as well. They could be angry without repercussion. If they were delighted with our service, they could express it without appearing to curry favor. If it was a bad hair day and they felt lousy, they could still express themselves without having to worry about how it might reflect on them. Although the identity of the SA person remained a secret, even to most of the staff, answers or updates from other people were signed. Among the strategic reasons for the signatures was to recognize staff, encourage users to get to know library staff, and promote full and helpful answers.

WHAT USERS WANT

Following is a sampling of user feedback gathered from the pages of the 1988 SA Book volume.

Students were quick to jump on some extreme policies in the mid-1980s. For example, our Food and Drink Posse was much complained about: "What's the purpose for having idiot 'drink and food patrols' around the library at night. It's just a hassle. Who really cares if the guy takes your ID#?"

Other "hard to defend" examples:

- Roping down the lists of current course reserves to a desk. Doing so, we prohibited photocopying, something most users desperately wanted.

- Removing mice from the online catalog terminal keyboards. Presumably, we thought fewer terminals would "freeze up." Once this complaint made the rounds, the mice were reinstated within the day.

- Not allowing undergraduates the graduate student privilege of borrowing bound periodicals even if they were taking graduate level classes.

- Leaving the book stacks dark at all times, causing users to grope for light switches. (The oil shortages of the previous decade were irrelevant to these undergraduates, who were more concerned about their personal safety than with conserving electricity.)

Then there were the perennial requests for us to improve long-standing problems, such as getting books back to the shelves quickly: "Hey, have you guys given up or what? What is the deal with all the unshelved books? Hire some more shelvers!"

These frequent complaints helped us get funds for shelf reading and reshelving. When improvements occurred, users complimented the improvement. Another "success" measure was the drop off in complaints about the condition of the book stacks.

It is always easier to argue for improvements with student complaints in hand:

- Fix the damned copiers or at least put signs on them!

- Extra toilet paper, please!

- Have you changed toilet paper, or have I grown calluses?

We used these suggestions to leverage improvements from the university, to improve photocopying service on campus and ensure that housekeepers were fully supplied with good quality and quantities of paper goods. Circulation seemed to catch most of the flak, but other parts of the organization had their share of complaints. Students questioned how books could be in bookstores but not on the library's shelves, why some books had not been ordered, why some service points were persistently rude to users, why a nearby sister institution always had university press books before we did, and so on. And when we did something right, users took notice:

> Opening the [old front] door was the smartest move Duke has made since admitting [basketball player] Danny Ferry. Thank you. Thank you. It was so sensible I am shocked at Duke's change in behavior. Using Common Sense! Thank you. Sorry about that [backhand compliment] I am really glad they did this.

Although we could not immediately implement all student ideas, many suggestions helped us, over time, to improve our services:

> Put catalog terminals in the stacks.

> How about putting some dictionaries in the computer clusters so those of us who can't spell won't have to lug them around.

> Why is the closing bell so loud and grating that it makes me wet my pants when it goes off?

> [Let us] renew books by phone.

> We need a lounge area with a soda machine, coffee machine, and snack machine so that people can relax during studies.

> Why is the heat still on when it is April 27 (and 80 degrees outside)?

> Why won't the Xerox machines print on legal size paper?

An odd phenomenon occurred: Suggestions that had nothing to do with the library started to appear in the book. We found ourselves referring complaints and questions about dorm living, food quality in the dining halls, the registration process, sports, good and bad faculty members, and more. We forwarded all of these and were a little surprised when many responses came back with full explanations, good humor, and some resolve to change what was criticized. The pages of the SA Book became a way to tangibly and publicly praise staff, inside and outside the library. Our praise of good work done by electricians, plumbers, painters, and others was welcomed and remembered by other parts of the university. New requests for repairs were readily accepted and fulfilled in a timely way.

STYLE AND TONE

I made an effort to answer complaints, whether accusatory, harsh, or impatient, in open and nonjudgmental terms. Having a few days to contemplate an answer helped me gain objectivity and see the possibilities within a complaint.

Often it was a matter of walking the line between being stuffy or flip. My tendency to err toward the latter earned me several rebuffs from rightly offended readers:

> What is your job? Do you just sit in an office all day and write ridiculous answers to these questions?
>
> *Answer:* No, sometimes I stand up.

But it did seem that the more playful and whimsical my answers, the more readers the book attracted:

> How do I get to the tunnels? [the "off limits" campus heating tunnels]
>
> *Answer:* Indirectly, obliquely, occludedly, parenthetically, inscrutably, and circumlocutionally.
>
> Would it be possible, by your divine mercy, O Ye of the Suggestion Book, to be blessed with staplers by the photocopy machines?
>
> *Answer:* A few, we omnisciently thought, were already in place. Ubiquitously, we'll ascertain what's what.
>
> Since so many undergraduates insist on copulating in Perkins, you should be a pal and throw some mattresses here and there in the stacks—if you can't beat 'em. . . .
>
> *Answer:* Your comment suggests:
>
> (a) that the end of the semester is upon us, and,
>
> (b) that you are extraordinarily perceptive and have anticipated the library's Christmas party fund raiser: Rent-a-Sealy.
>
> Will you marry me?
>
> *Answer:* Leave a picture and last year's tax form 1040 and your proposal will be given all due consideration.

And there were times to shift into the Dear Abby mode:

> It is summer and I'm hating life because I was dumb enough to take classes in the summer. Do you have a suggestion?
>
> *Answer:* Take a walk in the forest: wade in the creeks. Give yourself at least four hours for solitude and exploring the forest's floor.

PROBLEMS AND CHALLENGES

There's no denying it, a SA Book takes work. Perhaps due to guilt from having so much fun in the role as the anonymous Suggestion Answer Person, I wrote answers for most questions away from the office, on the weekend, on holiday breaks, at the coffee shop, etc. I did it as a pleasurable extra, an add-on to my "regular" work. (As I look back, it was probably among my most important work.) If I delayed answering, while on vacation or excessively lazy or "out of steam," someone inevitably complained: "What's taking so long [to answer]? I don't want to study, I need distraction."

The mechanics of getting the answers onto paper and distributed further aggravated any delay I caused. The SA Book process can be "high maintenance," involving a lot of copying and distributing. And because the SA Book was located in a public area, there was some risk of vandalism. A few pages would disappear each semester, never to be seen again. Once the entire notebook disappeared. Another time, the two bound volumes of the first thousand pages (photocopies) were absconded with. We surmise they are in a landfill or gracing someone's shelf of college memorabilia. Occasionally, coarse language appeared on the pages. Fortunately, the SA Book was self-criticizing and largely self-policing. If the language deteriorated someone would eventually ask for a halt:

> Why can't people have any class when writing suggestions to the library? Is it necessary to demonstrate such high levels of crassness?
>
> What happened to the good ol' days when people made humorous suggestions instead of petty complaints? Oops. I hope that wasn't another complaint.
>
> *Answer:* Often the complaints, once we work on them, help us do our work better. Besides, even the complaints have their humorous side. However, don't believe the canard that library staff laugh riotously as each day's selection of suggestions/complaints is passed around prior to being filed circularly.

Although I never censored expletives, I did "censor" attacks on individuals by "whiting out" the name and other identifying information in the complaint. Our response always recommended that the writer talk with the individual concerned or with the head of that person's department. At the same time, we would share the full text of the criticism with the named individual and his or her supervisor. Usually, there was cause for the expressed anger and the feedback was valid, if painful to receive.

If there was a second complaint about an individual, describing a believable incident, we knew we had a problem. A few staff took these criticisms to heart, resolving to improve. Some denied the complaints—the user was wrong;

they were right. In cases like that, the supervisor had the obligation (and some documentation!) to do something about it. I valued, for obvious reasons, getting updated answers with quality information from the people closest to the suggestion or question. But it was interesting to see how many of us (myself included) could explain in a clear way our reasons for doing something the way we did. For example, the why of splitting a prolific author's publications into two locations in the stacks can be explained in a technically rational and believable manner. Although that explanation satisfied us, I doubt it satisfied the user.

Too often we did not take time to reflect on the implicit criticism in a question about why we did something the way we did it. Because the student made the effort to ask, the issue probably was problematic for that person. In spite of that, we rarely contemplated changing the policy or going back and changing the outcome. Too often our glib and rational answers remind me of something Justice Sandra Day O'Connor said in 2001 when disagreeing with a Supreme Court decision: The Court "cloaks (a) pointless indignity with the mantle of reasonableness."

Sometimes referred suggestions came back with defensive responses. Or the responses were dismissive or obfuscating. An example is this ill-tempered retort from a branch librarian: "A stupid question deserves a stupid answer." The question was about how Saran Wrap got its "cling." The librarian missed an opportunity to show off library resources and how librarians add value to information seeking.

When the responses were unimaginative or humorless I would edit them, although it was my preference to insert the response as received. Many excellent updates (signed by the authors) were inserted into the book without emendation. Their answers were informative and educationally intriguing, giving readers a glimpse into the answer-seeking process.

Undeniably, there were some staff members who were discomfited by the SA Book. Our giving a voice to the user questioned the staff's absolute certainty of knowing what was best. When users pointed out the absurdity of a policy developed without user input or of a practice that no longer made much sense, this questioned the wisdom of the involved staff. Complaints about branch libraries could bring to light some odd practices. One writer spotlighted a subject branch's unstated policy of not lending books to all university students. This caused immediate and vigorous backpedaling and a rapid turnaround. Non-majors could now borrow books.

SUPPORT

Administrative support is essential for a SA Book to survive and to be influential. This level of support varied among my administrative colleagues, but I was fortunate to have several directors as champions. A surprise supporter was our library advisory board (akin to a nonlibrarian "board of visitors"). They delighted in the book, reading it whenever they came to campus, and unfailingly made it known at each meeting of the board just how much they liked it and learned from it. Besides the warm praise of the board members, it was always pleasing when out of the blue strangers who had somehow discovered I was the SA Book author would tell me about their enjoyment and appreciation of the book.

Another source of support was the campus student newspaper. Every two or three years an article would appear praising the library's openness to students and the wit and wisdom in questions and responses.[3]

CONCLUSION

Is it worth it? Yes!

We gained hundreds of improvements in facilities, services, policies, and staffing. We also gained insights into how we are perceived and what our users want from us. And we had the opportunity to display the humorous, imaginative, and human side of our profession. Our desire to save the time of the user was facilitated. Our desire to help students was made manifest.

Sources

The thirty-six chapters in this book are based on essays written and published elsewhere. The original essays first appeared in the sources cited below in chronological order. All of the chapters have been edited, revised, and otherwise updated, and many contain new material.

1992. "Productivity in Libraries? Managers Step Aside!" *Journal of Library Administration* 17: 23–42. http://www.informaworld.com

1994. "Sherlock's Dog or Managers and Mess Finding." *Library Administration & Management* 8: 139–49.

1998. "Lessons for Libraries from a Self Managing Team: The Orpheus Chamber Orchestra Experience." *Library Administration & Management* 12: 142–46.

1999. "*'She's Just Too Good to Be True, But She Is':* Recognition Ceremonies and Other Motivational Rituals." *Library Administration & Management* 13: 212–15.

1999. "'I've Closed My Eyes to the Cold Hard Truth I'm Seeing' Making Performance Appraisal Work." *Library Administration & Management* 13: 87–89.

2000. *"'I'm So Low, I Can't Get High'*: The Low Morale Syndrome and What to Do about It." *Library Administration & Management* 14: 218–21.

2001. "A Reason for Rain: Hoop Lessons for Library Leaders." *Library Administration & Management* 15: 39–43.

2001. "'To Save the Time of the User': Customer Service at the Millennium." *Library Administration & Management* 15: 179–82.

2001. "'Where Are the Snows of Yesteryear?' Reflections on a 'Suggestion Box' That Worked." *Library Administration & Management* 15: 240–43.

2002. "She Took Everything But the Blame": The Bad Boss is Back." *Library Administration & Management* 16, no. 3 (Summer): 156–58.

2002. "'From the Gutter to You Is Not Up': Worst and Best Practice." *Library Administration & Management* 16: 92–94.

2002. "Prestissimo Leadership." *Library Administration & Management* 16: 34–37.

2003. "Teams in Libraries." *Library Administration & Management* 17, no. 3 (Summer): 144–46.

2003. "A Zabarian Experience." *Library Administration & Management* 17, no. 1 (Winter): 40–42.

2003. "Seeking First to Understand . . ." *Library Administration & Management* 17: 99–100.

2003. "Leaving the Comfort Zone." *Library Administration & Management* 17, no. 4 (Fall): 196–97.

2004. "Sacred Teams." *Library Administration & Management* 18: 42–44.

2004. "Leading from the Middle: 'I'm the Boss'." *Library Administration & Management* 18, no. 4 (Fall): 205–7.

2004. "The Stove Side Chat." *Library Administration & Management* 18, no. 3 (Summer): 157–58, 161.

2004. "You Have the Resources." *Library Administration & Management* 18, no. 2 (Spring): 93–95.

2005. "A Gift from the Woods." *Library Administration & Management* 19: 94–97.

2006. "Balaam's Ass: Toward Proactive Leadership in Libraries." *Library Administration & Management* 20: 30–33.

2006. "Letting Go: A Reflection on Teams That Were." In *Teams in Technical Services*, edited by Rosann Bazirjian and Rebecca Mugridge, 155–69. Lanham, MD: Scarecrow Press.

2006. "Coaching for Results." *Library Administration & Management* 20: 86–89.

2006. "The Invisible Leader: Lessons for Leaders from the Orpheus Chamber Orchestra." *OD Practitioner* 38: 5–9.

2006. "You Can't Build a Fire in the Rain: Sparking Change in Libraries." *Library Administration & Management* 20: 201–3.

2006. "Southwest: The Unstodgy Airline." *Library Administration & Management* 20: 142–46.

2007. "On the Road, Again: Lessons along the Way." *Library Administration & Management* 21: 90–92.

2007. "*I'll Ask the Questions*': The Insecure Boss." *Library Administration & Management* 21: 193–95.

2008. "Komandas darbs (Teamwork): teorija un prakse." *Biblioteku Pasuale* [*Library World*] 43: 2–6. (Published in Riga, Latvia.)

2008. "Bridger and Me." *Library Administration & Management* 22: 100–102.

2008. "Deterministic, Highly Reductive, and Transient." *Library Administration & Management* 22: 148–49 and 154.

2008. "Rock Castle Gorge." *Library Administration & Management* 22: 44–46.

2008. "'I Can't Find You Anywhere but Gone' Revisited." *Library Administration & Management* 22: 48–51.

2008. "It's in the DNA": Infusing Organizational Values at Southwest." *Library Administration & Management* 23: 38–41.

2009. "The Spark Plug: A Leader's Catalyst for Change." *Library Leadership & Management* 23: 89–91.

2009. "Peer Coaching for the New Library." In *Strategies for Regenerating the Library and Information Profession.* Edited by Jana Varlejs and Graham Walton, 126–36. (The proceedings of the OFLA satellite conference "Moving In, Moving Up and Moving On: Strategies for Regenerating the LIS Profession." CPDWL/New Professionals Discussion Group, August 19, 2009, University of Bologna, ex-Convento di Santa Cristina.)

2009. "What? So What? Now What?" *Library Leadership & Management* 23: 143–46.

Notes

CHAPTER 1

1. A reference to Fred Emery's research outcomes appears in John Lubans Jr., "Orchestrating Success (The Orpheus Chamber Orchestra)," in *People in Charge: Creating Self Managing Workplaces,* ed. Robert Rehm, 187–97 (Stroud: Hawthorn Press, 1999).

CHAPTER 2

1. John Briscoe, *Tadich Grill: The Story of San Francisco's Oldest Restaurant with Recipes* (Berkeley, Calif.: Ten Speed Press, 2002). This deftly illustrated book chronicles the Tadich Grill. The author first ate at Tadich's when he was five years old.

2. An affordable anthology, giving good insights into leadership studies, is J. Thomas Wren, *Leader's Companion: Insights on Leadership through the Ages* (New York: Free Press, 1995).

3. Robert E. Kelley, "In Praise of Followers," *Harvard Business Review* 66, no. 6 (November/December 1988): 142–48. There are remarkable congruities between Kelley's follower grid and the five styles of conflict resolution identified in the Thomas Kilmann Conflict Mode Instrument: (1) competing (alienated follower), (2) collaborating (effective follower), (3) compromising (survivor), (4) avoiding (sheep), and (5) accommodating (yes people).

CHAPTER 4

1. This case study looks back on a ten-year experiment with teams in technical services at Duke University. My roles during these years were Assistant University Librarian for Public Services, then AUL for Technical Services, Associate University Librarian, and ultimately, Deputy University Librarian. In 2000, I left the university.

CHAPTER 5

1. See http://www.cesarsway.com (accessed April 4, 2010).

2. The Jack London classic can be found at http://london.sonoma.edu/ Writings/CallOfTheWild/ (accessed April 4, 2010).

CHAPTER 7

1. Interview with Glen English, February 3, 2005. This and several other quotations in the text come from interviews with Southwest employees during the first half of 2005. Unless otherwise noted, the quote is from the person named in the segment.

CHAPTER 9

1. John Lubans Jr., "I Can't Find You Anywhere But Gone: Avoiding Marginalization," *Library Administration & Management* 14, no. 2. (Spring 2000): 67–69. This chapter incorporates many of the ideas I presented in a talk to the National Library of Latvia's International "Digital Libraries for Learning" Conference, November 19, 2007, in Riga, Latvia. My Internet use studies are at www.lubans.org. The student quotations in this chapter come from these studies.

CHAPTER 10

1. I interviewed SWA's Herb Kelleher (cofounder and chairman of the board) and Colleen Barrett (president) on January 28, 2008, at Love Field in Dallas, Texas. I also attended two leadership classes at SWA's University of People—its training and development academy—on January 29. Unless otherwise noted, quoted items, including the core values, are from my two-day visit.

CHAPTER 11

1. Mary Parker Follett concludes that, "to demand an unquestioned obedience to orders not approved, not perhaps even understood, is bad business policy." "The Giving of Orders," in *Scientific Foundations of Business Administration,* ed. Henry C. Metcalf (Baltimore, MD: Williams and Wilkins, 1926).

2. Deming's fourteen points appear in Peter R. Scholtes, *Team Handbook* (Madison, WI: Scholtes, 1990), 2–4.

CHAPTER 12

1. Quadrant illustration is by John Lubans Jr.

CHAPTER 13

1. To learn more about the basketball team studies, see my Web site at Lubans.org.

CHAPTER 14

1. While reading Ray Oldenburg's, *The Great Good Place,* 3rd ed. (New York: Marlowe & Co., 1999), Zabar's was never far from my mind. I've come to regard Zabar's as possessing many of the hallmarks of Oldenburg's "third place": access is free or inexpensive; food and drink are available—of course! The store is highly accessible, within walking distance for many in this city of millions; many customers and staff can be termed "regulars"—those who habitually congregate there. It is inviting and comfortable, as well worn as one's favorite shoes. And over time one will find new friends and old there.

2. David, Scott's counterpart, illustrates community: An older woman greets him at the service desk and they chat. She runs a typewriter store on Amsterdam, frequented by New York's many authors to buy ribbons and have repairs made to their Coronas. Her business is about to close, David suggests, maybe she would like to work at Zabar's? Whether she does, matters not; it is his gesture of friendliness that makes for community. Like someone said, Zabar's is full of decent people.

3. Rabbi Joy Levitt quoted in Tina Kelley, "A Lifetime Amid the Lox and Rugelach," *The New York Times,* May 31, 2008, www.nytimes.com/2008/05/31/nyregion/31zabars.html?ex=1369972800&en=b914fcecb95211a8&ei=5124&partner=permalink&exprod=permalink (accessed March 20, 2009).

CHAPTER 15

1. The picture was taken alongside the upper balcony of the Sydney Opera House. Simone heads up a line of 100 or more alternating faces—all musicians in the opera orchestra—fanned out like playing cards, many smiling in the bright daylight, some projecting out like alternating bumps on a Chinese New Year's serpent, narrowing down into a cello-spiked tail.

CHAPTER 16

1. I adapted this classroom activity from Tom Coens, Mary Jenkins, and Peter Block, *Abolishing Performance Appraisals: Why They Backfire and What to Do Instead* (San Francisco: Berrett-Koehler Publishing, 2000).

CHAPTER 17

1. A Juilliard music student quoted in Orpheus Chamber Orchestra literature in 2007.

2. Some additional recommended readings on coaching:

   Roger Hendrix. "Private, Private Conversation: When There's Nothing More to Be Said Is When Important Things Get Said." *Across the Board* (March/April 2005): 44–47.

   Ruth F. Metz. *Coaching in the Library: A Management Strategy for Achieving Excellence.* Chicago: ALA, 2001. 105pp.

   John Paul Newport, "Team USA's Management Victory Ryder Cup Captain Paul Azinger Used a Group-dynamic Philosophy with Lessons for Golf and Beyond." *Wall Street Journal*, September 27, 2008.

   Douglas Stone et al. *Difficult Conversations: How to Discuss What Matters Most.* New York: Penguin Books, 2000.

CHAPTER 20

1. Karl Wallenda, the patriarch of the Flying Wallendas, made the 1,200-foot-long Tallulah Falls Gorge walk in July 1970 in front of 35,000 spectators. He died in San Juan, Puerto Rico, in March 1978 at age seventy-three, after a fall of 123 feet. The cause of the fall was a loose guy wire connection, not a slip of the foot.

CHAPTER 21

1. For example, seen on a New York City bus in March 2006: Each of the first few seats was labeled with "Please won't you [the "o" in "you" is heart-shaped] give this seat to the elderly or disabled?" This approach probably works better—it certainly feels better—than the regulatory and nonempathetic "Seat reserved for the handicapped."

What alternatives might Adam Smith (or Barbara Tjikatu) have to offer the Maplewood (NJ) Public Library for solving its problem with fractious middle schoolers? See the story about Maplewood's extreme enforcement measures related by Tina Kelley in "Lock the Library! Rowdy Students Are Taking Over," *New York Times,* www.nytimes.com/2007/01/02/nyregion/02library.html?_r=1&oref=slogin (accessed January 3, 2007).

This discussion about "We Don't Climb" anticipated the spring 2008 publication of *Nudge: Improving Decisions About Health, Wealth, and Happiness* by Richard H. Thaler and Cass R. Sunstein, in which they suggest and demonstrate how indirect suggestion instead of overt direction may help people do the right thing.

2. For a glimpse of Mt. Conner—the false Uluru—take a look at www.furry.org.au/hiho/misc_stuff/album/chapter04/0411.html (accessed December 19, 2006).

3. Released into the public domain and available at http://en.wikipedia.org/wiki/Image:Brolga1.jpg (accessed December 19, 2006).

CHAPTER 27

1. For a useful discussion of facilitation techniques, see chapter 7, by Michael A. Gass and Cheryl A. Stevens, "Facilitating the Adventure Process," in *Adventure Education: Theory and Applications,* ed. Richard G. Prouty, Jane Panicucci, and Rufus Collinson, 101–23 (Beverly, MA: Project Adventure, 2007). (701 Cabot St., Beverly, MA 01915).

2. John Lubans Jr. 2007. "'Thank God and Greyhound, She's Gone' (to a Workshop) and Other T&D Matters." *Library Administration & Management* 21, no. 1 (2007): 35–37.

CHAPTER 28

1. See, for example, "Creative Climate: Organizational Aspects Influencing Creativity," *Journal of Library Administration* 10, nos.2/3 (1989): 15–26; and "The Creative Library Manager," *Library Administration & Management* 1 (January 1987): 6–7.

2. The concept of "'within available resources" differs from the glibly stated exhortation to "do more with less." My experience is that mess finding eliminates complexity and results in improvements and more, not fewer, resources.

3. More recently and not irrelevantly, I've become attuned to how country and western (C&W) song titles often describe the mess-finding condition; if nothing else, C&W music is about life's messes: "I've closed my eyes to the cold hard truth that I'm seeing" or "How can something that sounds SO good, make me feel so bad?" More relevant to this essay is "How come my dog don't bark when you come around?"

4. These and more "first steps" from various problem-solving formulas can be found in Ernest B. Archer, "How to Make a Business Decision," *Management Review* 69 (February 1980): 54–56.

5. Edward de Bono's 1970 book, *Lateral Thinking*, includes a chapter on the differences between vertical and lateral thinking. It was first published in East Grinstead (UK) by Ward Lock Education.

6. Many of the basic "continuous improvement" tools, including the Pareto chart, are discussed in *The Team Handbook*, by Peter R. Scholtes and others (Madison, WI: Joiner and Associates, 1992).

7. A definition of "customer": the next person in the process. Every process has at least one customer. This comes from the presentation by Sue Rohan at the TQM in Higher Education Conference in San Francisco on February 12, 1993.

8. The amount of time at work spent doing "real work" activities is discussed by Tim Fuller in "Eliminating Complexity from Work: Improving Productivity by Enhancing Quality," *National Productivity Review* (Autumn 1985): 27–44. One telling observation is that "time unavailable for work is as high as 25 percent in large organizations." He further reduces the amount of time available, because of "rework" or non-value-added complexity, to about 35 percent! In 2009 there were even more distractions by way of the Internet. The Internet has made us more productive, to be sure, but it comes with numerous distractions, if permitted: Twitter, YouTube, FaceBook, etc.

9. This is one of several creativity-inducing activities in James L. Adams, *Conceptual Blockbusting* (Stanford, CA: Stanford Alumni Association, 1974), 85–86.

10. A resource for better understanding statistics is Edward R. Tufte, *The Visual Display of Quantitative Information* (Cheshire, CT: Graphics Press, 1983).

11. SOAP comes from *The Outward Bound Wilderness First-Aid Handbook* by Jeff Isaac and Peter Goth, with very helpful illustrations by Laura Winninger (New York: Lyons & Burford, 1991). Pages 30–42 discuss the Patient Assessment System, including SOAP.

12. Scholtes et al., *Team Handbook,* 8–46. I encountered a brief discussion of "Ask 'Why?' Five Times" in Peter R. Scholtes, "Total Quality or Performance Appraisal: Choose One," in *The Practical Guide to Quality* (Madison, WI: Joiner and Associates, 1993), 99–100.

CHAPTER 29

1. Thus Allen B. Veaner sums up "business management derivates." He elaborates on the topic in "Paradigm Lost, Paradigm Regained? A Persistent Personnel Issue in Academic Librarianship, II," *College & Research Libraries* 55 (September 1994): 389–404. Although admittedly critical of business fads, he does not "suggest that we cannot learn from business and industry or should not apply appropriate business techniques to managing academic libraries. "The key is in the words *appropriate* and *proper*" (398).

CHAPTER 32

1. Stanford University undertook in 1986 a study of twenty-five large research library technical service departments to look at "staffing efficiency." The results were shared among the twenty-five participants in mid-1987. The data are relevant to research library productivity in showing per capita output at each of the twenty-five institutions.

2. The term KITA comes from this classic article: Frederick Herzberg, "One More Time: How Do You Motivate Employees?" *Harvard Business Review* 6S (September/October 1987): 109–20.

3. Books like the following suggest the positive direction of change: Thomas T. Peters, *Thriving on Chaos, Handbook for a Management Revolution* (New York: Knopf, 1987); Peter R. Scholtes et al., *The Team Handbook: How to Use Teams to Improve. Quality* (Madison. WI: Joiner Associates, 1988) (inspired by "The Deming Way," a readable look at "TQM"); and especially Marvin R. Weisbord, *Productive Workplaces: Organizing and Managing for Dignity. Meaning and Community* (San Francisco: Jossey-Bass, 1987).

CHAPTER 36

1. The French poet Francois Villon (1431–1463) is the source of the "Where are the snows of yesteryear?" (*"Où sont les neiges d'antan?"*) question in the title. I used it to "prime the pump" as the first entry on the first page of the Suggestion Answer Book in 1982.

   As mentioned, this chapter is based on a recent perusal of suggestions and answers for the year 1988. If someone would like to do an archeological dig into the more than 2,500 or 7,500 entries, from 1982 to 1999, let me know.

   I did try an e-version of the Suggestion Answer Book. But it never caught on. The online version had neither the cachet of paper and ink—the old technology—nor the ease of flipping pages and seeing the unique handwriting, emendations, and responses on each of the pages. However, with the recent popularity of blogs and twitter, it is possible that an e-SA Book might be more favorably received and possibly surpass a paper and ink version.

2. Location matters. My chosen spot for the book was in the library's spacious lobby across and away from the door. A SA Book peruser could linger without being disturbed. The location provided a modicum of privacy and was out of the traffic flow.

3. More recently, after I retired, the local newspaper singled out the historic and ongoing SA Book for one of its community awards: "For many reasons—the years spent toiling in obscurity, bringing the center of the Earth to Durham and, most important, proving that even a prestigious, high-pressure academic institution can have a sense of humor, Duke's Answer Person is the recipient of this week's Durham Grit Award. Long may he or she provide the answers to life's most serious—and silly—questions" (*Durham Herald Sun*, June 4, 2005).

References

"800! Duke Tops N.C. State in 87–86." 2008. GoDuke.com, March 1. http://www.goduke.com/ViewArticle.dbml?SPSID=22724&SPID=1845&DB_OEM_ID=4200&ATCLID=1401499 (accessed April 5, 2010).

Ahuja, Anjana. 2006. "After More than 200 Years, Science Admits It: Adam Smith Was Right." Science Notebook, *The Times,* March 27, www.timesonline.co.uk/tol/comment/columnists/anjana_ahuja/article696969.ece (accessed April 5, 2010).

Barrett, Colleen. 2000. "Corner on Customer Service: Southwest Airlines' 'Muscle'." *Southwest Airlines Spirit* (June): 12.

Blanchard, Ken, and Barbara Glanz. 2005. *The Simple Truths of Service—Inspired by Johnny the Bagger.* Napier, IL: Macmillan Media & Simple Truths.

Brafman, Ori, and Rom Brafman. 2008. *Sway: The Irresistible Pull of Irrational Behavior*. New York: Random House.

Burns, James MacGregor. 1978. *Leadership*. New York: Harper & Row.

Carrigan, Dennis P. 1989. "Letters: The 'Dismal Science' Revisited." *College and Research Libraries* (July): 485–86.

Casciaro, Tiziana, and Miguel Sousa Lobo. 2005. "Competent Jerks, Lovable Fools and the Formation of Social Networks." *Harvard Business Review* 83, no. 6: 92–99. For a very useful summary see http://hbswk.hbs.edu/item/4916.html (accessed April 5, 2010).

Coens, Tom, and Mary Jenkins. 2002. *Abolishing Performance Appraisals: Why They Backfire and What to Do Instead.* San Francisco: Berrett-Koehler Publishers.

Davis, Stan, and Bill Davidson. 1991. *2020 Vision: Transform Your Business Today to Succeed in Tomorrow's Economy.* New York: Simon & Schuster.

Doyle, Sir Arthur Conan. 1953. "Silver Blaze." In *The Complete Sherlock Holmes,* vol. 1. Garden City, NY: Doubleday.

Flaherty, James. 1999. *Coaching—Evoking Excellence in Others*. Boston: Butterworth/Heinemann.

Follett, M. P. 1978. "The Giving of Orders." In *Classics of Public Administration,* edited by Jay M Shafritz and Albert C Hyde, 37. Oak Park, IL: Moore Publishing.

Follett, Mary Parker. 1996a. "Coordination." In *Prophet of Management: A Celebration of Writings from the 1920s,* ed. Pauline Graham, 188. Boston: Harvard Business School Press.

Follett, Mary Parker, with commentary by Warren Bennis. 1996b. "The Essentials of Leadership." In *Prophet of Management: A Celebration of Writings from the 1920s,* ed. Pauline Graham, 163–181. Boston: Harvard Business School Press.

Freiberg, Kevin, and Jackie Freiberg. 1998. *Nuts! Southwest Airlines' Crazy Recipe for Business and Personal Success.* New York: Broadway Books.

Fuller, Tim. 1985. "Eliminating Complexity from Work: Improving Productivity by Enhancing Quality." *National Productivity Review* (Autumn): 27–44.

Gallwey, W. Timothy. 1997. *The Inner Game of Tennis.* New York: Random House.

Golding, William. 1962. *Lord of the Flies.* Introduction by E. M. Forster. New York: Coward-McCann.

Goldsmith, Marshall, et al. 2003. *Global Leadership: The Next Generation.* New York: Prentice-Hall.

Grote, Dick. 2002. *The Performance Appraisal Question and Answer Book: A Survival Guide for Managers.* New York: AMACOM

Gulick, Luther, and Lyndall Urwick, eds. 1937. *Papers on the Science of Administration.* New York: Institute of Public Administration, 3–13.

Hackman, J. Richard. 2002a. *Leading Teams: Setting the Stage for Great Performances.* Boston: Harvard Business School Press. (Especially the chapter on expert coaching, pp. 165–96.)

Hackman, J. Richard. 2002b. *Nobody on the Podium: Lessons About Leadership from the Orpheus Chamber Orchestra.* VHS. Reference #C15–02–16449. Boston: Kennedy School of Government.

Henri, Robert. 1984. *The Art Spirit: Notes, Articles, Fragments of Letters and Talks to Students, Bearing on the Concept and Technique of Picture Making, the Study of Art Generally, and on Appreciation.* New York: Harper & Row, 169.

Herzberg, Frederick. 1964. "The Motivation- Hygiene Concept and Problems of Manpower." *Personnel Administration* 27, no. 1: 3–7.

Herzberg, Frederick. 1987. "One More Time: How Do You Motivate Employees?" *Harvard Business Review* 65 (September/October): 109–20.

Hill, Hamlin. 1963. "Introduction." In *A Connecticut Yankee in King Arthur's Court,* by Samuel Langhorne Clemens. San Francisco: Chandler Publishing.

Holland, Bernard. 2008. "An Ensemble Finds Unity with a Seasoned Soprano." *The New York Times,* April 3, E4.

Hoopes, James. 2003. *False Prophets: The Gurus Who Created Modern Management and Why Their Ideas Are Bad for Business Today.* Cambridge, MA: Perseus Books Group.

Hubbard, John. 2007. "Going Virtual: Technology & the Future of Academic Libraries." University of Wisconsin-Milwaukee, Library Council of Southeastern Wisconsin Annual Conference, May 16. www.librarycouncil. org (accessed April 4, 2010).

Huntford, Roland. 1986. *Shackleton.* New York: Atheneum.

Isaksen, S. G., and D. J. Treffinger. 1985. *Creative Problem Solving: The Basic Course.* Buffalo, NY: Byerly Limited.

Ishikawa, K. 1985. *What Is Total Quality Management?* Translated by D. J. Lu. Englewood Cliffs, NJ: Prentice-Hall.

Jennings, Lois. 1992. "Regrowing Staff: Managerial Priority for the Future of University Libraries." *The Public Access Computer Systems Review* 3: 4–15.

Jensen, Michael. 2007. "The New Metrics of Scholarly Authority," *The Chronicle of Higher Education* 53, no. 41 (June 15): B6, http://chronicle. com/weekly/v53/i41/41b00601.htm (accessed June 18, 2009) (subscription.)

Katz, Daniel, and Robert L. Kahn. 1966. *The Social Psychology of Organizations.* New York: Wiley & Sons, 14–29.

Katzenbach, Jon R., and Douglas K. Smith. 2001. *The Discipline of Teams: A Mindbook-Workbook for Delivering Small Group Performance.* New York: John Wiley & Sons.

Kelleher, Herb. n.d. *The Art of Coaching in Business.* DVD. Baltimore, MD: Greylock Associates.

Kellerman, Barbara. 2004. *Bad Leadership: What It Is, How It Happens, and Why It Matters.* Boston: Harvard Business School Press.

Kellerman, Barbara. 2008. *Followership: How Followers Are Creating Change and Changing Leaders.* Boston: Harvard Business School Press.

Kelley, Robert E. 1988. "In Praise of Followers." *Harvard Business Review* 66 (November–December): 142–48.

Kellogg, Alex P. 2001. "N.J. Court Allows Rutgers Athletes to Sue over Being Forced to Run Naked." *Chronicle of Higher Education* (July 27): A37.

Kennedy, Larry W. 1991. *Quality Management in the Nonprofit World*. San Francisco: Jossey-Bass.

Kotter, John P. 1996. *Leading Change*. Boston: Harvard Business School Press, 161–73.

Kouzes, James M., and Barry Z. Posner. 2003.*The Leadership Challenge*. San Francisco: Jossey-Bass.

Kuller, Alison Murray, ed. 1986. *Readings from the Hurricane Island Outward Bound School*. Rockland, ME: HIOBS, 59. (The geology quote comes from an unnamed editor at Time-Life Books.)

LaFasto, Frank M., and Carl Larson. 2001. *When Teams Work Best: 6,000 Team Members and Leaders Tell What It Takes to Succeed*. Thousand Oaks, CA: Sage Publications.

LeBoeuf, Michael. 1982. *The Productivity Challenge: How to Make It Work for America and You*. New York: McGraw-Hill.

Lewin, Kurt. ca. 1938. *Experimental Studies in Social Climates of Growth*. 16mm. Available from Penn Slate Audio Visual Services, Film no. 32519,16.

Lewis, Michael. 2009. "The No-Stats All-Star." *New York Times Magazine,* February 15, 2009, MM26, www.nytimes.com/2009/02/15/magazine/15Battier-t.html (accessed April 5, 2010).

Litwin, G. H., and R. A. Stringer. 1968. *Motivation and Organizational Climate*. Boston: Harvard Business School Press.

Lubans, John, Jr. 1996. "'I Ain't No Cowboy; I Just Found This Hat': Confessions of an Administrator in an Organization of Self Managing Teams." *Library Administration & Management* 10: 28–40.

Lubans, John, Jr. 1999. "Feedback for Duke Women's Basketball Team Captains." Unpublished paper, November 28. (Photocopy. 5pp.).

Lubans, John, Jr. 2001. "A Reason for Rain: Hoop Lessons for Library Leaders." *Library Administration & Management* 13: 39–43.

Lubans, John, Jr. 2002. "Orchestrating Success." In *People in Charge: Creating Self-Managing Workplaces,* by Robert Rehm. Gabriola Island, BC: New Society Publishing.

Lubans, John, Jr. 2004a. "Leading from the Middle." *Library Administration & Management* 18: 205–7.

Lubans, John, Jr. 2004b. "Leading from the Middle: I'm the Boss." *Library Administration & Management* 18, no. 4 (Fall): 202–7.

Lubans, John, Jr. 2006a. "Letting Go: A Reflection on Teams That Were." In *Teams in Technical Services*, ed. Rosann Bazirjian and Rebecca Mugridge, 155–69. Lanham, MD: Scarecrow Press.

Lubans, John, Jr. 2006b. "Southwest: The Un-stodgy Airline." *Library Administration & Management* 20, no. 3: 142–46.

Lubans, John, Jr. 2007. " 'Thank God and Greyhound, She's Gone,' (to a Workshop) and Other T&D Matters." *Library Administration & Management* 21, no. 1: 35–37.

Marshall, Peter. 1992. "Taoism and Buddhism." In *Demanding the Impossible: A History of Anarchism,* 53–60. London: HarperCollins.

McClam, Erin. 2005. "Ex-WorldCom Exec Gets Prison, House Arrest." August 5. www.mlive.com/newsflash/business/index.ssf?/base/business-46/1123248455162090.xml&storylist=mibusiness (accessed April 5, 2010).

Mooney, Marta. 1982. *Productivity Management.* (Conference Board Research Bulletin No. 127.) New York: Conference Board.

OCLC. 2006. *Perceptions of Libraries and Information Resources.* Dublin, OH: OCLC.

O'Toole, James. 1996. *Leading Change: The Argument for Value-Based Leadership.* New York: Ballantine Books.

O'Toole, James, and Edward E. Lawler III. 2006. "The Choices Managers Make—Or Don't." *The Conference Board Review* 44, no. 5: 24–29.

Ranganathan, Shiyali R. 1957. *The Five Laws of Library Science.* Bombay: Asia Publishing House.

Rehm, Robert, et al. 2002. *Futures that Work.* Gabriola Island, BC.: New Society Publishers. (Includes several cases of the future search with not-for-profits, along with much practical information about the process.)

Saunders, George. 2000. *Pastoralia/Stories.* New York: Riverhead Books.

Schweitzer, Vivien. 2006. "Orpheus Goes to School." *Symphony* 57, no. 2: 38–41.

Senge, Peter. 1990. *The Fifth Discipline; The Art and Practice of the Learning Organization*. New York: Doubleday Currency.

Sevareid, Eric. 2010. BrainyQuote.com. Xplore Inc. www.brainyquote.com/quotes/quotes/e/ericsevare113022.html (accessed April 2, 2010).

Shamp, Jim. 2005. "Wake Forest Tells How It Avoided Fluid Mix-Up." *The Herald-Sun* (Durham, North Carolina), July 2.

Shelor, Leslie. 2006. "A Typical Mountain Woman (Ruby Underwood)." http://blueridgegazette.blogspot.com/2006_02_01_archive.html (accessed April 5, 2010).

Solzhenitsyn, Aleksandr. 2004. *We Never Make Mistakes: Two Short Novels*. Translated by Paul W. Blackstock. New York: Norton.

Southwest Airlines. 2008a. *Employee Customer Relationship Video*. DVD. Dallas, TX: SWA. 13 minutes.

Southwest Airlines. 2008[?]b. *9/11: Lessons in Leadership (Freedom Isn't free.)* DVD. Dallas, TX: SWA. 60 minutes.

Streibel, Barbara J., et al. 2003. *The Team Handbook*. Madison, WI: Oriel Inc.

Strickland, Bryan. 2005. "Krzyzewski's Private Sessions Have Inspired Dockery, Melchionni." *The Herald-Sun,* December 21.

Strickland, Bryan. 2007. "Step in, Step Back." *The Herald Sun* (Durham, North Carolina), May 28, C1 and C6.

Stueart, Robert D., and Barbara B. Moran. 2002. *Library and Information Center Management*. Greenwood Village, CO: Libraries Unlimited, 252–67.

Taira, Koji. 1988. "Productivity Assessment: Japanese Perceptions and Practices." In *Productivity in Organizations: New Perspectives from industrial and Organizational Psychology,* 58. San Francisco: Jossey-Bass.

Tommasini, Anthony. 2008. "The Pluses and Minuses of Lacking a Conductor." *The New York Times*, October 18. www.nytimes.com/2008/10/18/arts/music/18orph.html (accessed April 5, 2010).

Total Quality Management: A Guide for the North Dakota University System. 1991. Fargo: North Dakota State University.

Trump, Donald, and Bill Zanker. 2007. *Think Big and Kick Ass in Business and Life*. New York: HarperCollins.

Tuckman B. 1965. "Developmental Sequences in Small Groups." *Psychological Bulletin* 63: 384–99.

Useem, Jerry. 2005. "America's Most Admired Companies." *Fortune* 151: 66–70.

Vogl, A. J. 2006. "The Future Is Now: Interview with John Naisbitt." *The Conference Board Review* 44, no. 5: 56.

Waldhart, Thomas J., and Thomas P. Marcum. 1976. "Productivity Measurement in Academic Libraries." In *Advances in Librarianship,* ed. M. J. Voigt and M. H. Hams, vol. 6, 53–77. New York: Academic Press.

Weisbord, Marvin R. 1987. *Productive Workplaces: Organizing and Managing for Dignity, Meaning and Community.* San Francisco: Jossey-Bass.

Wendt, Jana. 2006. "Simone Young." *The Bulletin* (Australia) 124, no. 32 (August 2).

Whyte, David. 1996. *The Heart Aroused: Poetry and the Preservation of the Soul in Corporate America.* New York: Doubleday.

Wodehouse, P. G. 2000. *Most of P. G. Wodehouse.* New York: Simon & Schuster.

Index

About the Author

JOHN LUBANS JR. lives in Durham, North Carolina. He writes and teaches about management and other topics related to libraries, drawing upon his many years of frontline and administrative library experience at public and private universities. He has recently received a Fulbright lecturing grant (effective February 2011) to teach library management and leadership at the University of Latvia in Riga. He can be reached at Lubans1@nc.rr.com, and his blog about this book is at http://blog.lubans.org.

Recent Titles in the
Beta Phi Mu Monograph Series